EUGENE CLYDE BROOKS

Publication of this book was assisted by grants from E. C. Brooks, Jr., and the Ford Foundation.

© 1960, Duke University Press

Library of Congress Catalog Card Number 60-13604

Cambridge University Press, London, N.W. 1, England

Printed in the United States of America
by the Seeman Printery, Inc., Durham, N. C.

EUGENE CLYDE BROOKS
EDUCATOR AND PUBLIC SERVANT

Willard B. Gatewood, Jr.

DUKE UNIVERSITY PRESS   *Durham, N. C.*   1960

Wingate College Library

To my son

Discarded

Discarded

Preface

Eugene Clyde Brooks was once described as a Southerner with "a deep sense of social and human values" who was "trying to build before it is too late." The justification for such a description lay in his intimate association with various reform movements during the first three decades of the twentieth century. Although Brooks rendered valuable services to many causes, his chief contributions were in the field of education. He was, in fact, a decisive figure in the educational advancement of his native North Carolina during a period that was probably the most significant in the educational history of the state. Between 1898 and 1934 he occupied almost every position on the educational ladder, and a striking feature of his career was the success that he achieved in each capacity. At one time or another during this period he was a teacher, principal, superintendent of city schools, clerk in the State Department of Public Instruction, professor of education in Trinity College, State Superintendent of Public Instruction, and president of North Carolina State College of Agriculture and Engineering. He edited a teachers' magazine for seventeen years, published seven books that won him a reputation as a versatile author, and figured prominently in several educational organizations of national and regional importance. He also directed the campaign for better schools initiated in 1902 by Governor Charles B. Aycock which was probably the most extraordinary educational movement in the history of the state. For the next seventeen years Brooks made numerous contributions to education, particularly through his efforts to improve teacher qualifications and school standards. As a professor in Trinity College he gave the institution a pre-eminence in North Carolina in teacher training. He not only inspired a generation of school men in his regular college classes, but established the first extension course for teachers in service in the state.

In 1919 Brooks became State Superintendent of Public Instruction in North Carolina. His comprehensive reorganization of public education in the state attracted national attention. The outstanding features of his program included the establishment of a uniform teacher certification plan and salary schedule, a sweeping change in the method of financing public schools, a remarkable improvement in the quality of the teaching personnel and county school administration, the creation of a $10,000,000 loan fund for the construction of schools, a rapid expansion of facilities for Negro education, and the codification of public school laws.

Brooks left the State Superintendency in 1923 to become president of North Carolina State College, where he remained until his permanent retirement in 1934. During his administration the college underwent a spectacular physical transformation and was converted from a trade-school to a technological and professional institution of recognized standing. While president of the college, Brooks led a movement for reforms in county government that came to fruition in legislative acts passed in 1927 and 1931. His efforts were, in large measure, responsible for a veritable revolution in the administration of county fiscal affairs. At the same time he served as secretary of the North Carolina Park Commission and played a key role in the establishment of the Great Smoky Mountains National Park, one of the major projects in conservation and recreation in the East.

Brooks's personal qualities were largely responsible for his success and advancement. He was a forceful, vigorous individual with an abundant physical energy, a perceptive mind, and a rare sense of humor. His unusual oratorical and forensic abilities proved to be decisive factors in more than a few of the hard-fought contests of his career. Above all, Brooks possessed many talents in human relations. In fact, one of his most valuable assets was a thorough understanding of men and their psychology—an understanding that he utilized to great advantage on numerous occasions, especially in dealing with the legislature. Tact, diplomacy, and persuasive eloquence coupled with a fierce tenacity of purpose generally characterized his procedure for overcoming opposition.

In addition to his personal traits, Brooks was assisted in his career by several influential friends and unusual circumstances. His close friendship with State Superintendent James Y. Joyner was a significant factor in his rise to prominence and was at least partially responsible for his appointment as Joyner's successor. Moreover, on several occasions Brooks moved into new positions that offered him extraordinary opportunities to demonstrate his abilities and to make significant contributions. For example, he was the first superintendent of the Monroe Graded Schools, the first director of Aycock's educational campaign, and the first professor of education at Trinity College. He became State Superintendent at a time when the educational movement of the past two decades—a movement in which he had played an important part—came to fruition. He assumed the presidency of North Carolina State College largely for the purpose of executing a reorganization program that had already been outlined and approved by the trustees. The fact that he came into these positions under such circumstances neither lessened the difficulty of the tasks nor detracted from the significance of his achievements.

This biography could never have been written without the cordial co-operation and assistance of numerous individuals. Mrs. E. C. Brooks of Raleigh and Mr. E. C. Brooks, Jr., of Durham responded to all my requests promptly and generously. My gratitude to them can scarcely be conveyed by a simple acknowledgment. Professors William T. Laprade and Richard L. Watson, Jr., of the Department of History of Duke University followed the project from its inception until the final, revised manuscript reached the press. They read the entire manuscript, gave invaluable criticisms, and provided constant encouragement. Professor Hugh Lefler of the University of North Carolina gave me the benefit of his rich understanding of North Carolina history and offered many timely suggestions. Many former associates of Brooks were interviewed personally; to them I am deeply indebted for the information that they so freely gave. The staff members of the libraries at Duke University, the University of North Carolina, and North Carolina State College were always generous in their assistance. I am especially grateful for the aid of Dr. Mattie Russell, Curator of Manuscripts at Duke University, and Mr. Houston G. Jones, North Carolina State Archivist. *The North Carolina Historical Review,* through its managing editor, Dr. D. L. Corbitt, has granted permission to publish portions of this study which appeared in a modified form in that journal. The members of the Duke University Press have been helpful in numerous ways. Without the aid, encouragement, and patience of my wife, Lu Brown Gatewood, this biography would never have been published.

WILLARD B. GATEWOOD, JR.

North Carolina Wesleyan College
Rocky Mount, North Carolina

Contents

Illustrations

EUGENE CLYDE BROOKS

THE LIBRARY LAWS OF NORTH CAROLINA MAKE
IT A MISDEMEANOR TO WILLFULLY DAMAGE OR
KEEP PUBLIC LIBRARY PROPERTY, SUBJECT TO
A $50 FINE ON CONVICTION.

TEARING PAGE CORNERS IS SERIOUS DAMAGE;
FAILURE TO RETURN BOOKS IS INTERPRETED
AS KEEPING PUBLIC PROPERTY.

One: EARLY LIFE, *1871-1903*

[1]

In the first decade of the eighteenth century, John Lawson, the
English Surveyor-General, traveled through the province of Carolina. In his account of this exploration, published in 1709, he described the eastern area inhabited by the belligerent Tuscarora Indians as consisting of vast swamps and marshes, dense forests of lob-
lolly pine trees, and lazy tributaries of the Neuse River. Between the
time of publication of Lawson's travel account and the outbreak of
the American Revolution, the area underwent a significant change.
During this period North Carolina became a separate province and
passed from the control of the Lords Proprietors to the English
Crown. The population increased, settlements gradually moved up
the eastern rivers, and the Indian menace was removed. The scattered villages and broad cultivated acres presented a picture radically
different from Lawson's description.[1]

Those settlers who participated in this transformation of the
colony of North Carolina included persons by the name of Brooks.
Members of this family had settled in the area as early as 1649. A
John Brooks, one of those "discenting [*sic*] persons called Baptist,"
received land grants in Craven County during the first half of the
eighteenth century. He later joined the westward movement and
settled in Pitt County. Later still, several of his kinsmen were granted
lands in Craven County, and by 1775 various branches of the Brooks
family had settled throughout the coastal plains region of North
Carolina. With the outbreak of the American Revolution members

1. John Lawson, *History of North Carolina,* ed. Frances Harriss (Richmond, 1951),
pp. 58-60; Hugh Lefler and Albert Newsome, *North Carolina: The History of a
Southern State* (Chapel Hill, 1954), pp. 69-70; D. L. Corbitt, *The Formation of North
Carolina Counties, 1663-1943* (Raleigh, 1950), pp. xii-xv.

of the family in this area cast their lot against the Crown and joined
the rebel forces.[2]

After the Revolution one branch of the family continued to live
along the Neuse River in Craven County on fertile lands that had
been granted to Joseph Brooks in 1769. One of Joseph Brooks's
descendents, a namesake, who married Margaret Jones, was a man
of some means, especially after their inheritance of a considerable
sum of money from her father in 1837. Their second child, born
on July 20, 1843, was a son, Edward Jones Brooks. The child grew up
on his father's farm and received a rather adequate formal education.
He later taught school near his home and throughout his life manifested a keen interest in education.[3]

Shortly after the beginning of the Civil War, Edward Brooks
joined a cavalry outfit in the Confederate Army called the Pamlico
Volunteers, and ultimately rose to the rank of Ordnance Sergeant
of Company I of the Second North Carolina Regiment. He served
throughout the war and was twice captured by the enemy. He bore
for life the scars from wounds received in the battle at Antietam.
One of these, a grotesque mark on his face, accounted for the beard
that he wore after the war.[4]

With the collapse of the Confederacy, Brooks started a bleak trek
back to Craven County. En route he visited relatives near Edward's
Bridge in Greene County, where he first learned that his father and
brother, who had also joined the Confederate service, had died in
the battle at Fort Fisher. His visit in Greene County was not totally
shrouded by this tragic news, however, for during this time he renewed an acquaintance with his distant cousin, Martha Eleanor
Brooks, then an attractive seventeen-year-old girl. This cousin was
undoubtedly sufficient reason for extending his stay, but after a brief
courtship, he returned to his father's plantation in Craven County.
The ubiquitous signs of defeat, coupled with the loss of his father

2. J. Montgomery Seaver, *Brooks Family History* (Philadelphia, n.d.), p. 24; Ida
Brooks Kellam, *Brooks and Kindred Families* (n.p., 1950), pp. 7-8.
3. Kellam, *Brooks and Kindred Families*, pp. 144-146; memorandum by Mrs. Mary
Edmonds Brooks Cobb, Oct. 6, 1956.
4. Roll of Honor, North Carolina Troops, 1861-1863, State Department of Archives
and History, Raleigh, North Carolina; John W. Moore, *Roster of North Carolina
Troops in the War Between the States* (Raleigh, 1882), I, 73; Walter Clark, *Histories of
the Several Regiments and Battalions From North Carolina in the Great War*, I (Raleigh, 1901), 158-175; interview with Mr. E. C. Brooks, Jr., July 12, 1956; memorandum
by Mrs. Mary Edmonds Brooks Cobb, Oct. 6, 1956.

and brother, probably made his home a lonely place; he therefore returned to Greene County shortly afterward to resume his courtship of Martha Brooks. In time he won her hand in marriage, but only upon promising her mother that he would never take his bride to live in Craven County, which was then considered a fertile breeding ground for malaria and typhoid fever.[5]

Brooks married his cousin Martha on January 21, 1869, and they made their home in Greene County. Three years later they moved several miles south into Lenoir County and settled near the place where the English Surveyor-General, John Lawson, had crossed Contentnea Creek. Their farm was located in the rural community of Bethel in Contentnea Neck Township about a mile from the present town of Grifton. Contentnea Neck township lay in that northeastern corner of Lenoir County between the Neuse River and Contentnea Creek bordering Pitt and Greene counties. It contained rich farm and timber lands as well as large swamps.[6]

Brooks's early married life fell within the chaotic period of Reconstruction. The combination of an impoverished people, a corrupt Republican government, and an uneasy relationship between Negroes and whites produced a situation unfavorable to the political success of an ex-Confederate soldier who supported the Democratic Party. So long as the state remained under Republican domination Edward Brooks possessed few outlets for his political ambitions.[7]

By 1877 the Democrats had completed their return to power in North Carolina and had introduced constitutional changes that assured their control of the state. One such change empowered the legislature to appoint justices of the peace, who in turn chose the county commissioners and approved the action of the commissioners in all important matters. In addition to their judicial duties, the justices controlled the county election machinery and the appointment of registrars and judges in voting precincts. The Democrats' "redemption" of the state precipitated a rise in the fortunes of Ed-

5. "Item from the Papers of Eugene C. Brooks in His Own Handwriting," Eugene Clyde Brooks Papers, Duke University Library, Durham, North Carolina. Hereinafter cited as Brooks Papers (DUL).

6. Brooks Family Bible (in the possession of Mrs. E. C. Brooks, Raleigh, North Carolina); "Dr. E. C. Brooks," *The State* (June 19, 1937), p. 3; *Kinston Free Press* (Kinston, North Carolina), Industrial Issue of 1906; *Pearce's Map of North Carolina* (New York, 1876).

7. For an account of Reconstruction in North Carolina, see J. G. deR. Hamilton, *Reconstruction in North Carolina* (Raleigh, 1906).

ward Brooks. In 1883 he became a justice of the peace in Lenoir
County, a post which meant influence and prestige. Henceforth, he
was called "squire" or "judge," titles commonly applied to justices
in the area.[8]

By this time Brooks had become one of the significant figures in
his community. The fees that he collected as a justice enhanced his
wealth and enabled him by 1894 to expand his original landholdings
by 163 acres. Even so, his farm was considered only average size by
local standards. Thus, the popular respect for him was by no means
based upon his material possessions; rather it stemmed from his
honest, efficient execution of his official duties and his active participation in the civic life of the community. Brooks not only held
the highest offices in the local Masonic lodges; he also figured prominently in the educational progress of Lenoir County. As a member
of the county board of education, he was a constant advocate of better
schools at a time when public education received little popular support.[9]

In 1892 Brooks became a candidate for the State House of Representatives on the Democratic ticket. The Lenoir County Democrats
opened their campaign in August at Rose of Sharon in Contentnea
Neck Township where they encountered strong opposition from the
Populists. One observer noted that "times are serious, and disaster
may be before us if the Democrats do not prevail in the coming
election." Late in September, 1892, a group of prominent young
politicians, including Charles B. Aycock and Josephus Daniels, in-
vaded Lenoir County to aid the Democratic candidates. In the November election Brooks defeated his opponent by only fifty-one votes;
but with this slim victory he reached the apex of his political career.
His tenure in the legislature was not attended by any special dis-

8. Paul Wager, *County Government and Administration in North Carolina* (Chapel
Hill, 1928), pp. 22, 222-223; W. W. Dunn to E. J. Brooks, Aug. 21, 1883, E. J. Brooks
Papers, Duke University Library, Durham, North Carolina; Eugene C. Brooks, "The
Education of a North Carolinian," p. 23, Eugene C. Brooks Papers in the possession of
Mr. B. L. Smith, Greensboro, North Carolina. Hereinafter cited as Brooks Papers
(BLS).
9. Deeds and Mortgages of Lenoir County, Book 5, pp. 461-462, Book 9, p. 145,
Book 17, p. 519. Office of the Register of Deeds, Lenoir County Courthouse, Kinston,
North Carolina; Tenth Census of the United States, Agriculture Schedule, Lenoir
County, North Carolina, p. 17, State Department of Archives and History, Raleigh,
North Carolina; interview with Mrs. Anna Pittman Purvis, June 10, 1956; *Kinston Free
Press*, Sept. 8, 1892; Grifton Lodge No. 452 To Whom It May Concern, March 24, 1894,
Brooks Papers (DUL).

tinction, perhaps because he was so often absent from the sessions, owing to sickness in the family.[10]

[2]

On December 3, 1871, while they were still living in Greene County, the Brooks's first son was born. They named him Eugene Clyde Brooks, but usually called him "Genie" and later "Gene." Before the boy was a year old, the family moved to their new home in Lenoir County. He and his older sister Lucy along with six younger brothers and sisters spent their early years in the rural community of Bethel.[11] One of Genie's earliest recollections concerned an accident that befell him at the age of four. Even then liking to go to the nearby woods where the men chopped wood, he had begged his father for a little ax. After much persuasion, Squire Brooks gave him a hatchet. Genie immediately started toward the woods to demonstrate his skill in hewing trees. He ran along the path with his head held high and his hatchet clutched tightly. Suddenly he tripped over a vine and fell to the ground. The hatchet slipped from his grip and completely severed the little finger from his left hand. He rushed home, received medical attention, and then returned to the scene of the accident, where he found his finger and buried it with a fanfare comparable to the state funerals for Santa Anna's leg.[12]

Brooks's childhood companions included his brothers and sisters, numerous cousins in the area, and the children of such neighboring families as the Barwicks and Pittmans. At an early age he and his brothers began to share in the chores around the farm, but they always had adequate time for recreation. In the summer they enjoyed baseball, swimming, and fishing; and in the fall they organized bird-hunting parties. Other forms of recreation included card-playing

10. *New Bern Weekly Journal* (New Bern, North Carolina), Aug. 25, 1892; *Kinston Free Press*, Nov. 10, 1892; *Journal of the House of Representatives of North Carolina, 1893*, pp. 11, 33, 75, 224, 371, 490.

11. E. C. Brooks, "Eugene Clyde Brooks: An Autobiographical Sketch" (typewritten), D. H. Hill Library, North Carolina State College, Raleigh. Three of the eleven children born to Edward and Martha Brooks died in infancy. The Brooks children in the order of their births: Lucy, 1870; Eugene Clyde, 1871; Margaret, 1873; Hugh Cecil, 1875; Seldon, 1877; Luther, 1880; Mary Edmond, 1882; Martha Eleanor, 1884; Jesse Pittman, 1886; Walter Spivey, 1888; Glenn, 1895. Memorandum of Mrs. Mary Edmonds Brooks Cobb, Oct. 6, 1956.

12. "Dr. E. C. Brooks," *The State* (June 19, 1937), p. 3; memorandum by Mrs. Mary Edmonds Brooks Cobb, Oct. 6, 1956.

and Saturday night gatherings of community young people at the Brooks home for the quadrille and the Virginia Reel. Brooks's parents, particularly his mother, a jovial woman known as "Miss Pattie," were extremely popular among the younger set, and their home, a comfortable eight-room bungalow, was a kind of community social center.[13]

Among Brooks's closest associates were the children of the Negro tenant families. He gained a first-hand knowledge of Negroes in the heart of one of the "black belt" counties. His community of Contentnea Neck possessed a greater concentration of Negroes than any other township in Lenoir County. The Brooks boys frequently visited Negro homes, where they stuffed themselves with hog jowl, turnip greens, and corn bread until "their bellies bulged out like melons." The relations between white and Negro children in the area were usually quite harmonious, but occasionally young Brooks and his friends insulted Negro children on their way to school, and "fights would ensue." Severe punishments always awaited Brooks after one of these clashes, because his parents would not condone disrespect toward anyone. His association with the Lenoir County Negroes undoubtedly molded his attitude toward them in general and influenced the direction of his later efforts in their behalf.[14]

The popularity of the Brooks family in the Bethel community rested mainly upon their quality of neighborliness. Young Brooks with his father and brothers aided neighbors without charge in "wheat threshing, log rolling, and house raising." Whenever his father slaughtered a calf or pig, Brooks took part of the fresh meat in the family buggy and distributed it among friends. This spirit of community co-operation found additional expression in services to neighbors in distress. On one occasion Henry Cannon, a nearby farmer, was stricken with a severe case of typhoid fever and was unable to cultivate his crops. Squire Brooks assembled the neighbors and soon "put the fields in excellent condition," while his wife and Gene assisted Mrs. Cannon in nursing the sick man. Such instances

13. Interview with Mrs. Anna Pittman Purvis, June 10, 1956; Eugene C. Brooks, "A Half Century Ago," p. 2. Brooks Papers (BLS); memorandum by Mrs. Mary Edmonds Brooks Cobb, Oct. 6, 1956.

14. *Kinston Free Press*, Industrial Issue, 1906; Brooks, "A Half Century Ago," p. 1; Brooks, "The Education of a North Carolinian," p. 5.

of voluntary co-operation among the farmers of Contentnea Neck made an indelible impression upon young Brooks.[15]

Religion was another strong influence in his early life. His father, who "stood at the head of his church relations," impressed upon him the rules of Christian conduct and taught him to respect law. "Any man has the right to insult you," he warned, "when you are beyond the pale of the law." Martha Brooks, a devout member of St. John's Episcopal Church in Pitt County, was undoubtedly responsible for her son's interest in Bible stories and his attendance at the monthly church meetings. Her greatest ambition was that her son should become a minister. Although Brooks did not fulfil this ambition, he retained an interest in religious affairs throughout his life.[16]

During his early years he was deeply impressed by the fiery preachers who visited the community and thundered against card games, dancing, and especially athletic contests held on Sundays. The fear of God's wrath was a constant theme of their sermons. They explained the acceleration of the mortality rate in Bethel by tuberculosis, typhoid fever, and malaria as the work of a God whose wrath had been aroused by the sins of the victims or their ancestors. Mothers prayed to a dreadful God, while amid unsanitary conditions disease spread rapidly from one member of their families to another. These doctrines of a wrathful God evidently were not wholly lost upon young Brooks. He later wrote that "one boy in the neighborhood, seeing the wrath of God, terrible in its visitation," decided to enter the ministry in order that he might warn people of God's anger and that he himself might escape it. Perhaps this is a reference to himself, for in 1890 he declared his intention of becoming a minister.[17]

Not only did Brooks listen to the rantings of local preachers, but he heard the discussions of farmers gathered at Bethel's country store. Certainly, this community center made a vivid impression upon him. The store at Bethel contained the post office, a small alcove for the stock of liquors, and "long benches . . . in front for visitors." The

15. Brooks, "The Education of a North Carolinian," pp. 29-31.
16. Brooks, "A Half Century Ago," p. 2; Grifton Lodge No. 452 To Whom It May Concern, March 24, 1894, Brooks Papers (DUL); memorandum by Mrs. Mary Edmonds Brooks Cobb, Oct. 6, 1956; interview with Mrs. Anna Pittman Purvis, June 10, 1956.
17. Brooks, "A Half Century Ago," p. 1; Brooks, "The Education of a North Carolinian," p. 8; Eugene C. Brooks to John F. Crowell, July 15, 1890, Trinity College Papers, Duke University Library, Durham, North Carolina.

traveling salesmen with their covered wagons full of patent medicines, tobacco products, and other merchandise brought news to Bethel from various parts of the state. The store was also the scene of political meetings and debates. At the age of five, Brooks was introduced to politics as he sat near his father at the store listening to the heated discussion about the elections of 1876. The disputed presidential election of that year stirred the Bethel farmers to "talk of war."[18]

One of Brooks's most delightful childhood experiences was a visit with his maternal grandmother at Edward's Bridge, where his uncle, Sam Brooks, was building a store. He was permitted to carry meals to his uncle and watch the construction of the building. After its completion, the store made life "full of interesting events" for young Brooks, who now decided to become "a storekeeper." The failure of his uncle's business caused him such great disappointment that he must have been near tears as he witnessed the selling of the merchandise at public auction. Despite his uncle's misfortune, Brooks retained his love for the country store and later declared that it presented "a cross section of North Carolina life and I loved life."[19]

As a son of a justice of the peace, Brooks had a peculiar vantage point from which to observe local politics during the period following Reconstruction. The justices were the real centers of political power in the counties in this period. Their restoration to power in 1876 was occasioned by the Democrats' desire "to rescue the eastern counties from the extravagance and danger of negro and carpetbag rule." According to Brooks, the party guardians in Lenoir County "were not wanting in political cunning when they desired to remove a man of the opposite political faith." He recalled the fate of a justice of the peace in an adjoining township whose "friends" tricked him into resigning, then blocked his nomination to another office that he desired. Brooks formed his earliest opinion of politicians from such maneuvers and later expressed displeasure with references to himself as a shrewd politician.[20]

One of the most important occasions for the people of Contentnea Neck township was a legal case important enough for jury trial. The

18. Brooks, "The Education of a North Carolinian," p. 34.
19. *Ibid.*, pp. 34-35.
20. *Ibid.*, pp. 23-34; Wager, *County Government in North Carolina*, p. 59; interview with Mrs. E. C. Brooks, June 19, 1956.

court usually convened in the shade of an oak tree with the presiding J. P. seated at a table flanked on one side by the jurors. A crowd of almost a hundred people generally attended such trials; among them were salesmen displaying "fruit trees, lightning rods, stomach remedies, etc." Young Brooks looked forward to attending these trials and thoroughly enjoyed the excitement. He greatly admired lawyers, whose dignity was enhanced by silk hats and Prince Albert coats. After hearing one celebrated lawyer plead a case, Brooks became convinced that "law was the greatest profession" and that he "was destined to become a lawyer."[21]

Not all courts held by the justices created such popular interest as the jury trials. Brooks's father "had to handle all sorts of petty cases, but the most perplexing were the friction and abuses involving domestic relations—friction between husband and wife." He often heard "their troubles," then advised them privately in order to spare the family the legal fees that they could ill afford. Years later, Brooks recalled one couple who regularly disturbed the peace with their family brawls. He described the man as a drunkard and a shrewd horse trader and the wife as a "slatternly quarrelsome woman." One night, after an especially violent row in which the wife had been badly abused, Squire Brooks decided to terminate these disturbances by an immediate trial. Within a few minutes the culprit was brought to the Brooks home, where the back porch served as a courtroom. The Squire began "to outline the case, to name the penalty which might mean a jail sentence, the effect on his [the culprit's] crops, and a heavy fine with its effect on the family." Soon the man and his wife were weeping, whereupon Squire Brooks offered to stop the proceeding if the man promised to cease beating his wife and remain sober and the woman promised to "strive to be a better wife." They agreed and "made their marks" on two elaborate documents.[22]

The justices of the peace in Lenoir County assembled on the first Mondays in January and June at the county seat to hold sessions of the inferior court. This meant that Squire Brooks had to travel to Kinston, which was fifteen miles from his home. Young Gene accompanied his father on these trips and looked forward to the "drive to

21. Brooks, "The Education of a North Carolinian," p. 26.
22. *Ibid.*, pp. 24-26.

Kinston on First Mondays." By the time he and his father reached Kinston their buggy was filled with hitch-hikers. Young Brooks usually sat in the courtroom while the court was in session, and what he saw further bolstered his determination to become an attorney. But the courtroom was by no means the only place of interest for him in Kinston. The ice factory and the North Carolina and Atlantic Railroad were for Gene Brooks objects of great fascination. Occasionally, he was able to see these Kinston marvels other than on first Mondays, because he sometimes rode to Kinston in his father's wagons sent for farm supplies when low water prevented river transportation between Grifton and New Bern.[23]

The town of Grifton also played an important role in Brooks's early life. Indeed, this was a town that he was able to observe in the process of growth. He later declared that as a youth he watched the decline of certain communities in favor of others possessing "more of the factors that promote progress." According to him, the financial failure of the country store was usually the first sign of a community's decline. Certainly, he witnessed the "passing" of the once prosperous community of Edward's Bridge, which first lost its store, then its school and church. This was followed by the removal of its families to the thriving community of Bethel. During Brooks's adolescence Bethel underwent a similar change in favor of nearby Bell's Ferry. This hamlet, located on the banks of Contentnea Creek in Lenoir and Pitt counties, grew rapidly for a few years after the federal government made the Contentnea navigable. Steamboats traveled regularly between New Bern and Bell's Ferry. Frank Pittman started the first passenger boat service between the two towns; and his young relative, Gene Brooks, probably made his first trip to New Bern aboard the *Cobb*.[24]

Bell's Ferry, containing such industries as saw-milling and cotton-ginning, soon became a commercial center for a rather wide area. In 1883 the village was incorporated; six years later its name was changed to Grifton. The growth of the town, especially after the erection of Methodist and Disciple churches there, "drew interest

23. *Ibid.*, pp. 26-27; W. W. Dunn to E. J. Brooks, Aug. 21, 1883, E. J. Brooks Papers; Brooks, "A Half Century Ago," p. 2. See also George Nowitzy, *Norfolk: The Marine Metropolis of Virginia and the Sound and River Cities of North Carolina* (Norfolk, 1889), pp. 180-183.
24. Brooks, "The Education of a North Carolinian," pp. 32-33; *Kinston Free Press*, Industrial Issue of 1906; interview with Mrs. Anna Pittman Purvis, June 10, 1956.

from Bethel." The units of the Masonic lodge and Farmers' Alliance at Bethel soon moved to Grifton, while the large general store near the wharf, owned by a Cicero Griffin, profited from the failure of the country stores at Edward's Bridge and Bethel. Despite the apparent decline of Bethel, the Brooks family remained there until Squire Brooks purchased a house in Grifton about the turn of the century.[25]

One economic advantage of Cicero Griffin's store over many rural stores was its large stock of alcoholic beverages. By 1880, when the liquor question had become a state-wide issue, many local acts of the legislature prohibited the sale of alcohol in country stores near schools and churches. At that time Cicero Griffin possessed a kind of monopoly on the sale of liquor in the area. According to Brooks, people in his locality considered liquor necessary as medicine, "and nearly everybody took his dram and joked about prohibition." The agitation about the liquor question in Lenoir County, especially among church groups, was not chiefly concerned with the medicinal uses of alcohol, but with the "sorry social spectacle" produced by numerous drunkards. But in 1881 Contentnea Neck and Lenoir County joined other areas in defeating the state referendum on prohibition. Thus, Cicero Griffin continued his profitable liquor trade. His open bar with its convenient distillery was frequently the scene of riotous gatherings and noisy brawls.[26]

One autumn day in the late 1870's Brooks walked to Grifton on an errand for his father and, after transacting his business, wandered into the bar at Griffin's store. His encounter there with two notorious drunkards proved to be his introduction to the liquor problem and reinforced the instruction in the evils of alcohol that he had already received from his sober parents as well as at school and church. In the classroom he studied works by prohibitionists and entered declamation contests on temperance subjects. His personal sobriety and support of prohibition movements in later life apparently owed much to his early experiences with the liquor problem in Lenoir County.[27]

25. *Kinston Free Press,* Industrial Issue of 1906; *Laws and Resolutions of the State of North Carolina, 1883,* pp. 762-763; Brooks, "The Education of a North Carolinian," p. 33; memoranda by Mrs. Glenn Brooks Mayberry, Oct. 6, 1956, and Mrs. Mary Edmonds Brooks Cobb, Oct. 6, 1956.

26. Brooks, "The Education of a North Carolinian," pp. 15-17; Daniel Whitener, *Prohibition in North Carolina, 1715-1945* (Chapel Hill, 1945), pp. 60, 233.

27. Brooks, "The Education of a North Carolinian," pp. 17-19.

For nineteen years the social, political, and economic activities of the rural community of Bethel formed a significant part of Brooks's education. He later insisted that "the forces that promote development are so many that only a few have been classified . . . as educative, but the unclassified are and have been more influential than the classified." Indeed, he felt that these unclassified educational forces in Contentnea Neck were far more influential in his early development than the formal education that he received from schools that compared favorably with similar institutions in other parts of the state.[28]

[3]

The public schools in Lenoir County as elsewhere in North Carolina were exceedingly poor during the late 1870's. In fact, little progress was made in the field of public education in the state from 1876 to 1890, the period of Brooks's early education. This was an era in which people were preoccupied with other needs and interests. Only a small group of individuals remained loyal to the cause of public education, and their efforts were frustrated by a poverty-stricken people unwilling, perhaps unable, to pay the taxes necessary for efficient schools. This popular apathy or hostility was fostered by various legacies of Reconstruction and by the continuing idea that public schools were charity institutions.[29]

Brooks's formal education began in a private school located on the family farm. A public school was conducted somewhere in the community, but according to Brooks, "it was too common for us to attend." Therefore, Squire Brooks and several relatives established a private school, first in an abandoned store building and later in a vacant log house on the Brooks property. They employed the Squire's sister-in-law as the teacher. In this so-called dame's school, young Brooks, his older sister, and their cousins began their formal education.[30]

28. *Ibid.,* p. 1.
29. *Ibid.,* p. 20; M.C.S. Noble, *A History of the Public Schools of North Carolina* (Chapel Hill, 1930), pp. 383-397.
30. Brooks, "The Education of a North Carolinian," p. 7.

After several years of private education, Gene Brooks attended Phillips Public School, which was located almost two miles from his home. This free school was a log structure about sixteen feet square, with a large fireplace at one end, a door at the other, several windows with wooden shutters, and long plank benches without backs. The school had no sanitary facilities or drinking water, and the nearest residence was a mile away. The children at the school quenched their thirst from a nearby stream, and Brooks found "it thrilling to lie down flat and let the water ripple past your nose and mouth . . . or dip it up in your cap." Unfortunately, he found the school work uninteresting and largely unintelligible because of the long hours of recitation. So intense was his dislike for it that he contrived all sorts of schemes to avoid going to school at all. About the only part of the school activities that he enjoyed was the frequent play periods necessitated by crowded conditions.[31]

At Phillips School, Brooks was introduced to his first reader. Previously, his main burden had been Webster's Blue Back Speller. His efforts in learning to spell caused him "days of anguish" and resulted in his being slapped by the teacher. The fact that he "simply could not spell" posed difficulties for him in reading, while the punctuation exercises caused him almost as much pain as a spelling bee. "I read nothing that impressed me," he later confessed, "and I was censured for bringing *John Halifax* to school." However, he did like the exercises in sentence diagramming and was proficient in arithmetic and geography, his favorite subjects. In spite of his difficulties in certain fields, one of his teachers at Phillips School often referred to him as "the brightest pupil" that she ever taught.[32]

About 1880 Squire Brooks and other prominent men in the Bethel Masonic lodge began considering means to improve the educational opportunities of their children. After several months of planning, they organized Bethel Academy and incorporated it under a board of trustees. Tuition rates were one dollar a month per pupil for the primary subjects and three dollars for advanced subjects, including algebra and Latin. For several years the school had one teacher, and never more than two. The academy attracted students

31. *Ibid.*, pp. 10-11; memorandum by Mrs. Mary Edmonds Brooks Cobb, Oct. 6, 1956.
32. Brooks, "The Education of a North Carolinian," pp. 7, 11; interview with Mr. John G. Dawson, Sept. 7, 1956.

not only from Bethel community, but from surrounding counties as well. Such students lived with families in the vicinity of the school.[33]

Squire Brooks as chairman of the academy trustees apparently bore the burden of establishing the school. He supervised the construction of the building and corresponded with President Kemp Battle of the University of North Carolina about securing a capable teacher. Upon Battle's recommendation, the trustees hired J. D. Murphy, a recent University graduate, as the first teacher in Bethel Academy. After establishing the school, Squire Brooks's duties consisted mainly of collecting the monthly tuition fees from the patrons. "Professor" Murphy as well as his successors lived in the Brooks home.[34]

Families with several children in school could not easily afford to pay the tuition fee. Therefore, Squire Brooks sought to remedy this difficulty by supporting a measure that would convert the academy into a free public school. In the Legislature of 1883 W. T. Dortch of Wayne County introduced a local option bill that Squire Brooks heartily endorsed. The Dortch Bill, which was enacted into law, provided that ten voters could request the county commissioners to put the question of a local school tax to a popular vote. When approved by the voters, the tax could not exceed twenty-five cents on the $100 valuation of property and seventy-five cents on the poll. Taxes collected from one race were to be used exclusively for the schools of that race. With the passage of the act, Squire Brooks immediately prepared to call an election in the Bethel school district. The election in the summer of 1883 resulted in the conversion of Bethel Academy into a public school. It had operated on this basis only five months, however, when the opponents of the local tax petitioned the county commissioners to call another election. Squire Brooks at once consulted State Superintendent of Public Instruction John C. Scarborough and assured him that the opposition was made up of "the ignorant and small taxpayers" who had created such a stir that the local tax "might be defeated." At this point the State Supreme Court settled the matter at least temporarily by declaring the Dortch

33. Brooks, "The Education of a North Carolinian," pp. 3, 12-13; *Kinston Free Press,* Industrial Issue of 1906.
34. Brooks, "The Education of a North Carolinian," pp. 12-13.

Act unconstitutional. Bethel Academy then resumed operation as a private school.[35]

The academy was located in the heart of Bethel community about a mile and a half from the Brooks farm. The building contained two stories: the upper story was a Masonic hall; and the lower floor, a large room with "high homemade desks." The academy stood in a grove of large oak trees near the Disciple and Primitive Baptist churches, a blacksmith shop, and a country store. For nearly ten years after the establishment of the school, Bethel was "the most cultured community in Contentnea Neck."[36]

Gene Brooks received the major portion of his precollege training in Bethel Academy. He left Phillips School and was present at the opening of the academy, which remained in much confusion for the first week owing to the presence of only one teacher to handle all the duties of the occasion. Thus, not until the fifth day did young Brooks recite his lesson; and then only upon his own request, evidence that his attitude toward school had changed. When he asked Mr. Murphy to listen to his recitation, the teacher "laughed, moved his false tooth up and down," praised his love of knowledge, and promised to grant his request.[37]

For eight years Brooks attended Bethel Academy, and after his initial difficulty apparently had few complaints about the infrequency of his recitations. His demonstration of intellectual ability in various fields won him the respect of both students and teachers. He excelled in mathematics and Latin and won several medals for his forensic skills. His education at the academy was broadened by his association with students from "distant" places in surrounding counties and by his visits in their homes. Reflecting upon his education at the academy, Brooks insisted that the value of classroom instruction was "almost zero," but "one distinct aid . . . in my educational work was the memory of the difficulties, the handicaps, the joys, and the successes of my youthful school days."[38]

35. *Ibid.; Public Laws and Resolutions of North Carolina, 1883*, pp. 225-229; E. J. Brooks to J. C. Scarborough, June 3, 1884, Correspondence of the State Superintendent of Public Instruction, State Department of Archives and History, Raleigh, North Carolina. Hereinafter cited as S. P. I. Correspondence. See also *North Carolina Supreme Court Reports*, February Term, 1885, XLIX, 514.

36. Brooks, "The Education of a North Carolinian," p. 12.

37. *Ibid.*, p. 13.

38. *Ibid.*, pp. 7-9; *North Carolina Education*, XVI (June, 1922), 13; *Trinity Chronicle* (Trinity College Newspaper), Sept. 18, 1907.

Upon graduation from Bethel Academy, Brooks decided to enter Trinity College, a small Methodist institution in Randolph County. In 1887 the energetic and able John Franklin Crowell became president of this struggling college, and during the seven years of his administration the school underwent a remarkable transformation.[39] In the midst of this new era for Trinity, Brooks applied for admission. In mid-summer, 1890, he corresponded with Crowell concerning admission and the possibility of receiving financial aid. Brooks wrote that a small loan from Trinity was necessary for him to begin his college education, since "short crops and other misfortunes" made financial assistance from home impossible "for the present."[40] He might have added that the education of his sister Lucy, who read her valedictory at Greensboro Female College in 1890, had placed an additional expense upon the family. He assured Crowell that he desired "to enter the ministry," if he should go to college.[41]

President Crowell granted his request for a loan, and Brooks matriculated at Trinity College in September, 1890. The first glimpses of college life in such a distant place as Randolph County must have been rather frightening to him. But this "big country boy" possessed a pleasing personality that immediately won him a wide circle of friends on the campus. He was enthusiastic about his studies and responsive to the stimuli provided by the remarkable faculty at Trinity during Crowell's administration.[42]

Brooks concentrated his attention upon the liberal arts and seems to have abandoned the idea of becoming a minister shortly after he arrived at Trinity. Nevertheless, he retained his interest in religious affairs, particularly through the Young Men's Christian Association and the Methodist Church, which he joined while a student. But the various courses in history, economics, and English apparently consumed the major portion of his time and attention. His grades indicated that he excelled in these fields. During his freshman year he studied Roman history under Professor John Spencer Bassett,

39. See Nora Chaffin, *Trinity College, 1839-1892: The Beginnings of Duke University* (Durham, 1950); John F. Crowell, *Personal Recollections of Trinity College, North Carolina, 1887-1894* (Durham, 1939).
40. Eugene C. Brooks to John F. Crowell, July 15, 1890, Trinity College Papers.
41. *Ibid.*; Grifton Lodge No. 452 To Whom It May Concern, March 4, 1894, Brooks Papers (DUL).
42. Edwin Mims to W. B. Gatewood, Jr., April 19, 1956; interview with Mrs. Anna Pittman Purvis, June 10, 1956; E. C. Brooks to W. P. Few, Sept. 29, 1928, William Preston Few Papers (in the possession of the President of Duke University).

English under Professor J. L. Armstrong, and physiology under Professor W. H. Pegram. In his second year Brooks studied Greek, Latin, history, and mathematics and made superior grades in each. On January 1, 1892, he received permission to go "home to teach till April." The records do not disclose any information about his teaching position, but presumably it was in one of the schools in Contentnea Neck.[43]

Brooks returned to school in September, 1892, and resumed his studies at the new Trinity College plant in Durham. He took a room in the attractive College Inn, one of the new buildings. In this new environment he completed the last two years of his college education. In this period three professors wielded an especially significant influence upon him. One of these, Jerome Dowd, a professor of economic and mercantile sciences, became one of his favorite teachers and stimulated his interest in economic questions. Another was Edwin Mims, a young instructor in English, whose course in literature left a lasting imprint upon Brooks. He later insisted that Mims "kindled him." However, no member of the faculty had a greater influence upon him than Stephen B. Weeks, professor of history and government. Brooks took every course that Weeks offered and later said of him: "To him more than any other teacher the writer is indebted for his interest in history and historical research. As a teacher he was not generally popular. But that small group of men at Trinity College . . . received at his hands an interest in the cause and effect in history that constitutes most of the permanent furnishings of the mind that come down from the undergraduate period."[44]

Brooks became a charter member of the Trinity College Historical Society organized by Weeks in 1892. Dr. Charles G. Hill, a Baltimore physician and a native North Carolinian, gave $100 to be used as annual prizes for the two best papers written by seniors on some phase of North Carolina history. The prize was first offered in 1893.

43. Instructors' Reports, 1890-1892, John F. Crowell Papers, Duke University Library, Durham, North Carolina; Report of Attendance, Grades, Progress, and Conduct, 1891-1892, Trinity College Papers; interview with Mrs. E. C. Brooks, May 9, 1956.
44. *Trinity College: Catalogue and Announcements, 1893-94,* p. 8; Grade Book, 1893-1906, Central Records Office, Duke University; Trinity College Book: Courses for 1894, Treasurer's Office, Woman's College, Duke University; Edwin Mims to W. B. Gatewood, Jr., April 26, 1956; Edwin Mims, "Sixty Years in the Classroom," *Greensboro Daily News,* March 11, 1956; E. C. Brooks, "Stephen B. Weeks," *North Carolina Education,* XII (June, 1918), 12.

In the following year Brooks's senior thesis on "The Legal Status of Slavery in North Carolina" won first prize.[45]

The Hesperian Literary Society was another campus organization that played an important role in Brooks's college life. As a member of the society, he gained experience in public speaking, an art that later won him wide acclaim. His skill as an orator placed him among the most frequent speakers of the society. His orations included such topics as "Evaluation in Politics," "The Power of Solitude," and "The Legacy of Nations." Brooks served the organization in various other capacities, especially as a member of its library and fund-raising committees. Among the items listed in his bill of $9.55 for 1891-1892 were fines for such offenses as "lounging," "throwing paper on the floor," and "passing between the president and the speaker."[46]

In addition to the Hesperian Society, Brooks took part in several other campus groups, including the Trinity football squad. In 1892 the secret scholastic order called 9019 considered him for membership, but finally rejected his name. One of his most beneficial extracurricular activities was his work in college journalism. Brooks and his friend, W. W. Flowers, edited the "locals department" of the *Trinity Archive*, the college magazine. In this capacity they acted as reporters of local gossip and news items. Brooks also wrote full-length articles for the *Archive*. One of these, entitled "What Is Man?," was written in a flamboyant style with the apparent intention of conveying the impression of philosophical profundity. A second article, "Should the State Do More for Education?," touched a question that was to confront him many times in the future. He argued that North Carolina should raise the level of its elementary schools to the same degree of efficiency that had been achieved by the state-supported colleges. This, he said, could be accomplished without oppressive taxation. He argued further that the federal government should aid public education, because its taxes were derived from all the people, while only property owners paid state taxes. These articles, despite their lack of literary merit, indicated his

45. Nannie May Tilley, *The Trinity College Historical Society, 1892-1941* (Durham, 1941), pp. 18, 104; *The Trinity Archive* (March, 1894), p. 31; J. F. Crowell to Charles G. Hill, June 19, 1894, J. F. Crowell Letter-Press Book, Duke University Library, Durham, North Carolina; Minutes of the Trinity College Historical Society, 1892-1901, p. 20, Duke University Library, Durham, North Carolina.

46. Minutes of the Hesperian Literary Society, 1892-1893, Hesperian Literary Society Treasurer's Book, 1891-1895, Duke University Library, Durham, North Carolina.

interest in education and journalism, two fields of endeavor that would constitute a major portion of his life's work.[47]

By the time of his graduation from Trinity Brooks held a position of esteem and respect among professors and students alike. President Crowell assured Mrs. Brooks that her son's college record justified her pride in him. Brooks was among eight seniors chosen to deliver orations at the graduation exercises in 1894. His address on "Centralization in America" was a plea for a central government controlled by a strong middle class that was "neither drunk with wealth nor embittered with poverty." Following his oration, the graduation program was concluded with the conferring of degrees. On June 14, 1894, Brooks, standing very proudly on the platform in Stokes Hall, received his Bachelor of Arts degree from President John Franklin Crowell.[48]

[4]

At one time or another in his early life, Brooks entertained ideas of becoming a preacher, a lawyer, and a merchant. While at Trinity College, however, he became interested in journalism and decided to enter that profession upon graduation. Not only had he gained experience in this work on the *Trinity Archive,* but President Crowell desired "to put Trinity men into journalism as fast as we can." Crowell himself had edited an educational magazine and seems to have encouraged Brooks's ambitions.[49]

Brooks began his search for a job several months before his graduation. His first prospect was a position as an assistant to John W. Jenkins, the new editor of the *Durham Globe.* Although the salary was meager, Crowell advised Brooks to accept the position if it were offered, but apparently the offer was never made. Shortly afterward, his second prospect for a job appeared when the editorship

47. E. C. Brooks to W. H. Wannamaker, Dec. 21, 1936, Brooks Papers (DUL); Records and Minutes of the 9019, Trinity College Papers; E. C. Brooks, "What Is Man?," *Trinity Archive,* Feb., 1893, pp. 189-192; E. C. Brooks, "Should the State Do More For Education?," *Trinity Archive,* Dec., 1893, pp. 8-11.

48. J. F. Crowell to Mrs. E. J. Brooks, March 7, 1894, Crowell Letter-Press Book; *Trinity College Commencement Program, 1894;* E. C. Brooks, "Centralization in America," E. C. Brooks to Charles Edwards, May 23, 1934, Brooks Papers (DUL).

49. Crowell, *Personal Recollections,* p. 62; William K. Boyd, *The Story of Durham: City of the New South* (Durham, 1927), pp. 253-254; J. F. Crowell to E. C. Brooks, March 14, 1894, Crowell Letter-Press Book.

of the *Orphan's Friend* became vacant. This journal was published under the supervision of the Superintendent of the Masonic Orphan Asylum in Oxford, North Carolina. Brooks desired this appointment and secured a strong recommendation from President Crowell, who praised his "good judgment and ample energy," his loyalty and excellent business sense, and his college record and "apt way of rendering himself of the greatest service in general." Since the orphan asylum was maintained by the Masons, it was important that Brooks have the support of a local Masonic society. The Grifton Lodge, of which his father was then secretary, fulfilled this need by assuring the Asylum Superintendent that he was a "young man of unspotted character with exalted aspirations, determined to excel in whatever he undertakes." Despite these recommendations, Brooks failed to obtain the editorship of the *Orphan's Friend*.[50]

His difficulties in securing employment can be partially explained by the general economic condition of the country following the Panic of 1893. Brooks seriously considered buying a weekly paper, but lacked the necessary capital, although according to Professor Jerome Dowd, "many newspapers can be bought for a song." Actually, Dowd advised him to gain at least a year of experience before trying to purchase a paper. At any rate, Brooks was still without a job at the time of his graduation from college. He returned to Lenoir County and probably secured temporary employment in a local mercantile establishment.[51]

Not until late in the summer of 1894 did he find work in his chosen profession. In August of that year Josephus Daniels, then chief clerk in the Department of the Interior, purchased the Raleigh *News and Observer*. Daniels was widely known in North Carolina and for several years had published the *Free Press* in Kinston, where he came to know the Brooks family. Moreover, he was then friendly toward Trinity College and President Crowell, who recommended Brooks for a position on the staff of the *News and Observer*. Since Daniels was to remain as chief clerk in the Interior Department, he

50. J. F. Crowell to E. C. Brooks, March 14, 1894, J. F. Crowell to the Superintendent of the Oxford Orphan Asylum, March 19, 1894, Crowell Letter-Press Book; Grifton Lodge No. 452 To Whom It May Concern, March 24, 1894, Brooks Papers (DUL).

51. Jerome Dowd to E. C. Brooks, May 9, 1894, Brooks Papers (DUL).

needed an assistant to aid him with his editorial and managerial duties. He selected Brooks for this position.[52]

Brooks immediately moved to Washington and took a room in the Daniels home at 1311 H Street. "I hope he will take a good deal of work off me," Daniels declared, "and get more business for the paper." On August 24, 1894, Daniels presented Brooks with a letter of introduction which authorized him to collect all moneys due the *News and Observer,* to solicit subscriptions and advertisements, and to represent the paper "in any and all capacities." Brooks apparently also assisted Daniels in writing his column, "The Washington Letter," and reported various political events under the name of Washington Correspondent. In February, 1895, Daniels, having resigned as chief clerk in the Interior Department, devoted his full time to the newspaper, thereby removing the need for Brooks's services.[53]

In anticipation of this change Brooks resigned from the staff of the *News and Observer* and became affiliated with the *Wilson Mirror* in Wilson, North Carolina, in January, 1895. He probably secured this position with the backing of Daniels, who had formerly published a newspaper there. The *Wilson Mirror,* edited by George Blount and Howard Herrick, was a large weekly paper with a subscription rate of one dollar a year. On December 26, 1894, Herrick announced his retirement and advertised his half interest in the newspaper for sale. Brooks and John Gold, a member of a prominent Wilson family, purchased Herrick's interest. But they could not overcome the difficulties of a bankrupt paper encountering stiff competition from the *Wilson Advance.* After three months they dissolved their connection with the *Mirror* and divided their profits equally.[54]

Brooks left Wilson a week before the *Mirror* ceased publication on May 2, 1895, and returned to Washington, where he remained for two years. He lived with the Daniels family until they moved

52. Joseph Daniels, *Editor in Politics* (Chapel Hill, 1941), pp. 85-101; *New Bern Weekly Journal,* Nov. 3, 1892; Chaffin, *Trinity College,* pp. 402, 430, 503-504; J. F. Crowell to E. C. Brooks, Aug. 4, 1894, Brooks Papers (DUL); Josephus Daniels to Mrs. Josephus Daniels, Aug. 11, 1894, Joseph Daniels Papers, Library of Congress, Washington, D. C.

53. Josephus Daniels to Mrs. Josephus Daniels, Aug. 23, 1894, Josephus Daniels To Whom It May Concern, Aug. 24, 1894, Daniels Papers.

54. Josephus Daniels, *Tarheel Editor* (Chapel Hill, 1939), pp. 182-188; *Wilson Mirror* (Wilson, North Carolina), Dec. 19, 26, 1894, May 2, 1895; interview with Mrs. E. C. Brooks, June 19, 1956; *State School Facts,* XIX (July, 1947).

back to Raleigh. Anticipating the failure of the venture in Wilson, Brooks had taken a Civil Service examination and received what the *Wilson Mirror* called "an appointment in the Treasury Department." But this position was not so grandiose as the *Mirror* suggested, for actually he had been appointed a watchman with an annual salary of $720. For Daniels' mother-in-law the most impressive feature of Brooks's new job was the "big long pistol" given to him "to use if necessary." Brooks was already an ambitious young man, and his position as a watchman could scarcely provide an adequate outlet for his aspirations.[55]

[5]

In 1897 Brooks returned to North Carolina, and the following January he secured an appointment as principal of the Kernersville Academy in spite of the fact that his teaching experience consisted only of a temporary job during his college days. The academy was "the central point" of Kernersville, a village in Forsyth County near Winston-Salem. The citizens of the town took great pride in their academy, which had been established in 1858 by a stock company and later brought under the control of the Methodist Church.[56]

Shortly after becoming principal, Brooks induced the trustees to enlarge the academy and to employ an additional teacher. He himself offered a variety of courses, including Latin and algebra. He was extremely popular with the students and townspeople and frequently participated in community activities. Under him the academy came to have the "flattering attendance" of fifty students, and one observer declared that through his influence the people of Kernersville were "more united on the subject of education than they had been in the years past."[57]

55. *Twelfth Report of the United States Civil Service Commission, July 1, 1894 to June 30, 1895*, Doc. No. 318, House of Representatives, 54th Congress, 2nd session, p. 87; *Wilson Mirror*, April 25, 1895; *Official Register of the United States Containing a List of Officers and Employees* (Washington, 1895), I, 51; Mrs. W. H. Bagley to Mrs. Josephus Daniels, April 27, 1895, Daniels Papers.

56. Brooks, "Autobiographical Sketch," p. 1; *Kernersville Messenger* (Kernersville, North Carolina), Sept. 8, 1898; D. P. Robbins, *Descriptive Sketch of Winston-Salem, Its Advantages and Surroundings, Kernersville, Etc.* (Winston, 1888), pp. 85-89; Adelaide Fries *et al., Forsyth: County on the March* (Chapel Hill, 1949), p. 132.

57. *Kernersville Messenger*, Sept. 8, 1898; interview with Mrs. E. C. Brooks, May 9, 1956; *Biennial Report of the Superintendent of Public Instruction in North Carolina, 1898-1900*, p. 134. Hereinafter cited as *Biennial Report*.

For Brooks, too, the year and a half in Kernersville proved to be decisive; for here he not only began his career in education, but met the young lady who later became his wife. Shortly after arriving in town, he became acquainted with N. W. Sapp, a prominent merchant and tobacco manufacturer as well as a trustee of the academy. Brooks taught one of Sapp's daughters and frequently visited in his home. There he met another daughter, Ida Myrtle, whom he found very attractive and charming. Soon he was seeing a great deal of her.[58]

In the midst of his courtship Brooks was offered the position of principal of the Ormandsville High School in Greene County, several miles from his childhood home. Under the circumstances it must have been a difficult decision for him to make, but he accepted the offer, which was to take effect in September, 1899. At the time, the state was under the control of a Republican governor elected by a combination of Republicans and Populists, known as Fusionists; and the eastern counties, including Greene, feared that the Negro would resume the place of political pre-eminence that he had held during Reconstruction. The Democrats, however, had regained control of the legislature in November, 1898. Brooks, of course, was a staunch Democrat and an admirer of Furnifold M. Simmons, the shrewd Democratic strategist.[59]

On September 4, 1899, Brooks assumed his new duties at the high school in Ormandsville, a village of forty inhabitants. Miss Bessie Harding was in charge of "primary work and music," while Brooks taught the advanced courses. The school attracted students from neighboring counties who came to live with families in Ormandsville. Parents were assured that the "moral as well as the mental instruction" would be "strictly looked after," and that their children would "meet the same parental care in this school as at home." Brooks himself lived with the Ormand family and took part in various community affairs. He undoubtedly participated in the special crusade initiated by the Greene County school superintendent to eradicate the local apathy toward education. The four months that he stayed in Ormandsville apparently were not marked by any extra-

58. Robbins, *Descriptive Sketch of Winston-Salem*, pp. 91-92; memorandum by Mrs. E. C. Brooks, Sept. 30, 1956; interviews with Mrs. E. C. Brooks, May 9, June 19, 1956.
59. *State School Facts*, XIX (July, 1947); interview with Mr. E. C. Brooks, Jr., July 12, 1956; William A. Mabry, *The Negro in North Carolina Politics since Reconstruction* (Durham, 1940), pp. 31-36.

ordinary experience, but he widened his circle of friends and fully enjoyed his life as a rural school teacher.[60]

Much as Brooks liked Ormandsville, he was always willing to consider a desirable promotion. Thus, in December, 1899, he accepted the position of principal of the Kinston Graded School. Kinston then possessed one of only twenty-seven such schools in the state. In contrast to the single room school with one teacher in charge of all pupils, the graded schools, which were generally supported by local taxation, classified children according to age and achievement, with a teacher for each grade. Such schools formed the few bright spots in the state's public educational system. The Kinston Graded Schools, established in the same year that Brooks became principal, contained nine grades with a term of eight months. Brooks's record at Ormandsville, which apparently impressed Kinston Superintendent L. C. Brogden, coupled with the fact that he was a "local boy," was largely responsible for his appointment. The position possessed obvious attractions other than a salary of fifty dollars per month, which was considerably more than his former salary. The local newspaper echoed the sentiments of the Kinston citizens when it declared that the trustees had "made a good choice in selecting Mr. Brooks principal."[61]

Brooks assumed his new duties in January, 1900. In addition to the administrative work, he taught classes in English and history in the high school. As elsewhere, he became "extremely popular" among students and townspeople alike. One of his students later recalled that he "was the most thorough teacher who ever taught me." He was especially interested in improving the library facilities of the graded school, and his efforts resulted in the building of a reputable school library. During his first few months in his new position, Kinston, like other towns in the state, was the scene of much political activity. The central issue was the constitutional amendment submitted to the voters by the Democratic legislature in 1900. According

60. *North Carolina Business Directory, 1897,* ed. Levi Ranson (Raleigh, 1897), p. 301; *Kinston Free Press,* Sept. 6, 1899; *Biennial Report, 1898-1900,* p. 112; memorandum by Mrs. E. C. Brooks, Oct. 24, 1956; B. L. Davis to W. B. Gatewood, Jr., Aug. 21, 1956.

61. Edgar Knight, *Public School Education in North Carolina* (Boston, 1916), pp. 323-324; Charles Dabney, *Universal Education in the South* (Chapel Hill, 1936), I, 189; *Kinston Free Press,* Jan. 15, 1900. Minutes of the Board of Trustees of the Kinston Graded Schools, Dec. 12, 20, 1899, Office of the City Superintendent of Schools, Kinston, North Carolina.

to Charles B. Aycock, the Democratic nominee for governor, the amendment was "drawn with the deliberate purpose of depriving the negro of the right to vote and of allowing every white man to retain that right." The amendment required that applicants for registration must have paid the poll tax and be able to read and write any part of the Constitution. It also included the "grandfather clause," which provided that no person who was entitled to vote before January, 1867, or the lineal descendants of such a person, should be denied the right to register and vote by reason of his failure to possess the literacy qualifications, provided that he registered before December, 1908. The Democrats coupled their pleas for the passage of the amendment with promises of a minimum four-month term for public schools in order to secure the white votes in areas where the Negro population was sparse. Aycock pledged his full support to universal education or, more specifically, to "the education of every illiterate white child in North Carolina." During the spring of 1900 the White Supremacy Club in Kinston, an effective Democratic propaganda agency, voiced strong approval of the suffrage amendment and provided public speakers to discuss the superiority of the "Anglo-Saxon race."[62]

There is little evidence that Brooks actively participated in these Kinston political gatherings, but there can be little doubt that he fully endorsed the amendment. Not only was he a strong supporter of Furnifold M. Simmons and Charles B. Aycock, the champions of the movement, but he undoubtedly recognized the importance of the strong political motivation to the existing agitation for public schools. Within two years he became associated with Aycock's efforts to fulfil the Democratic pledges regarding public education. Nineteen years later he wrote that "it was the suffrage amendment . . . providing an educational qualification for voting and the stirring campaign of Governor Charles B. Aycock that really aroused the

62. *Kinston Free Press*, Dec. 21, 1899, Feb. 24, March 30, April 16, 1900; interview with Mr. John G. Dawson, September 7, 1956; R. D. W. Connor and Clarence Poe, *The Life and Speeches of Charles Brantley Aycock* (Garden City, 1912), p. 81; Mabry, *The Negro in North Carolina Politics since Reconstruction*, p. 59; Lefler and Newsome, *North Carolina*, pp. 522-523; *News and Observer* (Raleigh, North Carolina), May 2, 1900; William B. Hamilton, "Duke University and the Schools: The First Century," *The Duke University Centennial Conference on Teacher Training*, ed. William B. Hamilton and William H. Cartwright (Durham, 1953), p. 10. Hereinafter cited as Hamilton, "Duke University and the Schools."

state to the necessity of providing an adequate public school system."[63]

Brooks resigned from his position in the Kinston Graded School
before the passage of the amendment and the election of Aycock.
Although the trustees had re-elected him principal, he could hardly
afford to reject an offer to become superintendent of the graded
schools in Monroe. Upon his departure from Kinston, the *Free Press*,
unsparing in its praise, declared that despite his short tenure, he had
won the confidence of the people.

The new position in Monroe would not be without its difficulties
for Brooks. The graded schools there had been organized in June,
1900. Two unsuccessful attempts had previously been made to pass
a local tax for such schools, and in 1900, when the tax was finally
enacted, there was still strong opposition to it. Thus, the successful
establishment of the Monroe schools required a man who combined
intelligence and energy with abundant tact. The school trustees
made a fortunate choice in selecting Brooks. One observer later recalled that the citizens of Monroe soon realized that he "was the
right man, at the right place, at the right time."[64]

Brooks succeeded in establishing the graded schools on a sound
basis and in eradicating the opposition to the local tax. In his work
he was supported by trustees, whom he described as "progressive
men" fully aware that "teaching is a progressive science." His main
problems resulted largely from inadequate financial resources. The
Monroe schools were maintained by a special poll tax of $1.20 and a
special property tax of forty cents on the $100 valuation of property.
The citizens considered this a heavy tax and desired to reduce the
rate, but Brooks managed to prevent any reduction and to secure
donations from the Peabody Fund to carry the schools "safely over
the critical period." Under his administration the school system contained a white school of ten grades and a Negro school of seven
grades. Both were in session thirty-six weeks and enrolled a total of
711 pupils. The average daily attendance in the white school was
356 pupils and in the Negro school, 129. The ten white teachers re-

63. Eugene C. Brooks, "North Carolina's New Educational System," *South Atlantic
Quarterly*, XVIII (Oct., 1919), 279. See also E. C. Brooks, "Charles Brantley Aycock,"
South Atlantic Quarterly, XI (July, 1912), 279-282.
64. Minutes of the Board of Trustees of the Kinston Graded Schools, May 3, June
30, 1900; *Kinston Free Press*, June 15, 16, 1900; *News and Observer*, June 4, 1902;
memorandum by Mrs. Virginia N. Crowell, July 31, 1956.

ceived an average annual salary of $430, while the Negro faculty of two, later increased to three by Brooks, was paid an average annual salary of $213.75. The total expenditures for Brooks's first year were $11,086.14, and by 1901 the value of the graded schools' property had increased to $20,000.[65]

Brooks received a salary of $1,000, which was more than double his Kinston salary. In Monroe he devoted five hours per week to teaching and twenty-five hours to supervision. A primary aim of his administration was to secure well-trained teachers. He absolutely refused to permit an incompetent person to remain on his faculty, a policy fully supported by the trustees. By the end of his first year in Monroe, Brooks realized that the salaries of his teachers were "insufficient to retain or secure the best teachers in the state." He therefore persuaded the trustees to raise these salaries and to employ no teacher without normal school training and at least two years of experience in graded school work. He continually reminded the trustees that teaching required skill and previous training in order for the profession to receive "a higher consideration in the estimation of the public mind."[66]

Brooks, moreover, constantly sought ways of improving the organization and facilities of the Monroe schools. After his first year he observed that several students, ranging from the first to the tenth grades, who failed to complete the entire work of their respective grades, had to spend the next year in the same grade or pass over the work that they had not finished. He induced the trustees to employ two assistant teachers to give "delinquent students an opportunity of advancing as their ability demanded" and "the quicker students an opportunity of passing from one grade to another without being held back with the whole grade until the end of the year." In addition to this successful innovation, he introduced music and drawing in the lower grades and made instruction in the industrial arts the basis of the curriculum in the Negro school. Brooks emphasized the necessity of an exchange of ideas among his teachers and insisted that

65. *News and Observer,* June 4, 1902; *Sketches of Monroe and Union County,* ed. A. M. Stack and B. F. Beasley (Charlotte, 1901), p. 61; *Biennial Report, 1900-1902,* pp. 234-235; *Biennial Report, 1902-1904,* pp. 74-75; T. F. Toon to E. C. Brooks, March 25, 1901, E. C. Brooks to J. Y. Joyner, March 11, 1902, S. P. I. Correspondence.
66. Stack and Beasley, *Sketches of Monroe and Union County,* pp. 61-62; interview with Mrs. E. C. Brooks, June 19, 1956; memorandum by Mr. John R. Welsh, July 4, 1956; *Biennial Report, 1900-1902,* p. 234.

the teachers should be informed of the latest educational developments. Mainly for this reason, he held twenty teachers' meetings annually. Moreover, he initiated in Monroe, as in Kinston, a movement for better library facilities, and by the end of his first year there the graded school library contained six hundred volumes. In 1901 the city aldermen established a public library, and Brooks persuaded them to make the library a part of the graded school with the superintendent as librarian. Under this arrangement the library received an additional two hundred books before he left Monroe. His activities in the library movement attracted the attention of the officials of the State Literary and Historical Association, and he was appointed to its committee on libraries in 1902.[67]

Brooks's efficient administration of the graded schools coupled with his attractive personality won him a place of "high esteem" with the people of Monroe. One of his students at Monroe who became a figure of national prominence later wrote: "He was a fine teacher and a splendid administrator and gave the new graded schools a good start. . . . I regard him as one of the greatest educational statesmen that North Carolina has produced and I shall always be grateful to him for the influence that he had on my life."[68] The same qualities that endeared Brooks to the people of Monroe were rapidly winning him a place of recognition in the educational circles of the state. In 1902 he was elected vice-president of the North Carolina Teachers' Assembly, the state-wide teachers' association organized in 1883. In the same year his former employer, Josephus Daniels, declared editorially in his influential newspaper that Brooks was "one of the most capable, successful, and cultivated educators in the state."[69]

In January, 1902, Daniels published in the *News and Observer* a series of articles by Brooks on "the public school question." These articles were especially pertinent at the time, in view of Governor Aycock's efforts to fulfil his campaign pledges concerning public education. Brooks wrote that the chief defects of the state school

67. Stack and Beasley, *Sketches of Monroe and Union County*, p. 62; *Biennial Report, 1900-1902*, pp. 234-235; *Biennial Report, 1902-1904*, p. 75; *News and Observer*, June 4, 1902; Alex J. Field to E. C. Brooks, March 25, 1902, Brooks Papers (DUL).

68. Memorandum by Judge John J. Parker, Sept. 15, 1956. See also John J. Parker to E. C. Brooks, April 2, 1930, Brooks Papers (DUL).

69. *The Morning Post* (Raleigh, North Carolina), June 14, 1902; Charles L. Smith, *The History of Education in North Carolina* (Washington, 1888), pp. 177-178; *News and Observer*, Jan. 5, 1902.

system were incompetent teachers, inadequate equipment, and "lazy" county superintendents, all of which resulted largely from the lack of financial support. According to him, much of the responsibility for insufficient school income lay with the State Supreme Court, which had ruled that public education was not a necessary expense. His bold criticisms of the court included its decision in the Barksdale Case of 1885, which held that county commissioners could not levy a special tax in excess of the constitutional tax limitation in order to maintain the constitutional requirement of a four-month school term. Brooks also severely criticized the public-school curriculum for its failure to take into account the social and economic environment of the children. "Education should equip for service," he declared, and agriculture, the chief source of state income, should have a prominent place in the school curriculum. "If education makes one dissatisfied with the country," he wrote, "then the education is wrong." He insisted that the entire school system must be changed in order to provide an effective program of rural education, which, he believed, required the consolidation of rural school districts into larger units.[70]

Shortly after the publication of these articles, Brooks had occasion to discuss various aspects of public education with James Y. Joyner, the new State Superintendent of Public Instruction. Joyner was appointed on February 24, 1902, following the death of T. F. Toon, an old Confederate veteran who had been elected on the Democratic ticket in 1900. Joyner was a native of LaGrange, a village in Lenoir County near Brooks's childhood home. He had been professor of English in the State Normal and Industrial College at the time of his appointment as State Superintendent. Shortly after Joyner took over his new job, Brooks invited him to speak in Monroe on the subject of consolidation of school districts. Brooks wrote: "I have been trying to interest the people around Monroe in a plan to consolidate contiguous districts, making the Graded School the high school of the several districts, but the force is not sufficient. I believe that you can do us good." Although Joyner was unable to go to Monroe, he assured Brooks that he would appreciate suggestions from him "about the work in the state."[71] Within a short time

70. *News and Observer*, Jan. 5, 12, 19, 1902.
71. E. C. Brooks to J. Y. Joyner, March 11, 1902, J. Y. Joyner to E. C. Brooks, March 15, 1902, S. P. I. Correspondence.

the two men became partners in charge of the most extraordinary educational campaign in the history of the state.

In the meantime Brooks had continued his romantic interests in the young lady whom he had met while teaching in Kernersville Academy. Fortunately, he was able to visit her in Kernersville rather frequently; otherwise she would have had great difficulty in determining his intentions, because his numerous letters were scribbled in his almost illegible handwriting. Despite this handicap in communication, Brooks made himself understood and married Miss Ida Sapp on December 19, 1900. The ceremony was performed in "the beautifully decorated parlors" of her home. The bride, described as "one of the most charming young ladies in Kernersville," was dressed in "an elegant gray traveling suit." Brooks, then twenty-nine years old, stood a little more than five and a half feet and possessed a rather rotund figure. His hairline was already receding, but his dark eyes retained a youthful twinkle. After a two-week wedding trip, the couple returned to Monroe, where Brooks resumed his duties in the graded schools.[72]

The vivacious young Mrs. Brooks immediately became a popular figure in Monroe. She liked people and conversed fluently, even with strangers. She took great pride in her husband's work and was desirous of his advancement. As Brooks's public appearances and other engagements increased, it was his wife who "got him there." Not only was she responsible for the preparation of food necessary for Brooks's rather excessive appetite, but also for the bountiful meals served to their frequent guests. She persuaded her husband to give up smoking a pipe only to find that he resorted to cigarettes. The increasing quantity of cigarettes that he smoked gave her reason to regret the decision about the pipe.[73]

The couple remained in Monroe two and a half years after their marriage. These were happy years for them. Their first child, a girl, was born on October 12, 1901. They named her Martha Eleanor after Brooks's mother. The second child, Eugene Clyde, Jr., arrived

72. *News and Observer,* Dec. 21, 1900; interview with Mrs. E. C. Brooks, Jan. 25, 1957; Medical Record of Dr. E. C. Brooks, Hist. No. 5162, 5/11/31, Duke Hospital, Durham, North Carolina.

73. Interviews with Mrs. E. C. Brooks, May 9, 1956, and Mr. E. C. Brooks, Jr., July 12, 1956.

on January 31, 1903. The third Brooks child, Sarah Voss, was born two years later in Goldsboro. Brooks, a devoted family man, took every step within his means to provide for the welfare and happiness of his wife and children. He was never interested in accumulating a large sum of money and gave little attention to the particulars of family finance except for an infrequent reminder to his wife about the payment of an insurance premium. Mrs. Brooks was the financial manager of the family and from the beginning of her married life shared a joint bank account with her husband.[74]

On March 10, 1903, Brooks resigned his position in Monroe to become an assistant to State Superintendent Joyner. In this office he would receive an annual salary of $1,500. The trustees of the Monroe schools regretted losing him, and their chairman, Dr. S. J. Welsh, attempted in vain to find means of matching the salary of his new position. Welsh told the trustees that even if they did manage to retain Brooks by such a salary increase, they would not be able to keep him long, because he was "better than a $1500 man." The *Monroe Journal,* undoubtedly expressing the sentiment of a majority of the townspeople, declared that Brooks was a "most competent and thorough schoolman" who had given "Monroe a school of which she is very proud." In April, 1903, Mrs. Brooks and the children moved to Kernersville for the summer and joined Brooks in Raleigh late in August.[75]

74. Brooks Family Bible; memorandum by Mrs. E. C. Brooks, Sept. 30, 1956; interviews with Mrs. E. C. Brooks, May 9, 1956, and Mr. E. C. Brooks, Jr., July 12, 1956. See also W. C. Dula and A. C. Simpson, *Durham and Her People* (Durham, 1955).

75. Memorandum by Mr. John R. Welsh, July 4, 1956; *Monroe Journal* (Monroe, North Carolina), March 17, 1903.

Two: THE RISE OF AN EDUCATIONAL LEADER, *1903-1907*

[1]

On January 15, 1901, "immense throngs of people" gathered on the Capitol grounds in Raleigh to witness the official return to power of the Democrats in North Carolina. At noon the stately Charles B. Aycock appeared on the flag-draped rostrum in front of the Capitol Building to deliver his inaugural address as Governor of North Carolina. After a bitter indictment of his predecessor's administration, Aycock launched into a discussion of the suffrage amendment, which he insisted did "no injustice to the negro" and possessed "no taint of the inequality provided against by the Fifth Amendment." Then, moving to the closely related subject of education, he reiterated his campaign pledge "to make at least a four months' term in each year in every school district in the State" and noted the "importance of educating white and black alike." He declared that an educational revival was absolutely necessary in order to make good the campaign promise to "poor and unlettered men" that their children who reached the legal age after 1908 would possess the literacy requirements for voting. When Aycock stepped from the rostrum on that sunny January day, white supremacy was assured for at least the next eight years.[1]

Those who were to lead the educational campaign that Aycock referred to in his inaugural address faced a tremendous task. At that time public education was in an exceedingly backward state. First of all, the state lacked a unified system of education; schools were purely local in character without uniformity of standards, courses of

1. *Morning Post*, Jan. 16, 1901; Poe and Connor, *Life and Speeches of Charles B. Aycock*, pp. 229-235; Mabry, *The Negro in North Carolina Politics since Reconstruction*, p. 73.

study, teacher qualifications, textbooks, equipment, and grades. There were more than 8,000 separate school districts, each of which was supposed to have a school; but 800 had no school at all. The average value of a schoolhouse was less than $200; 829 were log houses. Many schools closed in winter, because the children could not be kept warm. Most of them had one teacher and an average daily attendance of about thirty pupils. Out of a total school population of 674,215 in 1901-1902, only 314,817 white children and 149,-278 Negro children were enrolled in school. The average school term was 82.4 days for whites and 76.15 for Negroes. This average included the longer term schools of thirty-eight towns and eight local tax districts. The total value of all school property was $1,146,000, and the total expenditures for public education in 1901 were about $1,300,000. The average monthly salary of teachers was $26.78 for whites and $22.19 for Negroes. The amount expended per child in North Carolina was $3.17, whereas that for the United States as a whole was $20.29. The state ranked tenth in illiteracy, with 47.6 per cent of its Negroes and 19.5 per cent of its native whites classified as illiterate.[2]

During the fight for the suffrage amendment, the Democrats had promised to rectify these poor educational conditions. Obviously, they would concentrate upon the white schools. The Legislature of 1901 made an appropriation named the *second* $100,000 to distinguish it from the *first* annual fund of $100,000 begun in 1899 and distributed on the basis of school population. In order for a county to receive aid from the *second* $100,000, called the equalizing fund, it must have reached the constitutional limit of taxation and still be unable to maintain a four-month school term. For twelve years after 1901, the size of this equalizing fund remained unchanged. In 1901 the General Assembly also made provisions for the establishment of rural libraries. Two years later, it reorganized the State Literary Fund by making available $200,000 as loans for building and improving schools. The same legislature took steps to make the Depart-

2. W. H. Plemmons, "Extension and Equalization of Educational Opportunity in the South," *Secondary Education in the South,* ed. W. C. Ryan, J. Minor Gwynn, and Arnold King (Chapel Hill, 1946), pp. 20-21; *Biennial Report, 1900-1902,* pp. 292-293, 334-335; Poe and Connor, *Life and Speeches of Charles B. Aycock,* pp. 114-116; Newsome and Lefler, *North Carolina,* p. 503; Mabry, *The Negro in North Carolina Politics since Reconstruction,* p. 74.

ment of Public Instruction equal in dignity and equipment to the other state departments.[3]

Shortly after the close of the legislature of 1901, Governor Aycock and State Superintendent Toon began mapping plans for carrying out the Democratic educational policy. They soon realized, however, that a general campaign to arouse public opinion in favor of public education would require considerable financial resources which the Governor did not have at his disposal. At this point an outside agency called the Southern Education Board came to Aycock's rescue. This organization, created late in 1901, grew out of the Conference for Christian Education in the South, which first met in Capon Springs, West Virginia in 1898. Later, the Conference underwent changes in leadership and scope of interest, and its name was changed to Conference for Education in the South. The movement soon won the support of numerous Northern philanthropists and Southern educators. The executive committee of the Conference, called the Southern Education Board, was responsible for creating public support for schools and for handling financial gifts. The Board was able to carry out its program through the generous financial assistance of John D. Rockefeller's General Education Board, George Foster Peabody, and others. The philanthropists acquiesced in Negro disfranchisement, and the Southern Education Board provided Aycock with the funds for his educational campaign.[4]

A convention in Raleigh on February 13, 1902, presided over by Governor Aycock, launched the campaign in North Carolina. This gathering of forty-three men, representing all phases of education in the state, was called at the suggestion of Charles D. McIver, president of the State Normal and Industrial College and a prominent member of the Southern Education Board. The conference adopted an address to the people entitled "A Declaration Against Illiteracy," which was a frank admission of educational conditions and a plea for popular support for public schools. The conference outlined a plan

3. Fred Morrison, *Equalization of the Financial Burden of Education Among the Counties in North Carolina: A Study of the Equalizing Fund* (New York, 1925), pp. 10-11; Knight, *Public School Education in North Carolina*, pp. 337-339.

4. Poe and Connor, *Life and Speeches of Charles B. Aycock*, pp. 118-119; Louis R. Harlan, *Separate and Unequal: Public School Campaigns and Racism in the Southern Seaboard States, 1901-1915* (Chapel Hill, 1958), pp. 79-81; Rose Howell Holder, *McIver of North Carolina* (Chapel Hill, 1957), pp. 212-213.

of the campaign that was to be conducted under the direction of the Central Campaign Committee for the Promotion of Public Education in North Carolina. This committee was composed of Aycock, McIver, and Toon, who was succeeded by James Y. Joyner when he became State Superintendent on February 24, 1902.[5]

[2]

Eugene C. Brooks, superintendent of the Monroe Graded Schools, was among those attending the Raleigh meeting in February, 1902. He participated in all three sessions of the conference, endorsed the "Declaration Against Illiteracy," and became a member of the committee "to request the clergy of the state to preach one sermon each year on the subject of education." The aims of the educational campaign as outlined by the conference were local taxation, consolidation of school districts, improvement of schoolhouses, and longer school terms. These aims, endorsed by conferences in Greensboro and Charlotte, were almost identical to those suggested by Brooks the previous month in his articles in the *News and Observer*.[6]

The appointment of Joyner as State Superintendent held new opportunities for Brooks. Joyner was impressed by his efficient administration of the Monroe schools and by his sincere interest in all public school questions. Brooks, moreover, availed himself of every occasion to cultivate Joyner's friendship and to share his progressive ideas with him. Undoubtedly Joyner's influence was responsible for Brooks's appointment as executive secretary of the Central Campaign Committee for the Promotion of Public Education when it opened its headquarters in Raleigh in June, 1902. E. W. Knight, an educational historian who later knew Brooks intimately, wrote: "Though a young man Mr. Brooks was rapidly becoming recognized as a wise and progressive school man, and to his work he brought rare industry, resourcefulness, sound judgment, and earnest-

5. Knight, *Public School Education in North Carolina*, pp. 331-332; Holder, *McIver*, pp. 214-215.
6. *Morning Post*, Feb. 14, 1902; Knight, *Public School Education in North Carolina*, p. 333.

ness which were soon to place him in the foremost ranks of educational leadership in North Carolina."[7]

The educational campaign in North Carolina actually began in
June, 1902. Brooks as executive of the Central Campaign Committee
was responsible for publicity and for finding speakers for local rallies.
He issued bulletins emphasizing the advantages of local taxation,
consolidation of rural school districts, and the improvement of school
buildings. He occasionally released statistical statements on school
conditions and wrote brief articles for newspapers and journals. In
an article in the *Progressive Farmer* on the consolidation of school
districts, he insisted that the merger of several small districts into one
district with one large school, an efficient faculty, and a longer term
was more economical and provided "better instruction." He maintained that "a fourth of the schools are run contrary to law," because
they were operating for less than four months a year, and their districts contained less than the minimum school population required
by law.[8]

Brooks's main concern, however, was to find outstanding speakers
who would address rural gatherings for the purpose of inducing a
vote for local taxes and for the consolidation of small school districts.
He succeeded in securing a large corps of volunteer speakers including men of every profession and business and of every political faith
and religious creed. The first local rally, held in Wentworth in Rockingham County, was rather typical of many others during the summer
of 1902. Through Brooks, the Rockingham County officials arranged
to have ex-Governor Thomas J. Jarvis and Dr. Charles D. McIver
speak on the occasion. Before an audience of two thousand people,
Jarvis, who would never again "solicit the suffrage of the state" for
himself, implored his listeners to improve their public schools
through local taxation in order to give their children a "glorious"
future. Then, after a bountiful picnic and a concert by the Third
Regiment Band from Reidsville, Dr. McIver stirred the crowd with a

7. E. C. Brooks to J. Y. Joyner, March 11, 1902, J. Y. Joyner to E. C. Brooks, March
15, 1902, S. P. I. Correspondence; Knight, *Public School Education in North Carolina*,
pp. 33-34.
8. E. C. Brooks, *What Is Being Done For the Improvement of the Schools* (pamphlet); *Morning Post*, July 3, 11, 26, 29, 1902; *Greensboro Patriot*, July 2, 1902; E. C.
Brooks, "Consolidation of School Districts," *Progressive Farmer*, XVII (July 15, 1902),
7.

forceful address on the practical advantages of local taxation and consolidation of districts.[9]

From his office in Raleigh, Brooks organized scores of similar rallies in about thirty counties during June and July, 1902. After correspondence or conferences with county school officials and other interested persons in various sections of the state, he would send speakers to address these local audiences. The successful management of this state-wide campaign was obviously no easy task; but according to Joyner, Brooks directed the entire program with skill and efficiency. Within three months after Brooks completed the summer campaign, fourteen rural districts had adopted local taxation by popular vote; and elections were pending in twenty-four other districts. Upon his departure for Monroe on August 10, 1902, the *Morning Post* declared that he had "done efficient and valuable work in the office of the State Superintendent and has had charge of planning the educational campaign."[10]

After his return to Monroe, Brooks remained in close touch with State Superintendent Joyner, who sent him final reports on the results of their summer work. Joyner insisted that their efforts had been successful and assured him: "You will always be a welcome visitor in my office."[11] Late in 1902 Brooks conferred with Joyner about the problem of grading and classifying public schools, which he had planned to discuss before the Association of County Superintendents but had not on account of illness. At the request of the county school officials, Brooks attempted to grade and classify a school at a Union County teachers' meeting. After studying the difficulties and possible solutions to the problem, he wrote Joyner:

No grading or classifying will be practical or put into operation by the poorly informed teachers which does not deal exclusively with the texts they are required to use, regardless of what supplementary literature the expert would be glad to see them use. I believe here is where the [teachers'] institute holders made serious mistakes: by, once a year, lecturing on literature that is new to them, the teachers, instead of taking up the text that the law requires them to teach. . . . As to grading: it seems to me that there should be some authority somewhere to say how many subjects shall be taught in each school, depending of course on the

9. Knight, *Public School Education in North Carolina*, p. 334; *Biennial Report, 1900-1902*, pp. 380-381.

10. *Biennial Report, 1900-1902*, pp. lx-lxi; *Morning Post*, Aug. 10, 1902.

11. J. Y. Joyner to E. C. Brooks, Oct. 20, 1902, S. P. I. Correspondence.

length of the term, etc., and what the courses shall include. If the school
has only seven grades or classes and each class has four recitations, that
gives twenty-eight recitations a day—enough to tax the ingenuity of an expert. Now classify according to readers. At the end of four months, the
time has been insufficient for the beginner to complete the first reader and
so on throughout the seven grades. . . . You see, to lay down a course of
study is easy, to finish it is another thing.[12]

Joyner welcomed these suggestions by urging Brooks to assist him in
preparing a "workable course of study." But he felt that there was
"not much chance" to perfect a standard course of study and method
of grading except through the county superintendents, who in many
instances were incompetent political appointees. Joyner concluded
his letter to Brooks by saying: "I shall always be glad to hear from
you and will appreciate any suggestions that you make, . . . for I
know your heart is in this great work."[13]

In the spring of 1903 Brooks resigned his position as head of the
Monroe Graded Schools in order to accept Joyner's offer to become
chief clerk in the department of loans, rural libraries, and course of
study in the State Superintendent's office. At the same time he retained his job as executive secretary of the Central Campaign Committee and managed to get an increase in salary from the Southern
Education Board for this work. The combined salary of these two
positions was about $1,500, which was considerably more than he was
paid in Monroe. Brooks wrote Joyner:

I had a talk with Dr. McIver in regard to salary. I requested him to
make the status of my position as strong this year as possible, even if he
made only a nominal appropriation after this year. My object in this was
that my change would appear to the greatest advantage and exalt my
position as much as possible; and he agreed then to add $400 to the
amount allowed me by the state and if possible he would make it $500.
That accounts for the newspaper reports that the position pays $1500.
You understand that the public values a man by the salary that he re-
ceives, and while publicity is being given, I prefer to go on record as a
$1500 man.[14]

The trustees of the Monroe Graded Schools permitted Brooks to
leave on May 1, 1903, provided he would return to "wind up the

12. E. C. Brooks to J. Y. Joyner, Nov. 11, 1902, S. P. I. Correspondence.
13. J. Y. Joyner to E. C. Brooks, Nov. 19, 1902, S. P. I. Correspondence.
14. E. C. Brooks to J. Y. Joyner, March 11, 1903, S. P. I. Correspondence.

work" in the schools in June. During this month he gathered information on local taxation for McIver's report to the Southern Education Board and prepared for the forthcoming educational campaign.[15]

The summer campaign of 1903 was more intensive than the one of the previous year. By April 13, 1903, Brooks had received so many requests for speakers at local educational rallies that he declared: "It seems the whole State is going to vote on graded schools from the letters I have been receiving." The request from Duplin County insisted that the people of that area were "asleep and had been for over a hundred years, and it will require someone with a stentorian voice to arouse them." The petition from Person County read: "This county needs about two Walter Pages. If you have any men of that stamp, please send them." The major obstacle to local taxation in Davie County was the "apathy and indifference" of the people; whereas in the black belt counties, it was "the Negro problem."[16]

In order to fulfil these numerous requests, Brooks enlisted the services of additional speakers, especially college presidents. Congressman Robert N. Page also consented to participate in the movement and declined any pay for his traveling expenses. Some county boards of education refused to sanction educational rallies, because they believed, quite wrongly, that the county rather than the Southern Education Board should bear the expenses. Such misunderstandings, which necessitated corrections, placed additional work upon Brooks. The most popular speakers were Aycock, McIver, and Joyner, whose oratory seemed to possess a magnetic appeal. The superintendent of Martin County schools explained that these three men with their exalted reputations could arouse the people, although "the educational interest has not reached that point where the people will come out to hear a speaker through their interest in education solely."[17] It was difficult for Brooks to determine the areas in which

15. J. Y. Joyner to E. C. Brooks, March 12, 1903, J. Y. Joyner to E. C. Brooks, April 8, 1903, S. P. I. Correspondence; *Monroe Journal*, March 13, 1903.
16. S. W. Clement to E. C. Brooks, June 25, 1903, N. C. Newbold to E. C. Brooks, July 11, 1903, J. D. Hodges to E. C. Brooks, July 8, 1903, P. J. Long to E. C. Brooks, July 15, 1903, R. F. Beasley to E. C. Brooks, Sept. 9, 1903, James Y. Joyner Papers, University of North Carolina Library, Chapel Hill.
17. E. C. Brooks to George T. Winston, Aug. 12, 1903, F. P. Venable to E. C. Brooks, June 26, 1903, Charles Taylor to E. C. Brooks, June 24, 1903, R. N. Page to E. C. Brooks, June 22, 1903, S. R. Bateman to E. C. Brooks, Aug. 26, 1903, R. O. Everett to E. C. Brooks, July 18, 1903, Joyner Papers.

these three men could be most effective. When he asked McIver to speak in Valdese in June, 1903, for example, McIver replied: "I am not willing in my present physical and mental condition of weariness to strain myself to go two or three hundred miles simply for the entertainment of a little neighborhood gathering unless they are in earnest about voting the tax or unless there is some movement that will guarantee an effort in that direction."[18] As a result of such circumstances, Brooks was forced to send other speakers to substitute for McIver, Aycock, or Joyner. The blame for a disappointing speaker usually fell upon him.[19]

From May through September, 1903, Brooks both managed the publicity of the educational campaign and actively participated in some of the local rallies. He published lists of the speaking engagements in several large newspapers and periodically released statements on the progress of local taxation and consolidation. For the first week in July he arranged seventy-three addresses by sixteen prominent citizens; for the second week he scheduled eighty-two addresses. He also provided propaganda literature to areas anticipating local tax campaigns and advised county officials on the legal procedure of holding such tax elections. In addition, he traveled over the state observing at first-hand the varying educational conditions in different areas and delivered addresses on local taxation and consolidation in Craven and Union counties. He also took part in the annual meeting of the Association of County Superintendents in Raleigh, where he became acquainted with other school officials throughout the state.[20]

The results of the educational campaigns of 1902 and 1903 indicated that the work of Brooks, Joyner, McIver, and numerous others had been successful. Eighty-eight local tax districts were established, bringing the total to 174 in sixty-three counties. The number of school districts was decreased under consolidation by nearly 400, more than double the reduction in 1901-1902. More than 676 new schoolhouses were built from 1901 until November, 1903, and the

18. Charles D. McIver to E. C. Brooks, June 19, 1903, Joyner Papers.
19. F. B. Rankin to E. C. Brooks, June 20, 1903, Joyner Papers.
20. Charles D. McIver to E. C. Brooks, July 5, 1903, Harry Howell to E. C. Brooks, June 23, 1903, J. P. Long to E. C. Brooks, ?, S. M. Brinson to E. C. Brooks, June 12, 1903, F. C. Allen to E. C. Brooks, June 23, 1903, Joyner Papers; *Morning Post*, May 2, June 28, July 4, 14, 1903; *State School Facts*, XIX (July, 1947); *Proceedings of the State Association of County Superintendents, 1903*, p. 27.

average length of the school term reached 16.7 weeks, "the high water mark in the history of the State." The average salary of teachers increased $1.58 per month for whites and forty-four cents for Negroes. In addition to this statistical evidence, the letters of appreciation from local officials must have stirred Brooks's pride in his work.[21] The superintendent of schools in Davie County, where even Joyner had failed to elicit any enthusiasm for public schools in 1902, wrote Brooks: "The speeches [in 1903] were fine, carrying conviction. Several representative men including old bachelors have said to me they have always opposed local taxation before hearing these men, and that now they favored it and would work for the principle."[22]

In the spring of 1904 Brooks announced that he was planning another vigorous campaign for the forthcoming summer. These plans were changed after he consulted the Central Campaign Committee, and on June 5, 1904, he announced that since the people would be preoccupied with political elections during the summer and fall, the Committee had decided "not to wage so vigorous an educational campaign as before." But he prepared lists of speakers available upon request from local school officials desiring to hold rallies. The summer campaigns in behalf of public education continued for several years, but the intensity of those initial campaigns directed by Brooks was never surpassed. The efforts of Aycock, Joyner, McIver, and Brooks between 1902 and 1905 started an educational movement in North Carolina that gradually turned the school ideal into a public opinion that expressed itself in taxation and ultimately produced a reputable system of public schools.[23]

At the same time that Brooks managed the educational campaigns, he carried out the duties of his permanent office in the State Department of Public Instruction. His title as chief clerk of the department of loans, rural libraries, and course of study did not mean that his work was confined to these fields. He was in effect Joyner's deputy and assisted with numerous projects undertaken by the State Superintendent's office. For example, he was responsible for the

21. J. Y. Joyner, *A Year's Progress in Public Education and the Work Yet to Be Done* (Raleigh, 1903), pp. 7-10, 13.
22. J. D. Hodges to E. C. Brooks, July ——, 1903, Joyner Papers.
23. *Morning Post*, April 10, June 5, 1904. See also Newsome and Lefler, *North Carolina*, p. 552.

educational exhibit at the State Fair in 1903 and for the distribution
of leaflets on school progress among the crowd there. Apparently he
relieved Joyner of many of those small, yet necessary, tasks that confront a State Superintendent.[24]

One important aspect of Brooks's regular duties concerned the
distribution of the State Literary Fund for building and improving
schools. This fund of $200,000, created in 1903, was derived largely
from the sale of swamp lands owned by the State Board of Education.
Loans from the fund were made to the county boards of education,
payable in ten annual installments, bearing interest at the rate of 4
per cent. Under the rules for the distribution of the State Literary
Fund only half of the cost of new schools or the improvement of old
schools could be borrowed, and no loans were made to districts with
less than sixty-five children of school age unless such districts contained unusually sparse population or insurmountable natural bar-
riers. In the distribution of the funds, Brooks was instructed to give
preference to rural districts, large districts formed by consolidation,
and districts with local taxation.[25]

As soon as the Legislature of 1903 established the State Literary
Fund, the counties began to request loans. The numerous inquiries
received by Joyner during March led him to insist that Brooks leave
Monroe by May 1. Shortly after Brooks went to Raleigh, he was
flooded with applications for loans; but the inadequate reports submitted by many counties delayed the distribution of the funds.
Finally, he began the apportionment of the loans on July 15, 1903,
in order that local school officials might build and improve their
schools before the beginning of the next school term. Within eight-
een months he had lent $120,580 to 70 counties to build 228 new
schoolhouses. The amounts of these loans to the individual school
districts varied from $30 to the Lovelace district in Wilkes County
to $5,000 to Randleman in Randolph County.[26]

Brooks's work also included supervision of the schoolhouses
constructed or improved through aid from the State Literary Fund.
In order to receive a loan, the local districts had to agree to build

24. *Morning Post*, Oct. 31, 1903.
25. *Biennial Report, 1902-1904*, pp. 16-18; *Morning Post*, June 2, 1903.
26. J. Y. Joyner to E. C. Brooks, March 12, 1903, J. Y. Joyner to E. C. Brooks, April
14, 1903, Joyner Papers; John Ferrell to J. Y. Joyner, Sept. 17, 1903, S. P. I. Correspondence; *Morning Post*, May 26, July 11, 1903; *Biennial Report, 1902-1904*, pp. 19, 568-570

schools which cost at least $250, in accordance with plans approved by the State Department of Public Instruction. Brooks was responsible for insuring the execution of these regulations. His efforts to promote the construction of schoolhouses according to "principles of modern school architecture" apparently were successful. In 1904 Joyner reported: "In nothing has progress been more marked than in the character of public schoolhouses." Brooks also worked closely with the Woman's Association for the Betterment of Public School Houses and Grounds, which was organized in 1902. The purpose of the Association was to arouse public opinion in favor of better school buildings and to issue estimates of the costs of constructing and improving schools. Brooks represented the Department of Public Instruction at the meeting of the Association in 1903 and participated in the discussions on school construction. He considered the organization a distinct aid to him in promoting a school program over the state.[27]

In June, 1903, Brooks attended the annual meeting of the Teachers' Assembly at Wrightsville Beach. In addition to being vice-president of the Assembly, he served on the Committee on Legislation and the Committee on Correlation, both of which were of considerable importance. He delivered an address on "School House Building," which demonstrated his ability to attain a certain eloquence even when speaking about architectural principles. He urged county officials to plan their school buildings with a view toward "the preservation of the health and that which pertains to the moral and aesthetic growth of the child." He then outlined in detail the plans for such a school. "I hold it as a fundamental truth," he concluded, "that no child should be taught in a building that is less decent than his home."[28]

The second part of Brooks's work in the State Department of Public Instruction concerned rural libraries. He had previously demonstrated his interest in libraries by his activities in Kinston and Monroe. In 1901 the legislature appropriated $5,000 to encourage

27. *Biennial Report, 1902-1904,* pp. 19-22, 568-570; *Morning Post,* May 7, June 2, 1903; E. C. Brooks, "Women Improving School Houses," *World's Work,* XII (Sept., 1906), 7937-7938; R. D. W. Connor, *The Woman's Association for the Betterment of Public School Houses in North Carolina* (Raleigh, 1906), pp. 1-44.
28. Eugene C. Brooks, "School House Building," Brooks Papers (DUL); *Program of the North Carolina Teachers' Assembly, 1903; Morning Post,* June 13, 1903; Charles L. Coon to E. C. Brooks, June 16, 1903; Joyner Papers.

the establishment of libraries in rural schools. According to this measure, when "friends" raised ten dollars and the county board of education contributed ten dollars, the state would then add another ten, which made a total of thirty dollars to start a small library. Brooks was in charge of distributing the state funds for this purpose and of compiling lists of appropriate books for rural school libraries. In selecting these books he secured the advice of Professor Mims, who had taught him literature in Trinity College. For those schools just starting libraries, Brooks compiled a list of eighty-four books, annotated and classified according to school grades, which could be purchased for thirty dollars. Another list of thirty-six volumes was designed for existing libraries that intended to expand their facilities under the legislative act of 1901. Brooks also published a pamphlet in which he outlined several methods for using a library effectively. He was responsible in part for the success of the rural library movement between 1902 and 1904, a period in which 410 libraries were established in rural schools with 50,675 volumes, bringing the total number in the state to 877.[29]

Closely related to Brooks's official activity for the improvement of public school libraries was his private interest in that direction. He had become a member of the library committee of the State Literary and Historical Association in 1902, a body that continued to attract his attention. A year later, he joined a group of prominent Raleigh citizens who were interested in North Carolina history. In December, 1903, they formed the North Carolina History Club with Secretary of State J. Bryan Grimes as president and Brooks as secretary. Other members included Clarence Poe, editor of the *Progressive Farmer;* George T. Winston, president of North Carolina College of Agriculture and Mechanic Arts; and H. G. Connor, Justice of the State Supreme Court. These men attempted to organize similar clubs in other cities in the state and assisted the Department of Public Instruction in the preparation of literature to be used in the celebration of "North Carolina Day" in the public schools, a day authorized by the legislature in 1901 for the consideration of state history. The

29. *Biennial Report, 1900-1902,* pp. 198-200; Edwin Mims to E. C. Brooks, June 18, 1903, Joyner Papers; E. C. Brooks, *Thirty Dollar Library: Selected and Graded* (pamphlet); E. C. Brooks, *A Fifteen Dollar Supplementary Library* (pamphlet); E. C. Brooks, *Suggestions As to the Use of the Library in School* (pamphlet); *Biennial Report, 1902-1904,* pp. 6, 24.

purpose of these annual programs was to arouse pride in the history of the state and inspire confidence in its future.[30]

The third aspect of Brooks's official duties in the Department of Public Instruction dealt with the course of study in public schools. In 1902 he had discussed with Joyner the problem of adjusting the courses to the length of the school term and to the textbooks required by law. A course of study for the first seven grades prepared by Brooks and his friend, Charles L. Coon, in 1904 sought to harmonize these factors. They emphasized the close correlation between the mechanics of reading, literature, and spelling taught in the first three grades and between geography, nature study, and formal history, which was to begin in the fourth grade. Their course of study was based upon state-adopted textbooks and included books for teachers and suggestions for daily programs in a seven-grade school with one teacher. Superintendent Joyner strongly recommended this course of study for adoption by every county board of education.[31]

In November, 1903, Brooks explained his ideas on the course of study before the Association of Colleges and Preparatory Schools of the Southern States. This organization, established in 1895, was dedicated to the cause of raising educational standards among colleges and secondary schools in the South. The guiding genius of the crusade was Chancellor James H. Kirkland of Vanderbilt University. At the ninth annual session of the association, which met at Trinity College on November 4-6, 1903, Brooks delivered an address on "Rural High Schools in the South." He insisted that most of the high schools in the South were little more than "four years of interregnum" between elementary school and college, "in which time the imagination of the teacher may run riot, inject anything under the sun that is not offensive to the patrons, and omit whatever his or her lagging spirit finds undesirable." He believed that this situation resulted largely from the lack of any clearly defined course of study. Since each school was "practically a law unto itself," it was impossible for any Southern state to have a uniform course of study

30. Alex J. Field to E. C. Brooks, March 25, 1902, Brooks Papers (DUL); *Goldsboro Daily Argus* (Goldsboro, North Carolina), April 27, 1906; W. J. Peele to E. C. Brooks, Nov. 24, 1903, Brooks Papers (DUL); *Morning Post,* Dec. 19, 1903; *Biennial Report, 1902-1904,* pp. 15, 196-197.

31. E. C. Brooks and Charles L. Coon, *Elementary Course of Study* (Raleigh, 1904), pp. 1-24.

supervised and enforced by a single authority. Nevertheless, Brooks thought that the high school curriculum should include instruction in "practical" as well as "purely intellectual" subjects. Emphasizing the fact that 80 per cent of the public high schools in the South were rural, he insisted that their courses of study should be geared to the needs of rural people and should devote especial attention to agriculture.[32]

The fifteen months that Brooks spent in the Department of Public Instruction contributed significantly to his rise to prominence. It provided him an opportunity to view the educational system of the state from a peculiar vantage point and to gain experience in handling administrative problems. His travels over the state as executive secretary of the Central Campaign Committee afforded him a first-hand knowledge of school conditions in various areas. As a functionary in the Department of Public Instruction, he participated in the activities of several influential educational organizations and became acquainted with local school officials in all parts of the state. Above all, he gained the enduring respect and admiration of Superintendent Joyner, a valuable asset for future years.

[3]

On September 26, 1904, the board of Trustees of the Goldsboro Graded Schools accepted the resignation of their superintendent, Thomas R. Foust, who became head of the Guilford County schools. The next day Brooks applied for the office vacated by Foust. The Goldsboro position carried a great deal of prestige in addition to a salary of $1,500. Goldsboro had established one of the first graded schools in North Carolina and by 1904 had developed a model school system under the guidance of a succession of able superintendents including Edwin Alderman, later president of three Southern universities; P. P. Claxton, a United States Commissioner of Education; and James Y. Joyner. Brooks undoubtedly considered the superin-

32. Eugene C. Brooks, "Rural High Schools in the South," *Proceedings of the Ninth Annual Meeting of the Association of Colleges and Preparatory Schools of the Southern States* (Nashville, 1904), pp. 102, 106-108.

tendency of the Goldsboro schools a definite promotion over his present job.[33]

At the time that Brooks applied for the position, several influential friends strongly recommended his appointment. Governor Aycock, a former trustee of the Goldsboro schools, wrote the board of trustees: "I know Mr. Brooks well and can say that he is an excellent man in every way and in my opinion well qualified for the position of Superintendent." In a similar vein Joyner praised Brooks's work and expressed regret in losing his "valuable services," but concluded: "My knowledge of Mr. Brooks and of his work warrant me in recommending him with confidence as one of the best equipped men for the work of a successful superintendent that I know." Nothing, however, surpassed the "unqualified endorsement" expressed by the trustees of the Monroe Graded Schools, who described Brooks as "a man in every way qualified to discharge the duties of a superintendent." Other letters of recommendation lauded his executive ability and personal character.[34]

Brooks was appointed superintendent of the Goldsboro schools early in October, 1904, and was succeeded in the Department of Public Instruction by R. D. W. Connor, principal of the Wilmington Graded School. After moving his family to Goldsboro on November 1, Brooks wrote Joyner: "I wish to take this opportunity to express again my appreciation because you let me come to Raleigh and because you assisted me in leaving."[35] Shortly after his appointment, Brooks assumed direction of the Goldsboro schools which employed twenty-two white and nine Negro teachers. Nearly three-fourths of the white teachers possessed college diplomas and normal training. There were five school buildings having a total value of $66,000, four for whites and one for Negroes. The schools were scheduled to open on October 10, 1904, but a diphtheria epidemic caused a postponement of two weeks. As a result of this delay the schools operated only 149 days in 1904-1905, an unusually short term for Goldsboro.

33. *Goldsboro Daily Argus*, Sept. 27, 1904; E. C. Brooks to the Chairman of the Board of Trustees, Sept. 27, 1904, Brooks Papers (DUL); *Biennial Report, 1904-1906*, pp. 71, 77; Knight, *Public School Education in North Carolina*, p. 313; Poe and Connor, *Life and Speeches of Charles B. Aycock*, pp. 112-114.

34. Charles B. Aycock to A. C. Davis, Sept. 27, 1904, J. Y. Joyner to the Trustees of the Goldsboro Graded Schools, Sept. 27, 1904, H. B. Adams to the Trustees of the Goldsboro Graded Schools, Sept. 27, 1904, Charles D. McIver to E. B. Borden, Sept. 27, 1904, Brooks Papers (DUL).

35. E. C. Brooks to J. Y. Joyner, Nov. 2, 1904, S. P. I. Correspondence.

Otherwise, Brooks's first year in Goldsboro seems to have been a successful one. During the year he used part of the school fund of $19,677.81 for repairing school property, holding teachers' institutes, and taking a school census. The four white schools had an enrollment of 1008 pupils and an average daily attendance of 707; the enrollment of the Negro school was 636 and the average daily attendance was 277. The schools closed on May 18, 1905. Dr. J. B. Carlyle of Wake Forest College was the commencement speaker at the white graded school. According to the *Goldsboro Argus,* "Mr. E. C. Brooks, the very efficient, popular, and lovable superintendent, delivered the prizes and diplomas." From this date until Brooks left Goldsboro the *Argus* fully endorsed his work and always described him in superlatives.[36]

During the summer of 1905 Brooks conducted several teachers' institutes in the vicinity of Goldsboro, while Mrs. Brooks and the children were in Kernersville. These summer institutes provided instruction for several weeks for teachers in service who were unable to attend one of the summer normal schools. The purpose of the institutes was to raise the qualifications of the teachers. In addition to his institute work, Brooks joined the local tax campaign conducted by the Central Campaign Committee under Executive Secretary R. D. W. Connor. He first addressed a large crowd at Ebenezer in Wayne County. The *Goldsboro Argus* declared that he was "an interesting and entertaining speaker using the castaway of logic in argument and the acme of ornateness in diction . . . and those who do not let prejudice overrule their judgment will be benefitted by having heard him." Other speaking engagements took him as far away as Fair Bluff in Columbus County.[37]

In 1905 the Goldsboro schools opened on September 11. Brooks had added courses in domestic science and vocal music in the high school and had reorganized the high school curriculum to provide two courses of study from grades seven through ten—"one leading to college and the other leading to a more practical life." His objective here was to make "the course of study . . . broad enough to attract

36. *Biennial Report, 1904-1906,* pp. 71, 77, 103, 123, 131, 152, 176, 183; *Goldsboro Daily Argus,* Oct. 10, 24, 1904, June 1, 1905.
37. *Goldsboro Daily Argus,* May 11, 19, June 4, 1905; John Duckett to E. C. Brooks, Aug. 5, 1905, R. D. W. Connor to E. C. Brooks, Nov. 2, 1905, S. P. I. Correspondence.

every child of school age." During his second year at Goldsboro, Brooks employed three additional white teachers and spent $200 for libraries, four times the amount spent his first year. Teachers also received a considerable increase in salaries. In 1905 he personally interviewed each new student, gave him an "admission card," and required that he be vaccinated. At the beginning of the second semester in January, 1906, seventy new students entered the graded schools, bringing the total enrollment well above that for 1904-1905.[38]

The improvements in the Goldsboro schools under Brooks attracted the attention of other school men. Professor N. W. Walker of the University of North Carolina toured the schools and was pleased with Brooks's work. William Underhill, principal of the Kinston Graded School, also inspected the schools and "was much impressed by the up-to-date methods used." In May, 1906, the *Goldsboro Argus* reviewed Brooks's work and concluded: "The Goldsboro Graded School is recognized as one of the foremost schools in the state and we have cause to be proud of the work of this noble institution. . . . Professor Brooks is an able, competent, and successful superintendent and he has as able a corps of teachers as can be found in the state." The solid foundation of the Goldsboro schools laid by previous superintendents, the liberal financial resources, and the support of a favorable public opinion enabled Brooks to practice his educational ideas in a way that would not have been possible elsewhere.[39]

After the closing of the schools in May, 1906, Brooks resumed his summer educational work. Mrs. Brooks and the children again spent the summer in Kernersville in order to escape the excessive heat of the coastal plain. After a brief visit with his parents in Grifton, Brooks traveled to Raleigh to attend the Teachers' Assembly. For the following several weeks he delivered a series of lectures in the summer school for teachers at North Carolina College of Agriculture and Mechanic Arts. Shortly before returning to Goldsboro early in July, he declared that this was "by long odds the most successful

38. *Biennial Report, 1904-1906*, pp. 192, 202, 217; *Goldsboro Daily Argus*, June 1, Aug. 29, Nov. 18, 1905, Jan. 2, 1906.
39. *Goldsboro Daily Argus*, Nov. 8, 9, 1905, May 14, 1906.

summer school ever held in the state." For the remainder of the summer, he probably conducted teachers' institutes.[40]

With the opening of the Goldsboro schools on September 10, 1906, Brooks again personally interviewed and placed each new student in a certain grade. The school year 1906-1907 witnessed a noticeable increase in the average daily attendance and an additional rise in teachers' salaries. The school fund at Brooks's disposal that year was almost $3,000 more than that for 1904-1905. Thus, he was able to raise salaries and to establish a book rental system, a considerable innovation by which students could rent books for small fees. Apparently, he never permitted his numerous administrative duties to interfere with his personal interest in and supervision of teaching and classroom problems. One teacher later said of him: "He had a sympathetic approach to the everyday problems and a delightful way of making a teacher do the best possible work. He seemed to know just what guidance and direction the individual teacher needed."[41]

While in Goldsboro, Brooks participated in local civic affairs and at the same time continued his activities in state organizations. He was a frequent speaker before the historical clubs in the town and shared with them the "stories and legends of North Carolina history which he knew so well." He was also deeply interested in the existing agitation over the liquor question and contributed liberally to a fund "to enforce prohibition." He conducted the work of the Child Study Department of the Goldsboro Woman's Club and presented a series of lectures to the Wayne County Teachers' Association. In 1906 he was elected a trustee of the Reformatory of the South, an organization that proposed to erect reformatories to accommodate 1000 children at a cost of $500,000. He played an "influential" role in the establishment of the Association of City Public School Superintendents, which was organized in 1904, and was scheduled to lead the discussion on "Reading" at its annual meeting in the following year.[42]

In December, 1904, Brooks received his first appointment to an

40. Interview with Mrs. E. C. Brooks, May 9, 1956; *Goldsboro Daily Argus*, June 20, 1906; *Raleigh Times* (Raleigh, North Carolina), July 3, 1906.

41. *Goldsboro Daily Argus*, Sept. 3, 18, 1906; *Biennial Report, 1904-1906*, pp. 14, 26, 42, 66; memorandum by Mrs. Clarence Wilkins, July 5, 1956.

42. *Goldsboro Daily Argus*, Nov. 8, 1905, Jan. 9, Feb. 12, April 19, 1906; J. Y. Joyner to Robert Ogden, Nov. 27, 1907, Joyner Papers; *Proceedings of the North Carolina Association of City Public School Superintendents 1905*, p. 8.

important national group, the Committee of Eight on History in the Elementary Schools. This committee was formed as a result of a discussion at the annual meeting of the American Historical Association in 1904, in which a conference on history in the elementary schools was conducted by Professor J. A. James of Northwestern University. Several persons read papers indicating approaches to the problem; and upon the request of the conference, the Executive Council of the Association appointed a committee of eight persons to recommend a history course for elementary schools. The committee was composed of outstanding historians, normal school professors, and public school officials, all of whom had manifested some interest in elementary school history. Brooks, apparently the Southern representative, had recently published (with Charles L. Coon) a course of study for elementary schools in which a prominent place was given to history.[43]

The appointing of a national committee to study a particular phase of the school curriculum was by no means an innovation in 1904. The practice had been employed for some years by the National Education Association and the American Historical Association, and the reports of these committees had, in some instances, wielded a strong influence over the program of studies in public schools. In 1896 the American Historical Association created the Committee of Seven which prepared a course in history for secondary schools. According to one authority, it was not until after 1900 that the forces aroused by the economic revolution of the nineteenth century began to seek means to equip the individual for the complex responsibilities of his social relationships. Citizenship became the keynote of the period, and history gained in popularity as particularly adapted to impart right social attitudes. An international viewpoint was encouraged, since the United States was a rising world power. Thus, against this background the Committee of Eight embarked upon its project to revise the history curriculum of the elementary schools.[44]

43. Committee of Eight, *The Study of History in the Elementary Schools: Report to the American Historical Association* (New York, 1909), p. v; *Annual Report of the American Historical Association for the Year 1904* (Washington, 1905), pp. 28-30, 55. Hereinafter cited as *Annual Report of A. H. A.*
44. See Henry Johnson, *Teaching of History in the Elementary and Secondary Schools* (New York, 1930), pp. 141-145; Bessie Pierce, *Public Opinion and the Teaching of History in the United States* (New York, 1926), pp. 43-44.

Brooks and the other members of the Committee held five meetings, sent out inquiries to officials in "typical" schools, and consulted
elementary teachers. Reports from the Committee were read at the
annual meetings of the American Historical Association in 1905 and
1906. The complete report published in 1909 stated: "Fundamental-
ly our plan is based on the proposition that the history teaching in
the elementary schools should be focused around American History.
But we do not mean to imply that American History signifies an
account of events alone that have occurred in America. Our aim is
to explain the America of today, its civilization, its institutions, and
its traditions." The European background to American history was
to receive special attention in grades six through eight. The Committee of Eight insisted that its course took into consideration "the
demands of the hour" and "the capacities of teachers." Recognizing
the needs of teachers, the Committee included in its report a full
syllabus for an eight-year course in history, with reference books and
modes of treatment. The work of the Committee revolutionized
history courses in many elementary schools in the United States.[45]

Brooks resigned his position in Goldsboro two years prior to the
publication of the Committee of Eight report in 1909 and accepted
the professorship in education in Trinity College. His administration
of the Goldsboro schools for three years was marked by higher teachers' salaries, expanded library facilities, a reorganized course of study,
and an increase in average daily attendance. His efficient operation
of the schools, coupled with his interest in community affairs, made
him popular with the citizens of Goldsboro. Five years after his
departure from the city, he was again offered the superintendency
of the graded schools. One trustee wrote him in 1912: "It is the
unanimous opinion of our people, especially of the members of the
Board who were serving when you were here, that your administration of our schools was the most successful we had ever had."[46]

45. Committee of Eight, *The Study of History in the Elementary Schools*, pp. ix-x,
98-99; *Annual Report of the A. H. A., 1905*, I, 22-23; *Annual Report of the A. H. A.,
1906*, I, 63-66; *Provisional Report on a Course of Study in History* (Washington, 1906),
pp. 1-39.
46. George C. Royall to E. C. Brooks, March 29, 1912, Brooks Papers (DUL). See
also memorandum by Mrs. Clarence Wilkins, July 5, 1956.

Three: THE COLLEGE PROFESSOR, 1907-1919

[1]

In the spring of 1907, Brooks was requested to establish and head a department of education at Trinity College. This institution, which had once been a state-chartered normal college, had not emphasized the training of public school teachers after coming under the control of the Methodist Church in 1859. In effect, Brooks was asked to revive its tradition of teacher training. To explain this request is by no means simple, considering the immediate past history of the college and the paucity of evidence available. Perhaps, a partial explanation lay with that paradoxical figure, John C. Kilgo, president of Trinity College.

When Kilgo became president of the college in 1894, the battle between state and denominational colleges in North Carolina was entering its fiercest stage. He joined the Baptists in their fight against free tuition at state-supported colleges, especially the University of North Carolina, and stumped the state in behalf of Christian education, which of course was to be secured at denominational, though not sectarian, schools. He insisted that all taxes available for education should go to the public schools rather than to the institutions of higher learning. Some considered his support of the legislative appropriation of $100,000 in 1899 to lengthen the public school term as an act hostile to the University. Yet Kilgo persuaded the Trinity trustees to endorse resolutions favoring the "free public schools" and raising the college's admission requirements, which naturally affected the high schools in the state. Moreover, a third of the Trinity graduates between 1894 and 1900 went into teaching, although the college offered no formal training for teachers. Kilgo later insisted that "the chief forces" behind the educational revival in North Carolina at the turn of the century were the religious denominations. A part of the paradox of this man was that he could retain a "skeptical and grudging attitude toward the public schools long after they had proved their usefulness," and at the same time contribute "a more practical and fundamental assistance to the rise of public education than all the efforts of all members of Trinity College before him."[1]

Shortly after the opening of the twentieth century, the denominational and state colleges reached a *modus vivendi,* and the public schools gradually improved under the impetus of increasing financial support. The Legislature of 1907 authorized the establishment of rural high schools and appropriated $45,000 annually for their maintenance. The growth of public schools naturally increased the demand for teachers; therefore the state expanded its normal schools at Cullowhee and Boone and established a new one in Greenville in 1907. President Kilgo undoubtedly saw in this situation possibilities for Trinity College. The high school law and other educational legislation arising from the Aycock campaign not only created a need for the training of public school teachers, but would eventually remove the utility of such college-affiliated schools as Trinity Park High School. Without doubt these factors played a significant part in Kilgo's decision to set up a department of education at Trinity College.[2]

Late in the spring of 1907 Kilgo wrote Brooks requesting advice on the establishment of such a department and strongly suggesting him as a candidate for the new professorship. The reason for the selection of Brooks can only be surmised. He was a Trinity alumnus and had retained a close contact with his *alma mater,* especially through alumni organizations. Moreover, his job in the State Department of Public Instruction and in Aycock's educational campaign, his experience as a teacher, principal, and superintendent, and his work with teachers' institutes eminently qualified him for the new

1. Luther L. Gobbel, *Church-State Relationships in Education in North Carolina since 1776* (Durham, 1938), pp. 132-171; Paul N. Garber, *John Carlisle Kilgo: President of Trinity College, 1894-1910* (Durham, 1937), pp. 47, 54-63, 82; Hamilton, "Duke University and the Schools," pp. 8-9; W. T. Laprade, "The Administration of President Kilgo," *Trinity Alumni Register* (April, 1922), pp. 5-18.
2. Gobbel, *Church-State Relationships in Education in North Carolina,* pp. 205-209; Knight, *Public School Education in North Carolina,* pp. 321, 340.

task at Trinity, although he had not been educated in a teachers' college. On May 27, 1907, Brooks wrote Kilgo:

I believe if Trinity College takes this move, and she will sooner or later, that it will be the most important step taken by the institution since it was moved from Randolph County. The work appeals to me strongly, in fact it is the kind of work that I have been planning since I entered the teaching profession.

If you think it probable that this department will be established and that my name will be considered favorably in connection with it, I would like to come to Durham and talk with you about the matter. At the outset this Department should be made equal in rank with any department in the institution. As to salary, it would I fear be impossible for me to consider a position on the terms mentioned in your letter. I tried for two years to live on that salary and found it impossible to do so. I mention that because if it is not possible to begin with $2000 I could not consider the proposition. This is what my present position here is paying me and I find at the end of each year, even on that salary, I am not becoming a plutocrat or bloated bond holder.[3]

Evidently Brooks and Kilgo had not discussed the matter prior to this exchange of letters. Kilgo's offer came "right out of a clear sky," according to Mrs. Brooks, who was glad to move to Durham to be nearer her parents' home and out of the summer heat of Goldsboro. Apparently the question of salary was settled satisfactorily, for Brooks was appointed to the newly established Chair of the History and Science of Education on June 4, 1907.[4]

Brooks purchased a lot and built a house in Durham near the college, which meant that he bore a considerable financial burden for several years. He had a room in it set aside solely for his own study and usually spent several hours there each night. After his son Gene entered the Durham schools, Brooks required him to come into the study to prepare his assignments. A bond of mutual confidence and intimacy always existed between the two. But when Gene rushed through his lessons too quickly, Brooks would give him a book to read. The boy soon decided that there was no need to hurry. Brooks also brought "dull" college students to the study in his home in order that he might give them special assistance.[5]

3. E. C. Brooks to J. C. Kilgo, May 27, 1907, Trinity College Papers.
4. Interview with Mrs. E. C. Brooks, May 9, 1956; *North Carolina Christian Advocate*, LII (June 13, 1907), 5; Schedule of Salaries, 1913-1915, Few Papers.
5. Interview with Mr. E. C. Brooks, Jr., July 12, 1956; *Trinity Chronicle*, Dec. 11, 1907.

In the meantime Brooks had established the Department of Education at Trinity College. According to the college catalogue, the purpose of the Department was " (1) to develop a greater appreciation of the school as an institution in the history of mankind; (2) to acquaint the student with the status of primary and secondary education of the present day; (3) to impart knowledge of educational psychology and methods of teaching; (4) to acquaint the students with the conditions and needs in North Carolina." For students desiring to elect the course in education, Brooks recommended that they take Professor William K. Boyd's Medieval Europe, Professor W. I. Cranford's General Psychology, and Professor W. H. Glasson's Social Institutions. These he considered necessary for a "full understanding of the influence of educational systems and methods in the development of our institutional life."[6]

In 1907-1908 Brooks offered three courses in education. One of these, the history of education, taught three hours per week, emphasized the purpose and effect of education from ancient Greece to the present. In this course Brooks was particularly concerned with the development of educational thought, the comparison of aims and methods in education, and the influence of social, political, and economic changes upon the curriculum. His course in educational psychology dealt chiefly with the application of psychological principles, the growth of the child, and methods of teaching. The third course offered by Brooks, entitled Secondary Education, was designed for teachers in service in Durham County and included a study of the high school curriculum and educational psychology. He met this class on Saturdays in order that Durham County teachers could attend. He was assisted by his colleagues in the subject fields: Boyd in history and William P. Few and Edwin Mims in English. In its first year the Department of Education enrolled six majors and twenty-two teachers in the Saturday classes.[7]

Brooks's work at the college immediately won him recognition from his former associates in the field of public education. In November, 1907, State Superintendent Joyner wrote Robert Ogden of the Southern Education Board that Brooks was destined "to do a great

6. *Annual Catalogue of Trinity College, 1907-1908* (Durham, 1908), pp. 90-91.
7. *Ibid.*, p. 91; Hamilton, "Duke University and the Schools," p. 11; *Trinity Chronicle*, Oct. 16, 1907.

work at Trinity," because he was "an enthusiastic schoolman" and "one of the most promising of the men engaged in public school work in the state." Joyner was convinced that Trinity College would become a "potent force" in the movement for better schools.[8] To be sure, Brooks remained in close contact with the public schools. He was in great demand as a speaker and availed himself of every opportunity to observe educational progress in various parts of the state. Between March 11 and May 13, 1908, he filled at least ten speaking engagements before teachers' associations in Forsyth, Guilford, and Caldwell counties, classes at the State Normal and Industrial College, and commencement audiences in Franklin and Johnston counties. Since these appointments kept him away from the college almost every weekend that spring, Professors Boyd, Mims, and Few conducted the Saturday classes for Durham County teachers.[9]

By this time Brooks had arrived at certain conclusions concerning the weaknesses of the public school system. He pointed out the existing defects in numerous addresses and publications. For example, at the meeting of the Association of Colleges and Preparatory Schools of the Southern States in November, 1908, he called for a realistic approach to actual problems confronting Southern schools, rather than futile discussions of academic questions. "We meet in our Southern associations," he declared, "and view with much alarm the number of electives in the high school and the possibility of a three-year college when we have neither a well-developed curriculum in the grammar schools, nor state systems of high schools, nor uniform college entrance requirements." Despite statements to the contrary, students in the second year of high school were permitted to enter many colleges. According to Brooks, this situation resulted from poorly organized high schools and the lack of aid from the colleges. He believed that the competition for patronage between colleges and high schools would continue "until the State Department of Education . . . established a sort of regency board over all, and requires the high schools to do their part in the great educational ladder and the colleges theirs." For him the real problem was the establishment of a uniform course of study in high schools and

8. J. Y. Joyner to Robert Ogden, Nov. 22, 1907, Joyner Papers.
9. *Trinity Chronicle*, March 11, 18, 25, April 22, 29, May 6, 1908.

a restatement, not necessarily an elevation, of college admission requirements. "Fix a standard," he implored the colleges, "and live up
to it." He emphasized that the problem of completing the educational ladder from the grammar school through the college level was
peculiar to the South, for the North had long passed this stage in its
development.[10]

Brooks was particularly concerned about the establishment of
high schools in North Carolina and sought to aid school officials in
achieving the maximum benefits from the high school law of 1907.
He pointed out several factors that he considered important to the
successful operation of high schools. First, there should be a strong
grammar school that adequately prepared students for high school
work. According to Brooks, 60 per cent of the high schools in the
state were "doing only two years' work," and "only a small per cent"
of the school children ever passed beyond the seventh grade. Second,
high schools should not suffer from a lack of organization. Brooks
insisted that the high school curriculum should be organized to fit
the mental capacity and needs of the child and that the recitation
method of teaching should give way to "quiet work in the classroom."
Moreover, the promoting and grading of children should take into
account their unequal capacities. Third, it was absolutely necessary
for more men to become high school teachers. In Brooks's opinion
at least half of the teachers should be men in order to attract more
male students and erase the common notion that the high school
was solely for females.[11]

Brooks's energetic efforts in behalf of public education during his
first year at Trinity College was prophetic of his future years as a
college professor. The academic cloister was by no means the sole
domain of this man of such diverse talents and interests; rather it
served as a home base. Within a year he had made notable progress
in establishing a real link between Trinity and the public schools.
President Kilgo's report to the board of trustees in June, 1908, indicated some of Brooks's achievements in his first year at the college.
Kilgo stated:

10. E. C. Brooks, "Problems of the Southern College," *Proceedings of the Association of Colleges and Preparatory Schools of the Southern States, 1907,* pp. 141-157.
11. E. C. Brooks, *Building a System of High Schools in North Carolina.* Bulletin of
the Trinity College Department of Education, No. 1 (Durham, 1908); *Trinity Chronicle,* May 13, 1908.

Mr. Brooks entered upon his work with enthusiasm and wisdom and has had remarkable success in getting the work organized. He has arranged and correlated the courses of study in his department with the courses of study in other departments, and has placed in the Library an excellent collection of books dealing with the subject of education. Under his direction and with the aid of the members of the faculty, there have been arranged courses opened to teachers who live near enough to Durham to attend weekly. This work was begun as an experiment, the aim of which is to benefit the teachers in the public schools. The results have been more than satisfactory, and with the experience of the present year the department will be able to arrange better courses for the future. Mr. Brooks has given much attention to securing information about educational work in our State and the amount of tabulated information which he has gathered is of great value.[12]

The obvious implication of Kilgo's statement was that through Brooks's efforts Trinity College was shifting from its narrow attitude toward public schools to a spirit of active cooperation.[13]

[2]

In the summer of 1908, Brooks conducted teachers' institutes in several counties. After a brief vacation with his family in Morehead City, he returned to Durham to prepare for the opening of the college in September. For the academic year 1908-1909, he expanded the work of his department by adding three new courses. Juniors and seniors were allowed to take his general history of education and a new course called "the science of education," which dealt with the evolution of the curriculum and the relation of the school to society. In addition to educational psychology, Brooks taught a course in school management and a Saturday class in secondary education for Durham County teachers. A history of culture covering the principal intellectual movements was offered jointly by the departments of education and history.[14]

One of Brooks's most successful experiments was his extension course for Durham County teachers, the first of its kind in North

12. *Report of the President of Trinity College to the Board of Trustees, 1908,* pp. 3-4.
13. Brooks, "Autobiographical Sketch," p. 2; Edwin Mims to W. B. Gatewood, Jr., April 26, 1956.
14. *Trinity Chronicle,* Sept. 16, Oct. 14, 1908; *Annual Catalogue of Trinity College, 1908-1909,* pp. 90-91.

Carolina. It was in fact so successful that in July, 1908, State Superintendent Joyner authorized Durham County teachers to substitute
extension work under Brooks for the summer institutes required by
law. Under his plan Brooks sent out weekly assignments to the
teachers and met with them periodically, at first weekly and later
monthly. On August 2, 1909, the Durham County Board of Education required teachers to participate in the program or lose their
jobs and be denied a teaching position in any county school for one
year. Brooks was employed to conduct the work at a salary of ten
dollars a month. So valuable was the program that the board continued it in the following year.[15]

In his extension course Brooks dealt with school methods based
on practical experience, geography centered on local conditions, and
literature pertinent to the upper grammar grades and high school.
The teachers received their instructions each week by correspondence
and returned weekly reports with answers to the questions on the
particular subject under study. For example, Brooks used the book
Checking the Waste between January and April, 1913. In his weekly
mimeographed letter to the teachers, he considered the book chapter
by chapter and outlined the main points in each. His questions
sought always to relate the printed material to local situations. At
monthly meetings he discussed the content of the courses and examined the teachers upon the completion of each book. In this manner
he covered a variety of books dealing with subjects valuable to the
teacher and in many instances included works that the teacher was
required by law to use in the classroom.[16]

On September 24, 1915, the Durham County Board of Education
ordered the publication of a weekly school bulletin to replace
Brooks's mimeographed letters. This bulletin also served as a mouth-
piece for the board and the county superintendent. In this new
bulletin Brooks continued his correspondence course for teachers on
such subjects as literature, nature study, geography, language, and
history. He urged teachers to form local clubs for the purpose of

15. Hamilton, "Duke University and the Schools," p. 11; *Durham County School
Bulletin,* Sept. 23, 1915; Minutes of the Durham County Board of Education, III, 76,
115-116, Office of the County Superintendent of Public Schools, Durham County
Courthouse, Durham, North Carolina.

16. *Trinity Chronicle,* Oct. 20, 1909. The Brooks Papers (BLS) contain a complete
file of the mimeographed letters sent out to Durham County teachers by Brooks between Jan. and April, 1913.

discussing among themselves the topics covered in the course. In order to speed up this development, he kept a record of all local clubs and published reports of their work in the *Durham County School Bulletin*.[17]

By 1913 Brooks realized the need for some changes in the organization of the extension course. Instead of the monthly meetings of all teachers, he organized the primary and high school teachers into separate groups in order that there might be some specialization in the work. At about the same time he became convinced that these teachers' meetings had become too mechanical and feared that the teacher might get no pleasure from his duties. So in 1914 he urged the teachers to organize meetings and study groups locally to "give them richer enthusiasm and supply them with more life."[18] He declared:

It was William James of Harvard who said that if we miss the joy in doing a thing we miss the whole thing. And much of the reading outlined for teachers is done in a mechanical way and is little above drudgery. . . . I am proposing therefore to the county associations that the superintendents divide their teachers into smaller groups . . . and insist on the members attending once a week if possible. The leading idea that I have in mind is to select so far as possible the subject matter for discussion in these clubs that will give the teachers pleasure. . . . There will be at least three classes of teachers—primary, grammar and high school.[19]

Brooks then outlined a specific course of study for each group. By this method he hoped to include a wider variety of topics and thus to attract greater interest from the teachers.

During his twelve years at Trinity College, Brooks succeeded in establishing a model program of teacher training in Durham County. In 1914 and 1915 he personally conducted weekly demonstrations in classroom teaching. Parents were invited to attend in order "to come into a closer contact with the school." In 1917 Durham County employed Holland Holton as assistant superintendent of schools in charge of teacher training, but it was made clear that "the work of Mr. Holton will in no way interfere with that of Prof. Brooks." Indeed, the two men became fast friends and co-operated

17. Minutes of the Durham County Board of Education, III, 331-332; *Durham County School Bulletin*, Oct. 15, 1915.
18. *Durham Herald*, Aug. 27, 1914.
19. *Durham Herald*, Oct. 16, 1914.

fully in the training of county teachers. In 1918 they conducted a model summer school for teachers without experience who intended to start teaching in the county and for those possessing low grade certificates.[20]

Brooks's extension work for teachers in Durham County attracted the attention of school officials throughout the state. S. B. Underwood, a Trinity graduate and Superintendent of the Kinston Schools, co-operated with the Lenoir County superintendent in organizing extension work for 1912 based on the Brooks plan. In the same year Brooks explained his program to the city board of education in Winston-Salem, which was considering a similar arrangement between its schools and Salem College. Here some misunderstanding had apparently developed, as the Winston-Salem board seemed to think that Durham County contributed to the financial support of the Trinity College department of education. Actually, as William P. Few, who succeeded Kilgo as president of Trinity, said, the college expected "no compensation . . . except the satisfaction of doing good." As the reputation of the extension work grew, teachers from the city of Durham as well as from Granville, Johnston, and Orange counties participated in the courses. How Brooks performed all these duties so successfully is difficult to see. Actually, he did have some assistance from his friend W. D. Carmichael, Superintendent of the Durham City Schools, who offered a course for several years. Brooks was able to expand the scope of his educational work in 1913, when one of his former students, Dr. Edgar Knight, joined the department of education of Trinity College.[21]

In the meantime the expansion of Brooks's activities was leading to friction with a professor of education at the University of North Carolina. On July 1, 1912, the Orange County Board of Education voted "to get Prof. E. C. Brooks to give the Orange County teachers the same course he is giving the Durham County teachers." State Superintendent Joyner promised to exempt these teachers from the summer institutes also, and Brooks promptly inaugurated a new extension course which he taught in Hillsboro each month. At the time, L. A. Williams, a professor of education at the University, was

20. *Durham Herald*, Dec. 5, 1914, Feb. 9, 1915, June 9, 1918, July 27, 1918.
21. *Report of the President of Trinity College, 1912*, pp. 4-5; E. C. Brooks to W. P. Few, March 3, 1914, W. P. Few to R. H. Latham, Feb. 27, 1914, Few Papers; *Trinity Chronicle*, Oct. 21, 1914; *Durham Herald*, June 28, 1913, March 23, 1914.

directing the training of teachers in service in the Chapel Hill schools. In 1915 he suggested that teachers living in Orange County near Chapel Hill come under his direction. Brooks apparently resented this intrusion upon his program. At any rate, friction developed between the two men, and Williams came to feel that he himself had been "too officious" in the whole matter. Brooks evidently thought so too, because he gave up his extension work in Orange County in December, 1915. The county superintendent begged him to reconsider, declaring that his work was "one of the greatest factors in the educational development of the county." Brooks refused to heed his pleas, and the Orange County Board of Education sought to continue its extension program "by help of the University if possible."[22]

[3]

By 1909 Brooks had come to realize the pressing need for teacher-training facilities to meet the demands of the public high schools that were established over the state following the passage of the high school law in 1907. Within four years more than two hundred high schools were in operation in ninety-three counties. Brooks felt that Trinity College should take the lead in providing facilities for the preparation of teachers of such schools. He insisted that Trinity had "made no provision for the teacher who is below the college academic work in scholarship, yet who is too old to take a complete college course." From this group, he declared, "the larger number of high school teachers is to be drawn." For him the "lack of scholarship" among teachers was a major obstacle to the establishment of efficient high schools, and as a result many such schools did not open because of the lack of qualified teachers or opened and failed "because they lacked any purpose other than the subject matter of dead textbooks." Brooks believed that no institution in the state provided for elementary teachers with a high school diploma and

22. Minutes of the Orange County Board of Education, July 1, 1912-March 6, 1916, Office of the County Superintendent of Public Schools, Orange County, Hillsboro, North Carolina; *Report of the President of Trinity College, 1915,* pp. 6-7; *Durham Herald,* Jan. 15, 1915; L. A. Williams to E. C. Brooks, Feb. 2, 1915, L. A. Williams to E. C. Brooks, Dec. 20, 1915, S. P. Lockhart to E. C. Brooks, Dec. 27, 1915, Brooks Papers (DUL); E. C. Brooks to J. Y. Joyner, May 20, 1916, S. P. I. Correspondence.

experience who desired to qualify for high school teaching without taking a complete college course. He urged Trinity to provide "special assistance" for these teachers and outlined in detail a plan for enlarging the Department of Education to include this group.[23]

The college adopted his plan and established the School of Education in 1910. Brooks did not propose to "convert Trinity College into a teachers' college," but as he said, "to make connection between the different departments of all secondary schools and the corresponding departments in Trinity College." Through the School of Education he attempted to establish this connection. The requirements for admission were the completion of a high school course of approved standing and some experience in teaching. There was no tuition; only a matriculation fee of nine dollars per term was required. Six groups of studies, "running through the freshman and sophomore years," each with a major and two minor subjects were available to the applicant. He was to choose as his major the subject that he planned to teach in high school from the subject fields open to him, which included history, science, mathematics, English, modern language, and classics. These studies were offered by professors in the appropriate departments. In addition, students took courses in educational methods offered by Brooks. The School of Education remained a part of Trinity College until Brooks's departure and undoubtedly fulfilled his desire to render service at a time when teachers were "bewildered and looking in every direction for assistance."[24]

In many ways Brooks was an unorthodox professor of education. He had not attended a teachers' college; therefore, his courses were largely the products of his own experience, studies, and liberal-arts background. As a teacher with depth and perspective, he not only exerted a great influence through his extension work, but inspired "a whole generation of school men" in his regular college classes. The size of these classes increased until it was necessary to hold them in a large room in the new East Duke Building. He generally used the lecture method of teaching, interspersed with frequent

23. Knight, *Public School Education in North Carolina*, p. 40; E. C. Brooks, "A Plan For Enlarging the Department of Education at Trinity College" (*ca.* 1910), Brooks Papers (DUL).

24. Brooks, "A Plan For Enlarging the Department of Education at Trinity College," Brooks Papers (DUL); *Annual Catalogue of Trinity College, 1910-1911*, pp. 153-159; *Durham Herald*, May 28, 1910.

discussions by students. His own experience in public education eminently qualified him to interpret the needs of prospective public school teachers. Probably because of this experience, educational theories without practical application had no place in his courses. Apparently, Brooks employed his oratorical abilities in his classroom lectures, because his students consistently described him as "dynamic and inspiring."[25] One observer later wrote: "Dr. Brooks was one of the most genial men ever to teach at Trinity. He had a wonderful sense of humor and told a story in an inimitable fashion. His classes were never dull or boring. His laugh was one of the most contagious that I ever heard."[26] One of Brooks's students recalled an occasion when a young man, suffering the effects of a "rough" weekend, fell asleep in a Monday morning class. Brooks stopped his lecture and when the silence became laborious, the student awoke with a start to find his professor staring down at him. Brooks bowed low and said: "Thank you, sir!"[27]

In his classes Brooks emphasized the necessity for teachers to demonstrate "initiative and originality" in their work and to learn how to express their ideas. He urged his students to participate actively in civic affairs—"to become community leaders." Three constant themes of his courses were the utilization of man's ideas, "education for service," and community leadership. This is not to say that he did not present specific information and instruction in the history of education, educational psychology, and the other courses that he taught; but rather that he clearly indicated how the content of each might be effectively applied in various situations which his students would encounter as teachers. Among the books which he regularly used in his courses were William James's *Talk to Teachers,* F. M. McMurray's *How to Study and Teaching How to Study,* and, oddly enough, Emerson's essay on "Self-Reliance." For his numerous demonstrations in methods of handling materials, he drew heavily on English and history.[28]

25. Hamilton, "Duke University and the Schools," p. 11; interviews with Mr. B. L. Smith, April 28, 1956, Dr. John W. Carr, Sept. 28, 1956, and Mr. A. S. Brower, Oct. 2, 1956.

26. Hersey E. Spence, "*I Remember*": *Recollections and Reminiscences of Alma Mater* (Durham, 1954), p. 52.

27. Interview with Mr. B. L. Smith, April 28, 1956.

28. Interviews with Dr. John W. Carr, Jr., Sept. 28, 1956, and Mr. B. L. Smith, April 28, 1956.

Brooks took especial interest in his students and their work. In private conference as well as in the classroom, he urged them to take a realistic approach to educational problems and to utilize their own ideas in solving them. He seemed to possess a knack for discerning the special talents and interests of a student and for guiding his development along appropriate lines. In some instances, he made it possible for such students to secure advanced training at outstanding universities. At times he contributed toward their expenses from his own meager funds. One of his "favorite students" was Edgar W. Knight, whom he assisted in pursuing graduate work at Columbia University. Dr. Knight joined the department of education at Trinity College and later went to the University of North Carolina. He became the principal authority on the educational history of the South. Numerous students who came under Brooks's influence at Trinity between 1907 and 1919 became prominent in the field of education. These included a State Superintendent, several division directors in the State Department of Public Instruction, and many county and city school superintendents. One student who came to Trinity in 1908 through Brooks's influence and took his education courses became governor of North Carolina in 1945.[29]

Brooks was interested in nearly all activities affecting Trinity College and figured prominently in faculty circles. He served on several important faculty committees, especially those concerned with admissions and student life, and was appointed to a variety of temporary committees which required considerable time and work. For example, he assisted in arranging meetings of state and regional organizations at Trinity, investigating athletic programs, and revising courses. He also played a significant role in alumni affairs and was "on continuous call as the perennial toastmaster" at local alumni gatherings. He was not only instrumental in organizing county alumni groups, but expounded the advantages of Trinity in nearly every section of the state. In these travels he "looked over" prospective students. Whenever the college undertook a financial campaign

29. Interviews with Mr. A. S. Brower, Oct. 2, 1956, and Mr. E. C. Brooks, Jr., July 12, 1956; A. S. Brower, "Eugene Clyde Brooks: Fifth President of North Carolina State College" (an address delivered on March 17, 1951); *Durham Herald*, June 28, 1913, Feb. 6, 1916; *Trinity Chronicle*, Sept. 18, 1912; Hamilton, "Duke University and the Schools," pp. 11-12; William T. Laprade, "The History of Trinity College," pp. 59-61 (manuscript written in 1922 and in the possession of its author); R. Gregg Cherry to Mrs. E. C. Brooks, March 15, 1951, Brooks Papers (DUL).

among the alumni, Brooks gave unstintedly of his time and oratorical talents. For several years he served as chairman of the executive committee of the general alumni association and was on the editorial board of the *Trinity Alumni Register,* which began publication in 1915.[30]

Throughout his career at Trinity, Brooks assisted in various projects undertaken by the Methodist Church. In 1908 the Western North Carolina Conference of the church appointed him to a commission on education which was to investigate the admission requirements, courses of study, and equipment of Methodist schools. Two years later, the North Carolina Conference of the Methodist Church accepted his plan for educational rallies in every county for the purpose of advertising Trinity College. From the standpoint of the college, these rallies apparently proved to be quite successful. Not only was Brooks a frequent speaker before such Methodist groups as Sunday School conventions and the Federation of Wesley Bible Classes, he also sought to improve the teaching personnel of Sunday Schools by adding to his department a course in the management and teaching of such schools. In addition to such college-related religious activities, Brooks was a lay leader in the Duke Memorial Methodist Church in Durham. He considered strong churches necessary to any progressive, well-balanced community and urged his students to take part in the church affairs of the locality in which they taught.[31]

Brooks manifested a keen interest in the extra-curricular activities of Trinity College students. For several years he was on the advisory board of the campus newspaper and was a frequent speaker before student organizations. In a short speech to the Hesperian Literary Society, which elected him an honorary member in 1915, he declared that "the greatest thing in the world is an idea, and the

30. *Annual Catalogue of Trinity College, 1912-1913,* p. 18; Minutes of the Faculty Meetings of Trinity College, Feb. 2, 1911-Nov. 22, 1918, Office of the Secretary of Duke University, Durham, North Carolina; Brower, "Eugene Clyde Brooks"; *Trinity Chronicle,* Jan. 20, 1909, Feb. 9, 1910; R. Gregg Cherry to Mrs. E. C. Brooks, March 15, 1951, Brooks Papers (DUL); *Durham Herald,* June 6, 1917, March 6, 1918; *Annual Catalogue of Trinity College, 1917-1918,* p. 156; *Trinity Alumni Register* (1915-1919).

31. *Trinity Chronicle,* Dec. 9, 1908, April 6, 1910; *North Carolina Christian Advocate,* LIII (Dec. 3, 1908), 6; E. C. Brooks, "Educational Days," *North Carolina Christian Advocate,* LV (April 10, 1910), 4-5; Gilbert Rowe to E. C. Brooks, March 4, 1910, Brooks Papers (DUL); *Durham Herald,* Sept. 6, 1917, April 8, 1918; *Annual Catalogue of Trinity College, 1914-1915,* pp. 109-110; interviews with Mr. B. L. Smith, April 28, 1956, and Mr. E. C. Brooks, Jr., July 12, 1956.

greatest man in the world is he who can best express that idea." At
the request of the Young Men's Christian Association, he delivered
a series of lectures in 1918 on race relations in the South in which
he emphasized the need for a change in the white man's attitude
toward the Negro—a change from "contempt to an attitude of interest and service." According to his view, better housing facilities
and educational advantages were special needs of the Negro. The
time was approaching, he concluded, when the Negro would no
longer serve "as an ox," and education of the race was an absolute
necessity. Another evidence of his interest in extra-curricular activities was his establishment of the Education Club in March, 1916,
primarily as a forum in which students could discuss current educational problems.[32]

Brooks was not only popular with the students, but with the
faculty as well. Among his closest friends were Mims, Boyd, and
William T. Laprade, who had come to Trinity in 1909 as professor
of history. Dr. F. N. Parker, professor of Biblical literature, was
another of Brooks's faculty friends, and the two men spent many enjoyable hours together playing chess. There developed an intimate
relationship between Brooks and Professor William K. Boyd, who
assisted him in the extension work and in the writing of his books.
Boyd later described Brooks as a person possessing "imagination,
fertility of ideas, and interest in the place of Trinity in the development of education in North Carolina." According to another
colleague, the host of students, stimulated by contact with Brooks,
found "more in the task of teaching than a temporary means of
earning a livelihood until they could find a more substantial place in
the world for a permanent vocation."   Not the least among Brook's
friends at Trinity was President Kilgo, whose guidance and support
were important factors in his success at the college.[33]

So popular had Brooks become by the time of Kilgo's elevation
to the bishopric in 1910 that he was considered as a possible suc-

32. *Trinity Chronicle*, April 12, 1911, Sept. 15, 1915, March 13, April 10, 17, Nov.
28, 1918; *Annual Catalogue of Trinity College, 1911-1912*, p. 136; *Annual Catalogue of
Trinity College, 1917-1918*, p. 140.

33. William K. Boyd, "Memoirs of a Book Hunter," William K. Boyd Papers, Duke
University Library, Durham, North Carolina; Laprade, "History of Trinity College,"
p. 23; interview with Mrs. E. C. Brooks, May 9, 1956; Edwin Mims to W. B. Gatewood, Jr., April 26, 1956; F. N. Parker to E. C. Brooks, March 10, 1914, E. C. Brooks
to J. C. Kilgo, Dec. 18, 1913, Brooks Papers (DUL).

cessor to the presidency of Trinity College. Brooks had then been at Trinity only three years. One patron of the college wrote him: "I would still be happier to see you president of Trinity, and there is some conjecture that you might be."[34] Another friend, Harry Howell, superintendent of the High Point schools, wrote him:

I do not know that I can do anything, but I am willing enough and would like to do anything desired. I had a talk with Dr. Peacock [a college trustee] yesterday. He admitted that you are the best man in the faculty for the place; but he said that anybody acquainted with things knows that the man whom the Dukes want will be elected. He said . . . that all recognize that for sometime yet the college must look to the Dukes for help and that they must not be offended. How do you stand there?[35]

Although Brooks undoubtedly stood well with the Dukes, his close friend and colleague, Dean William P. Few, was in better standing with them and had been groomed for the position by Kilgo. At any rate, Few was elected president of Trinity College on June 6, 1910.[36]

As already indicated, Few gave Brooks strong support in expanding the work of his department for eight and a half years. The two men shared a mutual confidence and admiration. Few had taken a sympathetic approach to public education for years and was in thorough accord with Brooks's work. Indeed, he seldom missed an opportunity to boast about Brooks to the board of trustees. In every annual report between 1911 and 1918 he singled out Brooks's accomplishments for special consideration. In 1914 Few told the trustees that Brooks had "made quite a name for himself as a teacher, an educational organizer, and lately as a writer." A year later, he informed the trustees: "Twice before in my reports I have called attention to the extension work done by our department of education under the leadership of Professor E. C. Brooks. . . . It is of so great significance that I feel justified at this time in giving a brief history of the movement." He then proceeded to describe in most complimentary terms Brooks's success in establishing and perfecting his extension courses.[37]

34. T. A. Holton to E. C. Brooks, May 17, 1910, Brooks Papers (DUL).
35. Harry Howell to E. C. Brooks, May 18, 1910, Brooks Papers (DUL).
36. See *The Papers and Addresses of William Preston Few: Late President of Duke University*, ed. Robert H. Woody (Durham, 1951), pp. 49-50.
37. Hamilton, "Duke University and the Schools," pp. 12-13; *Report of the President of Trinity College, 1914*, pp. 3-4; *Report of the President of Trinity College, 1915*, pp. 6-7.

As much as Brooks would have enjoyed the elaborate inaugural ceremonies for Few, he was unable to attend because of the death of his father several days earlier on October 31, 1910. He, of course, hurried to Grifton to be with his bereaved and ailing mother. He had barely recovered from this tragedy when his mother suffered a cerebral hemorrhage and died on November 27, 1910. Brooks as the oldest son in the family became administrator of the estate and was forced to spend considerable time complying with the necessary legal regulations. Within the specified time he settled these matters and sold the family farm in Contentnea Neck township. He was appointed guardian of his youngest sister, Glenn, then fifteen years old.[38]

[4]

After six years at Trinity, Brooks decided in 1913 to take graduate work in Teachers College, Columbia University. He received the Dean Fellowship, and Trinity College paid him a third of his salary, which enabled him to move his family to New York. Edgar Knight assumed his classroom responsibilities, but Brooks remained in close contact with the activities of his department. President Few himself performed such chores as renting Brooks's house and collecting the rent. Brooks secured an apartment at 417 West 120th Street. He entered his son in a nearby public school and secured a private tutor for his two daughters.[39]

The major portion of Brooks's work at Columbia University was under the direction of Paul Monroe, professor of education, and Edwin R. A. Seligman, professor of political economy. From his study Brooks intended to gain information for a proposed work on "the history of educational practice." He wrote that he was "pursuing two lines of study that meet in my investigations—the origin of our public school system and the affect of economics on educa-

38. Memoranda by Mrs. Mary Edmonds Brooks Cobb, Oct. 6, 1956, and Mrs. Glenn Brooks Mayberry, Oct. 6, 1956; interview with Mrs. E. C. Brooks, June 19, 1956; Medical Record of Dr. E. C. Brooks, Hist. No. 5162, 5/11/31, Duke Hospital; Deeds and Mortgages of Lenoir County, Book 41, p. 763; Carolina Home and Farm and Eastern Reflector (Greenville, North Carolina), Dec. 9, 1910.
39. E. C. Brooks to J. Y. Joyner, Nov. 3, 1913, S. P. I. Correspondence; Trinity Chronicle, Sept. 10, 1913; Schedule of Salaries, W. P. Few to E. C. Brooks, Oct. 8, 1913, E. C. Brooks to W. P. Few, Sept. 30, 1913, Few Papers.

tion." He was particularly interested in the economics course under Seligman, whom he considered the "tallest timber in these parts." Brooks's education classes were largely concerned with education in the Elizabethan Age and the evolution of the public school system in the United States. He also attended lectures by Professor James T. Shotwell on Roman history and by Professor John Dewey on the European Enlightenment.[40]

During 1913-1914 Brooks and President Few carried on regular and frequent correspondence. Few kept him informed of happenings at Trinity, while Brooks reciprocated with descriptions of life at Columbia. On September 30, 1913, Brooks wrote Few:

There is a queer aggregation of folks in my immediate neighborhood. It is needless therefore for me to explain by saying that Teachers' College is across the street from me. A college presidentress from Chile goes by with glasses and a queer shaped hat; the honest Japanese schoolboy is everywhere; a leathery faced pedagogue from Hawaii is trying to unravel the whole mystery; a sombreroed Mexican, unconscious of the trouble at home, has come this far to find it; old maids with cheek bones and no abdomens are thick as fleas . . . anyway the spinsters are here galore. But the strangest thing about it all is that these professors, instructors, and officers can pass one another with serious faces. But they seem to be in earnest notwithstanding the human menagerie that rages without a keeper.[41]

At this stage, however, Brooks was pleased with Teachers' College and with life in the big city.

During his year in New York Brooks found time to visit his old friend and mentor, John Franklin Crowell, who was then connected with Dow, Jones and Company. Brooks and his wife were also entertained by Mr. and Mrs. Benjamin N. Duke at their home on Fifth Avenue. On this occasion Duke asked Brooks to accept a responsible position in the American Tobacco Company. Brooks's friends, Clinton Toms and W. W. Flowers, had already moved from public school work into the Duke tobacco empire. Brooks, however, declined Duke's offer and assured him that his "future" was in the educational world.[42]

40. E. C. Brooks to J. Y. Joyner, Nov. 3, 1913, S. P. I. Correspondence; E. C. Brooks to W. P. Few, Feb. ?, 1914, Few Papers; E. C. Brooks, Notebooks, Brooks Papers (BLS).
41. E. C. Brooks to W. P. Few, Sept. 30, 1913, Few Papers.
42. J. F. Crowell to E. C. Brooks, March 19, 1915, Trinity College Papers; interview with Mrs. E. C. Brooks, June 19, 1956.

In the meantime the letters from Joyner and Few with news from North Carolina had made Brooks homesick for his usual place in the midst of the activities that they described. By April, 1914, he was "counting the days that intervene between now and my freedom." In a letter to Joyner he wrote:

I have heard so much about theory around Teachers College and seen so little evidence of practical results that I wonder—How long, O God, how long? My work has been chiefly in the field of economics, of live institutions, and the history of education. . . . I sometimes drop in to hear other heads of departments address their students and it reminds me very much of a local tax campaign, a teachers' institute or a section of the Teachers' Assembly—or better a combination of the three. But the most refreshing thing is the eagerness of the crowd for some light—that insatiable thirst for a satisfying draught. Are they getting it? I don't know. I am afraid not.[43]

Joyner was delighted that Brooks was eager to return to North Carolina and declared that his heart was set "a trembling" whenever one of his "strongmen" took advanced study, for fear that they would be lured away by higher salaries elsewhere.[44]

In the spring of 1914 Brooks and Few arranged through correspondence the work of the Education Department for the next academic year. They persuaded Knight to remain as a professor and provided for the purchase of additional books on education for the college library.[45] While still at Columbia, Brooks wrote Few: "Since coming here I have become convinced that my work at Trinity was along the right lines. . . . The direction I have been giving is the direction that educational philosophers and psychologists are taking and must take, and we at Trinity have brought educational theory and educational practice a little closer together than I find in many teacher training institutions."[46]

Shortly before the date that Brooks planned to leave New York, his wife suffered an attack of appendicitis and had to be hospitalized for some time. After her rather slow recovery, the family returned to Durham early in May, 1914. Brooks considered his year at Columbia University quite "valuable," but he was glad "to get hold of

43. E. C. Brooks to J. Y. Joyner, April 14, 1914, S. P. I. Correspondence.
44. J. Y. Joyner to E. C. Brooks, April 21, 1914, S. P. I. Correspondence.
45. W. P. Few to E. C. Brooks, Feb. 14, 1914, E. C. Brooks to W. P. Few, Feb. 18, 1914, E. C. Brooks to W. P. Few, April 14, 1914, Few Papers.
46. E. C. Brooks to W. P. Few, April ?, 1914, Few Papers.

things again" in North Carolina. He had already admitted that an "active life in the field is more agreeable to me than a life of supposed ease in a big university."[47]

[5]

While teaching in Trinity College, Brooks gained a wide reputation as a versatile author. By 1924 he had published seven books, several educational articles in national journals, and nine articles in the *Trinity Alumni Register* on the history of Trinity College under Braxton Craven; collaborated on two supplements to state-adopted textbooks; and served as contributing editor of the *Encyclopaedia for the Young* and as editor of *North Carolina Education,* a teachers' magazine. In 1918 Davidson College recognized his literary efforts by conferring upon him the honorary degree of Doctor of Literature.[48]

Brooks continued to maintain his interest in history and historical writing that had first been aroused by Stephen B. Weeks. He frequently participated in the activities of the Trinity College Historical Society and co-operated with Professor William K. Boyd in initiating a new publication by the Society called the *John Lawson Monographs.* He actually secured the autobiography of Brantley York, the first head of the institution that became Trinity College, which was published in 1910 as the first volume in the new series. The Society, however, was unable to finance the publication of the second volume of *Monographs,* the memoirs of W. W. Holden, Governor of North Carolina during Reconstruction. In order to overcome this difficulty, Boyd urged the college to finance the publication, but President Few told him that "this was impossible." After being told about the "disheartening situation," Brooks went to see Few, reiterated Boyd's

47. E. C. Brooks to W. P. Few, Feb. ?, 1914, E. C. Brooks to W. P. Few, April ?, 1914, Few Papers; E. C. Brooks to J. Y. Joyner, April 14, 1914, S. P. I. Correspondence.
48. *Durham Herald,* April 11, 1916; E. C. Brooks, "Seven, Eight, and Nine Years in the Elementary School," *The Elementary School Teacher,* XVI (Sept., 1913), 20-28 and XVI (Oct., 1913), 82-92; E. C. Brooks, "The Value of Home Study Under Parental Supervision," *The Elementary School Journal,* XVIII (Nov., 1917), 187-194; *Trinity Alumni Register,* I (April, 1915)–IV (April, 1918); *Alumni Catalogue of Davidson College, 1837-1924,* ed. Thomas Lingle, W. J. Martin, and Frederick Hengeveld (Charlotte, 1924), p. 267; E. C. Brooks, *A Comparison of School Systems* (Bulletin of the Trinity College Department of Education, No. 2).

proposal, and added that "in case Trinity did not publish Holden's
memoirs the University of North Carolina would." Few then agreed
that the college would underwrite the venture, and Holden's memoirs appeared as the second volume in the series in 1911.[49]

In the same year, Brooks published his first major works. One of
these, a *Geography of North Carolina,* written in collaboration with
Superintendent W. D. Carmichael of the Durham city schools, was a
supplement to Dodge's *Advanced Geography,* a state-adopted textbook. Brooks and Carmichael each received $500 from Rand-Mc-
Nally and Company for their thirty-two page work.[50] Several years
later Brooks collaborated on a similar work with I. O. Schaub of
North Carolina State College. At the suggestion of State Superintendent Joyner they prepared an Agricultural Supplement to Milne's
Progressive Arithmetic, another state-adopted textbook. In this book-
let the authors sought to relate "the work of the schoolroom more
closely to the business needs of the community" through lessons
combining agriculture and arithmetic.[51]

Much more important than these textbook supplements was
Brooks's *Story of Cotton and the Development of the Cotton States,*
which was published in 1911. In preparing this volume, Brooks received valuable assistance from two of his colleagues in Trinity
College, William T. Laprade and William K. Boyd, who possessed
the advanced training in historical research and writing that he
lacked. Their advice helped him to avoid embarrassing pitfalls and
to produce a work worthy of critical scrutiny. Brooks himself was
close to the subject of the book, for he had been reared in cotton
country and had lived in a textile center since 1907. This first-hand
knowledge enabled him to describe the agricultural and manufacturing aspects of the cotton industry with particular clarity and insight. Although the work failed to provide a comparable account
of the marketing of cotton and the role of brokers and exchanges in

    49. Boyd, "Memoirs of a Book Hunter," Boyd Papers; Tilley, *Trinity College His-
torical Society,* pp. 93-94; *The Autobiography of Brantley York* [John Lawson Mono-
graphs], ed. W. K. Boyd, with an Introductory Sketch by E. C. Brooks (Durham, 1910).
    50. Rand McNally and Company to E. C. Brooks, Feb. 21, 1911, Brooks Papers
(DUL); Eugene C. Brooks and William D. Carmichael, *Geography of North Carolina*
(Chicago, 1911), pp. 1-32.
    51. E. C. Brooks and I. O. Schaub, *Agricultural Supplement to Milne's Progressive
Arithmetic, Second Book* (New York, 1914), p. 305; interview with Mr. I. O. Schaub,
June 28, 1956.

price fluctuations, it actually established Brooks's reputation as an author of books for school children.[52]

The *Story of Cotton* was designed to complement history textbooks that emphasized political events at the expense of economic forces. Brooks contended that school children could not fully understand political and social changes without an appreciation of economic influences "working in the life of the people." Thus, his book emphasized the economic importance of cotton in the history of the United States and sought to relate it to other economic, social, and political phases of American life. According to Brooks, "cotton sectionalized the South" and projected the questions of slavery, tariffs, and territories into the national political arena. The latter part of the volume, dealing with the post-Civil War period, placed emphasis upon the rise of cotton mills in the South, the increasing use of scientific agriculture, and the numerous varieties and by-products of the cotton plant.[53]

The *Story of Cotton* was acclaimed throughout the country as an epochal work in historical literature for school children. Certainly, it appeared at an opportune moment, for its emphasis on the relationship between economic and political forces was in harmony with the sentiment of the Progressive Era. In the South the subject alone was sufficient to win the book wide recognition, but its popularity in the South was greatly augmented by the existing movement for agricultural high schools. Within a year after its publication, the volume was adopted as a textbook in five Southern states and authorized for use in numerous local school units. By September, 1919, a total of 81,421 copies of the *Story of Cotton* had been sold and an additional 35,000 copies were printed shortly thereafter. The book was one of the most financially successful works that Brooks ever wrote, and he sold his rights to it to Rand McNally and Company for $10,000.[54]

52. Eugene Clyde Brooks, *The Story of Cotton and the Development of the Cotton States* (Chicago, 1911), p. iv; interview with Dr. W. T. Laprade, Nov. 10, 1955; W. H. Glasson, "Review of *The Story of Cotton and the Development of the Cotton States*," *South Atlantic Quarterly*, XI (July, 1912), 290-291.
53. See Brooks, *The Story of Cotton*, 368 pp.
54. *North Carolina Education*, VI (March, 1912), 13. Hereinafter cited as *N C E*. See also *N C E*, VI (April, 1912), 11; *N C E*, VI (May, 1912), 11; E. Horn to E. C. Brooks, Nov. 23, 1914, A. C. Haley to ——— Buehring, March 22, 1914, Edwin Mims to E. C. Brooks, Nov. 16, 1914, F. H. Perry to E. C. Brooks, Sept. 24, 1919, Brooks Papers (DUL); interview with Mr. E. C. Brooks, Jr., July 12, 1956.

So popular was the *Story of Cotton* that the publishers persuaded Brooks to write a companion volume on corn. He began
preparation of the *Story of Corn and the Westward Migration* early
in 1912, but it was not published until 1916. The main thesis of this
work was that the "grain of the West stimulated the demand for
better communication" and made internal improvements a national
issue. Brooks attempted to show the relationship between corn and
national politics in much the same manner in which he had treated
cotton in the earlier work, but without the same degree of success.
He did not bring to this work that first-hand knowledge of his subject that so enhanced his study of cotton, and it failed to achieve the
recognition and financial success of its predecessor.[55]

Another of Brooks's interests was to acquaint North Carolina
school children with native poetry in order to stimulate their literary
activity in later years. In September, 1911, he began publishing a
series of poems by North Carolina writers in *North Carolina Education,* and the following year he reproduced these verses in a book,
North Carolina Poems, for use in the public schools. This small
volume contained 105 poems by 37 different authors. In general, the
subject matter of the poems fell into three categories: notable historical events, famous men in state history, and natural phenomena.
The book was so popular that it was sold out within a few months
after publication, and as late as 1935 Brooks was still receiving requests for copies of the volume.[56]

Shortly after entering Columbia University in September, 1913,
Brooks completed a work undertaken at the suggestion of his friend,
P. P. Claxton, United States Commissioner of Education. It was a
bulletin entitled *Agriculture and Rural Life Day: Material For Its
Observance,* which was to be used in public schools on days set aside
in many states "to emphasize the importance of agriculture to the
nation and to the world of mankind." It contained seven parts dealing with such topics as scientific farming and agricultural leaders
and included generous excerpts from Brooks's *Story of Cotton* and
his unpublished *Story of Corn.* The bulletin was released in October,

55. See Eugene Clyde Brooks, *The Story of Corn and the Westward Migration*
(Chicago, 1916), 301 pp.
56. *North Carolina Poems,* ed. Eugene Clyde Brooks (Raleigh, 1912); J. A. Bivins,
"A North Carolina Book That Stirs the Heart," *N C E,* VI (Nov., 1912), 10; E. C.
Brooks to W. F. Marshall, June 18, 1935, Brooks Papers (DUL).

1913, and elicited favorable comment from school men throughout the country.[57]

Brooks attended Columbia University primarily for the purpose of securing information for a proposed work entitled "The Influence of Education on the Institutional Life of the People: How it Has Attempted to Adjust the Individual to Life Around Him." He wanted to deal with "what actually happened in the educational world" rather than theory, and was especially interested in the relationship between economics and education. Although he managed to complete a large portion of this two-volume work, the title of which was changed to "A History of Educational Practice," it was never published; but it undoubtedly provided a useful body of material for his lectures at Trinity College.[58]

This manuscript embodied a comprehensive statement of Brooks's ideas on the history of education and revealed his aversion to inflexible educational theories and his enthusiasm for what he called the practical approach to education. Brooks agreed with Dewey that social utility should be the aim of education and that "any method is right if the teacher can deliver the goods."[59] He relied heavily upon Dewey in formulating the central thesis of his "History of Educational Practice," in which he wrote:

The history of educational practice is the history of the conduct of man in his struggle to control his environment. The primitive man no less than the enlightened man of today used his mind for this purpose, and mental activity is largely what it is today because of its utility—to man in the present and in the past. Dewey says: "the biological point of view compels us to the conviction that mind, whatever else it may be, is at least an organ of service for the control of environment in relation to the end of the life process." This interpretation of the function of the mind leads us to the conclusion that man's occupation gives direction to his entire mental life, determines the fundamental modes of action, and controls the formation of habits.[60]

Brooks insisted that every age possessed its own educational system and theories "based in one way or another on the idea of work"

57. Eugene C. Brooks, *Agriculture and Rural Life Day: Material for Its Observance,* Bureau of Education Bulletin No. 43 (Washington, 1913); E. C. Brooks to W. K. Boyd, Sept. 18, 1913, Boyd Papers; E. C. Brooks to J. Y. Joyner, Nov. 13, 1913, S. P. I. Correspondence.
58. *Trinity Chronicle,* Sept. 10, 1913.
59. E. C. Brooks, "Review of *How We Think*," N C E, VIII (Feb., 1914), 16.
60. E. C. Brooks, "A History of Educational Practice," 2 vols. Brooks Papers (BLS).

and that educational practices change "most when occupations
change." But not until the rise of a new generation "with a new mental pattern" did teachers and theorists implement this pattern and
even then sought to justify it through some previous principle.[61]

His third major work, *Woodrow Wilson as President,* which was
published in 1916, differed in character and purpose from any other
volume that he wrote. In 1916 the publishing house of Row, Peterson and Company was anxious to cash in on the forthcoming presidential campaign through the publication of a book on Wilson. F.
H. Perry, a company representative, was largely responsible for af-
fording Brooks an opportunity to employ his pen in the President's
behalf. Although Brooks actually wrote most of the volume, Perry
and J. B. Aswell, a Democratic congressman from Louisiana, assisted him by collecting the necessary materials in a form that could
be easily incorporated into a readable text. With this assistance
Brooks completed the volume in June and July, 1916, and the three
men agreed that Brooks alone should be designated as the author.
When the book was released late in August, Aswell at once brought
it to the attention of the Democratic campaign managers and his
colleagues in Congress.[62]

Woodrow Wilson as President was a large volume of 586 pages
with generous excerpts quoted from presidential addresses. It described Wilson as a practicing politician, his efforts to secure progressive legislation, his role in the Mexican controversy, and his
policy of neutrality during World War I.[63] Through the efforts of
the publishers, the book received favorable publicity in numerous
Democratic journals which generally heaped unqualified praise upon
it. More thoughtful reviewers were primarily critical of its obvious
evidences of hasty preparation.[64] Despite its publicity, the volume
did not attain the financial success anticipated by the publishers.
The length of the work may have reduced its popular appeal, but
more significant perhaps was its emphasis upon domestic issues and

61. *Ibid.*
62. Interview with Mrs. E. C. Brooks, May 9, 1956; F. H. Perry to R. K. Row, July
1, 1916, R. K. Row to F. H. Perry, June 28, 1916, J. B. Aswell to E. C. Brooks, July 1,
1916, Royalty Agreement, Aug. 25, 1916, Brooks Papers (DUL); *Durham Herald,*
Aug. 26, 1916.
63. Eugene C. Brooks, *Woodrow Wilson as President* (Chicago, 1916), 586 pp.
64. See *New York Times,* Oct. 22, 1916; "The Candidates," *The Nation,* CII (Oct.
12, 1916), 350-351; W. T. Laprade, "Review of *Woodrow Wilson as President,*" *South
Atlantic Quarterly,* XV (Oct., 1916), 388-390.

the Mexican controversy at a time when the public was preoccupied with the European conflict. Brooks realized that his book would enter a falling market and stated in the preface that the war had "so affected men's memories that Wilson's domestic reforms had been almost forgotten."[65] At any rate, not until 1919, when Wilson was fighting for the League of Nations, was there "a run on the book."[66]

In the same year Brooks published his fourth major work entitled *Education for Democracy,* which was the third volume in the "Patriotism Through Literature Series." The purpose of this series was "to cultivate in young people a sane, helpful, and exalted patriotism, and to teach them their obligations to the outside world." Brooks divided his book into four parts, and apparently wrote the first part, "The Spirit of Democracy in Government," in the white heat of patriotic fervor. His wholesale condemnation of Germany and glorification of American democracy would have qualified this section for publication by the Committee on Public Information. But amid this patriotic harangue Brooks managed to state quite soberly the central theme of the book: that co-operation was the essence of democratic government, and co-operation in all phases of formal school work was the foundation of educational democracy.[67]

The real core of *Education for Democracy* was placed in parts two and three, which contained a clear statement of Brooks's ideas on several phases of public education. He insisted that the educational ideal should be the same as that of the nation; therefore, a primary task of American teachers was to "lead youth toward a larger freedom" through practical instruction in democracy. He believed that autocracy prevailed in many aspects of the educational system, especially among school administrators, who "standardize and strain after national uniformity without ever consulting the needs of the community or the individual teachers." He was convinced too that teachers made "the acquisition of knowledge incorporated in the textbook the goal of instruction" rather than hav-

65. G. M. Jones to W. B. Gatewood, Jr., Jan. 15, 1957; Brooks, *Woodrow Wilson As President,* p. 5.

66. E. C. Brooks to Row, Peterson and Company, Jan. 2, 1920, E. C. Brooks to James Stewart, April 13, 1920, S. P. I. Correspondence. Despite the increased sales of the book, "about 50% of the one and only printing was destroyed for paper stock in the 1920's." G. M. Jones (of Row, Peterson and Company) to Willard Gatewood, Jr., Jan. 15, 1957.

67. Eugene C. Brooks, *Education for Democracy* (Chicago, 1916), p. 264; *N C E,* XIV (March, 1920), 16.

ing as a goal the production of self-reliant, responsible citizens equipped with knowledge useful in making a living. This goal, he argued, could be attained through greater emphasis on social studies and vocational subjects. For him, the curriculum as a product of society was constantly undergoing changes, and the teacher "who holds exclusively to the past and ignores the demands of the present is out of harmony with the age."[68]

The second book that Brooks completed after leaving Trinity College appeared in 1922 and was entitled *Stories of South America.* It was designed for instructing school children in the history, geography, and "flora and fauna" of the continental states of South America. Brooks first became interested in this subject while teaching at Trinity, where he actually "collected most of the material" contained in the volume. As early as 1916 he had urged schools to lay the intellectual foundations for hemispheric solidarity through a study of the culture and language of Latin America. One purpose of his little book, then, was to introduce the germs of Pan-Americanism into the classrooms of the United States.[69]

The *Stories of South America,* actually a series of related essays, opened with a discussion of Columbus and his discoveries in the New World. Brooks repeated the Black Legend about the Spanish cruelty to the Indians and their consuming lust for gold. But his fairly accurate descriptions of the Inca civilization, the feats of Pizarro, the Spanish colonial organization, and the racial mixture in Spanish colonies were presented in a manner likely to arouse the interest of school children. He was more sympathetic to the revolutionary and republican eras in South America than to the colonial period, and the chapters devoted to such revolutionary leaders as San Martin and Bolivar provided fascinating and sound accounts of their ideas and accomplishments. The sixty-three pages devoted to Portuguese America, or Brazil, gave particular attention to the "wonders" of the Amazon region. The last chapter of the book, with its emphasis on the Pan-American Union and Monroe Doctrine was, in effect, a plea for greater inter-American co-operation.[70]

68. Brooks, *Education For Democracy,* Parts II and III.
69. E. C. Brooks, *Stories of South America: Historical and Geographical* (Richmond, 1922), p. 5; Brooks, *Woodrow Wilson As President,* pp. 516-517.
70. Brooks, *Stories of South America,* 260 pp.

In some respects, the *Stories of South America* was superior to Brooks's other works for school children. This was undoubtedly true regarding style of writing and organization of contents. However, the volume would have been enhanced by a brief account of the Roman Catholic Church in South America, and would probably have gained wider recognition, especially in the Southwestern states, if it had not been restricted to continental South America, but had included Mexico and the countries of Central America. Nevertheless, according to one authority, the book was a distinct contribution to the historical literature for public schools and was "one of the earliest, if not the first, book on Latin America for use as a text in elementary and high schools."[71] The volume was a conspicuous financial success, and within four months after publication, 4,783 copies had been sold. Twenty years after the first printing it was still a popular text, and in 1942 the publishers urged Brooks to "bring it up to date and add a chapter on Mexico," but by that time his precarious health would not permit such an undertaking.[72]

Although Brooks published a small book in 1924 for use in North Carolina schools,[73] his reputation as an author rested principally upon those works that he prepared or wrote while teaching in Trinity College. He undoubtedly selected some of his subjects with a view toward their saleability in book form, but his contemporaries found in each of his works contributions to the current literature in education, history, or politics. Although he was not a flawless stylist—sometimes flamboyant prose interefered with the accuracy of his account—Brooks won wide recognition as a versatile and forceful writer, comparable to the reputation that he possessed as a powerful orator.

[6]

During his twelve years in Durham, Brooks by no means confined his educational activities to classroom instruction and exten-

71. Halford Haskins, "Review of *Stories of South America*," Brooks Papers (DUL). See also Halford Haskins to E. C. Brooks, Feb. 20, 1923, Brooks Papers (DUL); *Journal of the National Education Association*, XII (Oct., 1923), 336.
72. "Analysis of Sales, Johnson Publishing Company, February 28, 1923," R. Hill Fleet to E. C. Brooks, March 27, 1942, E. C. Brooks to R. Hill Fleet, April 21, 1942, Brooks Papers (DUL).
73. See below pp. 249-250.

sion work at Trinity College. In the summer he generally delivered lectures and conducted teachers' institutes in various parts of the state. For example, in the summer of 1909 he "lectured at the Appalachian Training School in Boone and conducted institutes in Yancey, Cleveland, and Rockingham counties." He continued this kind of summer work until 1913, when President Robert Wright of East Carolina Teachers' Training School induced him to teach in the summer school there. But he declined Wright's invitation to return the following summer.[74]

In the meantime, Brooks's friend of undergraduate days, Bruce Payne, had undertaken to rebuild an obscure institution in Tennessee into George Peabody College for Teachers. While Brooks was studying at Columbia University, Payne pleaded with him to accept a permanent position at Peabody. On April 26, 1914, Brooks wrote Few: "I have had my last round with Payne, and I think he is satisfied and so am I. I think too much of my work in North Carolina to change for an uncertainty."[75] These were sweet words to Few, who immediately replied: "I am a well-wisher of Payne, . . . but I am glad that you have put the quietus on him. You have a great field here and you have been, are still and will be one of the greatest forces for enlightenment and real progress that has ever influenced this state."[76] Payne, however, did persuade Brooks to teach in the Peabody summer school in 1914. The following summer he returned there at an increased salary and also offered a course at Vanderbilt University.[77]

In addition to institute and summer school work, Brooks continued to hold a permanent place in several state and regional organizations. Through these groups he not only made important contacts for himself, but solidified the link between Trinity College and the public schools. He had become a significant figure in the Association of Colleges and Preparatory Schools of the Southern States since his first speech before that body in 1903. He again ad-

74. *Trinity Chronicle*, Sept. 15, 1909; Robert Wright to E. C. Brooks, April 2, 1913, Robert Wright to E. C. Brooks, Jan. 12, 1914, Brooks Papers (DUL).
75. E. C. Brooks to W. P. Few, April 26, 1914, Few Papers.
76. W. P. Few to E. C. Brooks, April 29, 1914, Few Papers.
77. Bruce Payne to E. C. Brooks, Dec. 13, 1913, Carter Alexander to E. C. Brooks, Jan. 18, 1914, Bruce Payne to E. C. Brooks, Jan. 16, 1915, Wilbur Tillett to E. C. Brooks, July 23, 1915, Brooks Papers (DUL); Woody, *William P. Few*, p. 89; *Trinity Chronicle*, Sept. 17, 1917.

dressed the Association in 1907 and 1909, and was a member of the executive committee for five years, 1908 through 1913. This was an especially crucial period for the recently established high schools in the South, and various organizations, such as the Association of Colleges and Preparatory Schools, were attempting to raise them to certain standards. In 1911 Brooks and two other members of a sub-committee presented a report "recommending the appointment of a commission to regulate the accrediting system" of schools and colleges in the South. The report, adopted with few amendments, called for the establishment of a Commission on the Accrediting of Schools that consisted of two members from each state. These individuals were to prepare a list of schools in their state which fulfilled the requirements for accreditation set by the Association. This procedure was part of a general movement to raise the level of high school instruction, which was important of course to the maintenance of higher academic standards in colleges.[78]

Brooks and the state inspector of high schools, N. W. Walker, represented North Carolina on the accrediting commission. In 1912 Superintendent Edwin Pusey of the Goldsboro schools was added as a third member from the state, representing an accredited secondary school. For several years Brooks worked closely with Chancellor James H. Kirkland of Vanderbilt University and others in expanding and refining the accrediting requirements. At the annual meeting of the Association in 1912, Brooks explained the operation of the method for accrediting high schools and for certifying their graduates.[79]

Four years later, when the Association met at Trinity College, Brooks and four other members were appointed to submit a plan for a commission "to undertake the classification of institutions of higher learning." Their plan, adopted in 1917 with minor changes, called for the creation of a Commission of Higher Education with

78. E. C. Brooks, "A Comparison of School Systems," *Proceedings of the Fifteenth Annual Meeting of the Association of Colleges and Preparatory Schools of the Southern States, 1909,* pp. 65-84; *Proceedings of the Seventeenth Annual Meeting, 1911,* pp. 23-24; *Proceedings of the Eighteenth Annual Meeting, 1912,* p. 11; Holland Holton, "Establishing and Improving Standards For Secondary Education in the South," *Secondary Education in the South,* pp. 48-49.

79. J. H. Kirkland to E. C. Brooks, Dec. 27, 1911, J. H. Kirkland to E. C. Brooks, Jan. 11, 1912, Brooks Papers (DUL); *Proceedings of the Eighteenth Annual Meeting, 1912,* pp. 12, 30, 86-92; *Proceedings of the Nineteenth Annual Meeting, 1913,* p. 25.

thirty-nine members representing both colleges and secondary schools. The duty of the Commission was to prepare a statement of standards to be met by colleges which were members or prospective members of the Association; to inspect these institutions periodically; and to recommend dismissal of any school that failed to meet the standards. Brooks became a member of the commission and continued to hold this position as long as he remained at Trinity College.[80]

Another regional group in which Brooks participated was the Southern Sociological Congress. This body was concerned with such reforms as the abolition of child labor and the convict lease systems, the passage of compulsory school laws, state health programs, and the solution of the race question in a spirit of justice to both races. For three years Brooks was appointed by the governor as the official delegate to the Congress from North Carolina. Undoubtedly, he found many congenial minds among this group, which was striving for greater social justice in the South.[81]

While at Trinity College, Brooks played a prominent role in several state organizations that he had joined earlier. He manifested a particular interest in the State Library Association and the State Association of County Superintendents. He remained an active member of the North Carolina Association of City School Superintendents and Principals, and in 1909 he spoke to that group on the "Status of the Graded School in North Carolina." This address embodied three of his favorite subjects: "the physical and moral condition of the child," the course of study, and the grading of that course. He pleaded for a flexible curriculum geared to the capacities and needs of children and deplored the widespread existence of a "mere formal memorizing of unintelligent contents" by grade school pupils. At the annual meeting in 1909, he was appointed to a committee of five to investigate the course of study and to recommend adjustments that would provide "economy of time" and new courses "demanded by new conditions." Through the persistent efforts of Brooks

80. *Proceedings of the Twenty-Second Annual Meeting, 1916*, p. 26; *Proceedings of the Twenty-Third Annual Meeting, 1917*, pp. 20-21, 27.
81. *The Call of the New South: Addresses Delivered at the Sociological Congress*, ed. J. E. McCulloch (Nashville, 1912), pp. 7-9; W. W. Kitchin to E. C. Brooks, April 8, 1912, Locke Craig to E. C. Brooks, April 5, 1913, Thomas W. Bickett to E. C. Brooks, July 19, 1917, Brooks Papers (DUL).

and many others, the North Carolina schools gradually reorganized their curricula to meet the demands of the twentieth century.[82]

Brooks used another organization, the North Carolina Teachers' Assembly, to spread his ideas on public education throughout the state. By 1913 he could say that he had attended fourteen consecutive annual sessions of the Assembly. During that period his name rarely failed to appear on the membership list of at least two important committees each year. For example, in 1910 he was a key member of the platform committee that endorsed the enactment of stronger certification laws and a constitutional amendment for a longer school term. Moreover, he was a frequent speaker at the annual meetings of the Assembly. Such occasions provided him with opportunities to expound on the needs for greater in-service training of teachers. In 1909 he outlined a home study course for teachers based on his extension work at Trinity College, which the Assembly lauded as a "great success."[83] Brooks was elected president of the Teachers' Assembly for 1912-1913. In his inaugural address, entitled "The Need for a New Educational Content," which was delivered at the meeting in Greensboro on November 27, 1912, he outlined some of his ideas concerning the public school curriculum. "My criticism of the organized school," he began, "is that it is not broad enough to reach all the children." He then reiterated his plea for a broader and more flexible curriculum that would include physical training and home-making as well as the cultural subjects. According to him, the purpose of the school was "to bring the life of the world in such relationship to the life of the child that he may know how to live."[84]

82. *Trinity Chronicle,* Sept. 15, 1909; *Durham Herald,* Jan. 29, 30, 1910; *Proceedings of the North Carolina Association of City Public School Superintendents and Principals, 1909,* pp. 4-5, 18-23.

83. E. C. Brooks to J. Y. Joyner, Nov. 23, 1913, S. P. I. Correspondence; *Proceedings and Addresses of the Twenty-Seventh Annual Session of the North Carolina Teachers' Assembly, 1910,* pp. 11-12; *Proceedings of the Teachers' Assembly, 1909,* pp. 217-224; see also *Proceedings of the Teachers' Assembly, 1915,* pp. 291-294; E. C. Brooks, "How To Improve the Teacher in Service," *Training School Quarterly,* II (Oct.-Dec., 1915), 167-171.

84. E. C. Brooks, "The Need For a New Educational Content," Nov. 27, 1912, Brooks Papers (DUL). Brooks, as president of the Teachers' Assembly, shared prominently in the agitation that helped to secure the passage of several educational measures in 1913. These included an act providing for the six-month school term, the creation of an equalizing fund of $375,000, the establishment of rural life schools, and amendments strengthening the compulsory school attendance laws. *Durham Herald,* March 7, 14, 26, 1913.

[7]

While at Trinity College, Brooks was active in the civic affairs of Durham, even dabbling in local politics. In 1911 he was elected a trustee of the Durham Public Library, which had first opened in 1898, reputedly as "the first library in North Carolina open to the public without the payment of dues or fees." The demands upon the library had steadily increased until the need for larger quarters had become acute. In 1916 Brooks was a leader in the movement to secure a grant from the Carnegie Corporation for a new library building. Through the persistent efforts of another trustee, Thomas B. Fuller, the Carnegie Corporation agreed to give $32,000 for this purpose, if the city of Durham would provide an annual maintenance fund of $4,000. The trustees, although not in complete agreement, decided to request the county to share in the annual appropriation. Brooks appeared before the county commissioners in behalf of the scheme and persuaded them to pay one-third of the annual fund. After settling complicated legal questions, the library trustees finally met all the stipulations of the Carnegie Corporation in June, 1918. Three years later, the new library was opened to the public.[85]

On January 21, 1915, Brooks was elected a member of the Durham City Board of Education to succeed Julian S. Carr. His first assignment in this capacity was to find an architect to rebuild the Morehead School, which had been destroyed by fire, and to appear before the city aldermen in the interest of a bond issue necessary to cover the building expenses. Later he sponsored successfully motions for raising teachers' salaries, improving school sanitary facilities, limiting the number of pupils per class, and creating a textbook rental system. One of his last contributions before resigning from the board in January, 1919, was to call the members' attention to the fact that the slow collection of taxes forced the schools to pay about $1,500 a year in interest on money borrowed to meet current expenses.[86]

85. Boyd, *Story of Durham*, pp. 262-263; Minutes of the Board of Trustees of the Durham Public Library, June 9, 1916—July 6, 1921, Durham Public Library, Durham, North Carolina.
86. Minutes of the Board of Education of the City of Durham, Jan., 1915-Jan., 1919, Office of the City Superintendent of Public Schools, Durham, North Carolina; *Durham Herald*, March 7, 1917.

During the First World War Brooks joined various local campaigns for the promotion of the war effort. He was a popular "four minute speaker," and he served as chairman of a committee to provide speakers for the campaign to sell liberty bonds. Later, as a director of the Chamber of Commerce, he promoted all sorts of patriotic activities. In October, 1917, his old friend, P. P. Claxton, Commissioner of Education, called him to Washington to assist in compiling a monthly bulletin on "Community and National Life" that was to be distributed in public schools as a "part of the general educational campaign for efficiency and preparedness."[87]

Brooks's first entry into local politics occurred on April 11, 1913, when at the insistence of citizens from the first ward he announced his candidacy for the city board of aldermen. The *Durham Herald,* lavish in its praise, declared: "Prof. Brooks is the type of man that the city should have on the board of aldermen and it is believed that his candidacy will meet with the favor of the Democrats of the city. He is one of the recognized leaders in the educational life of the state, a man of national reputation along some lines, and a wide-awake and public-spirited citizen." Brooks was elected from the first ward without opposition, receiving 1,322 votes. He was promptly made chairman of the committee on the reorganization of city government, in which capacity he set in motion several schemes of reorganization. He did not stay on the board long enough to see the fulfillment of his ideas, however, for on July 1, 1913, two months after his election, he resigned in order to spend a year at Columbia University.[88]

After returning to Durham in 1914, Brooks resumed his activities in state and municipal politics. He was mentioned as a candidate for Congress against Major Charles Stedman, the perennial representative from the fifth district. But Brooks possessed enough political sagacity not to risk a contest with a Confederate veteran. In the fall of 1916 he helped to organize a Wilson-Bickett Club in Durham. He greatly admired President Wilson and strongly endorsed Thomas W. Bickett, the Democratic gubernatorial candidate. He had become

87. *Durham Herald,* Dec. 8, 1917, Feb. 1, 1918; *Trinity Chronicle,* Oct. 24, 1917. Brooks was also a member of the local Rotary Club and a director of the Durham Building and Loan Association. *State School Facts,* XIX (July, 1947).

88. *Durham Herald,* April 11, 27, June 28, 1913; W. L. Brogden to E. C. Brooks, July 2, 1913, Brooks Papers (DUL).

acquainted with Bickett through Mrs. Brooks's brother, Oscar Sapp, and apparently cultivated his friendship. In 1917 Brooks again became involved in municipal politics, when he was seriously considered as a successor to Mayor B. S. Skinner, who died in October, 1917. The board of aldermen, however, finally chose M. E. Newsom, Jr., to fill Skinner's unexpired term.[89]

[8]

It is not surprising that a man of Brooks's personality, energy, and ability was honored in various ways and tempted by greener pastures elsewhere. Fortunate was Trinity College that he received the honors but withstood the temptations. Within five years after coming to Trinity as the first incumbent of the Chair in the History and Science of Education, Brooks had established himself in the field of education. His reputation was based upon his pioneer efforts in extension work, his classroom influence, his broad experience in public schools, his leadership in educational organizations, and his publications. By this time he was also widely known as a raconteur— a talent that he utilized skilfully in winning friends. These accomplishments and personal characteristics obviously brought him attractive offers from a variety of sources.

In 1912 Commissioner P. P. Claxton urged him to accept a position in the Bureau of Education, but Brooks promptly refused the offer. Similarly, he resisted Bruce Payne's efforts to lure him to Peabody College in the following year. While at Columbia University, he declined an offer to head the State School for the Feeble-Minded at Kinston, and a year later he turned down an opportunity to become chairman of the Education Department in the State Normal and Industrial College. In 1918, however, he seriously considered the possibility of becoming city superintendent of the Atlanta, Georgia, schools, but the Atlanta school board decided to retain the incumbent.[90]

89. Interviews with Mrs. E. C. Brooks, May 9, 1956, and Mr. E. C. Brooks, Jr., July 12, 1956; *Durham Herald*, Sept. 22, 1916, Feb. 17, 21, 23, Oct. 24, 25, Nov. 6, 1917.
90. P. P. Claxton to E. C. Brooks, Aug. 12, 1912, E. C. Brooks to P. P. Claxton, Aug. 17, 1912, R. D. W. Connor to E. C. Brooks, Feb. 2, 1914, J. I. Foust to E. C. Brooks, April 24, 1915, Brooks Papers (DUL); E. C. Brooks to J. Y. Joyner, July 16, 1918, J. Y. Joyner to E. C. Brooks, July 23, 1918, S. P. I. Correspondence.

Upon the resignation of D. H. Hill as president of North Carolina College of Agriculture and Mechanic Arts in 1916, Brooks allowed his name to be considered for the vacancy. He declared that "if the trustees . . . are convinced that I am equal to the task . . . and if the faculty should look with no uncertain favor upon my election, then I am willing to be considered for this important position." O. Max Gardner, a prominent trustee, joined several other members of the board in the support of Brooks's election. But, after reviewing thirty-seven candidates, the trustees finally selected Professor W. C. Riddick of the faculty as president.[91]

Brooks would have to wait another seven years before assuming the helm of this institution. Two of those years he remained at Trinity College pursuing his numerous activities. During that time he served as state director of the National Education Association and as vice-chairman of the State Educational Commission, a survey group created by the legislature. Then, on January 1, 1919, he became State Superintendent of Public Instruction with offices in Raleigh, thus making it necessary for him to leave his intimate circle of friends at Trinity. Both he and his wife considered their years in Durham the "happiest period" of their lives and continued to maintain a close relationship with Trinity officials and faculty. In June, 1920, the college bestowed upon him a doctorate of laws, an honor duplicated by the University of North Carolina a year later.[92]

91. E. C. Brooks to R. H. Ragan, Feb. 17, 1916, O. Max Gardner to E. C. Brooks, April 20, 1916, O. Max Gardner to D. F. Giles, Feb. 10, 1916, Brooks Papers (DUL); *Durham Herald,* May 3, 1916.
92. E. C. Brooks to T. W. Bickett, Feb. 6, 1918, Governors' Papers (Bickett), State Department of Archives and History, Raleigh, North Carolina; *State School Facts,* XIX (July, 1947); Minutes of the Faculty of Trinity College, April 15, May 6, 1920; interview with Mrs. E. C. Brooks, May 9, 1956; *Alumni Directory, University of North Carolina, 1795-1953* (Chapel Hill, 1954), p. 104.

Four: EDUCATIONAL JOURNALIST, 1906-1923

[1]

Throughout his career at Trinity College, Brooks was an effective force for educational progress as editor of a magazine for North Carolina teachers. Under his guidance this magazine, first published in 1906, survived longer than any comparable periodical in the history of the state. Between 1874 and 1906 at least eight educational journals were published in North Carolina, but most of them found the struggle for existence too difficult and collapsed within a few years. In 1897 P. P. Claxton and Clinton Toms established the *North Carolina Journal of Education,* which in 1901 became the *Atlantic Educational Journal,* published in Richmond, Dallas, and St. Louis. This change left North Carolina without a teachers' journal for the next five years, the period of Aycock's campaign for better schools.[1]

During these years there was considerable discussion about establishing another journal devoted to public education. The leader in this effort was Henry E. Seeman, a Canadian by birth, who had manifested interest in educational publications in North Carolina for more than a decade. Though a printer by trade, he attended the annual sessions of the Teachers' Assembly, where he continuously urged the organization to sponsor a journal. Finally, he offered to finance and publish a teachers' magazine, if the educational forces of the state would promise to support it. In 1905 the State Association of County Superintendents and other groups affiliated with the Teachers' Assembly pledged their support to Seeman's enterprise.[2]

1. Knight, *Public School Education in North Carolina,* p. 364; Ruth Groom, "North Carolina Journals of Education," *N C E,* VIII (May, 1914), 8-10, 15; Charles L. Lewis, *Philander Priestley Claxton: Crusader for Public Education* (Knoxville, 1948), pp. 98-109.

2. Boyd, *Story of Durham,* pp. 253-254; E. C. Brooks, "Henry E. Seeman," *N C E,*

In July, 1906, a committee representing the Assembly met in Raleigh to hear Seeman explain the details of his proposition. After a full discussion the group decided to begin the publication of a teachers' journal. The Assembly was to select the editor and assist in securing subscriptions, while Seeman was to become publisher and financial manager. Brooks, who had been in Raleigh earlier that summer lecturing at North Carolina College of Agriculture and Mechanic Arts, had undoubtedly discussed the question of an educational journal with Superintendent Joyner and apparently had indicated his willingness to accept the editorship. Brooks's previous experience in journalism and his reputation among school men, coupled with Joyner's endorsement, were probably the major factors influencing the Assembly representatives, who appointed him editor of the new *North Carolina Journal of Education* that was to be published bi-weekly in Durham. Brooks was requested to give up the superintendency of the Goldsboro schools in June, 1907, in order to devote full time to his editorial work at an annual salary of $1,200.[3]

Brooks and Seeman spent "the greater part of July and August making plans for the new publication." The first issue of this new educational journal appeared on September 15, 1906, at an annual subscription rate of one dollar. The magazine had an impressive format, being divided into several departments, including articles of especial interest to school superintendents, primary teachers, the Woman's Association for the Betterment of School Houses and Grounds, and teachers in high schools, academies, and colleges. Other sections were devoted to "educational method," current events, feature articles, and personal items. Brooks announced that in addition to these regular departments, a series of useful articles by experienced teachers and announcements by State Superintendent Joyner, chairman of the advisory editorial board, would be published from time to time.[4]

XI (May, 1917), 17-18; E. D. Fowler, *The Seeman Printery: Fifty Years, 1885-1935* (Durham, 1935); "Two Score Years and Ten: A Half Century of Educational Journalism," *N C E,* XXIII (Sept., 1956), 17.

3. Brooks, "Henry E. Seeman," *N C E,* XI (May, 1917), 17-18. *Goldsboro Daily Argus,* July 23, 1906. Brooks's papers relating to the teachers' magazine have apparently been destroyed. Inquiries at the Seeman Printery and the North Carolina Education Association, the present owners of the magazine, failed to reveal the location of such manuscripts.

4. Brooks, "Henry E. Seeman, *N C E,* XI (May, 1917), 18; *Goldsboro Daily Argus,* August 31, 1906; "Two Score Years and Ten: A Half Century of Educational Journal-

In the first issue of the *Journal,* Brooks stated its editorial policy, which he consistently supported for the next seventeen years:

The policy of the Journal is, and will continue, to do everything to advance the cause of education, to call attention to work that is well done, and to discuss problems that are giving the teachers most concern. We believe the profession would be improved by raising the standards of teachers and that a high grade certificate should command a high salary in any county. In order to provide opportunities for the improvement of teachers we believe each county should establish free township and county high schools. We believe the State should provide for a longer school term by so amending the Constitution that the county commissioners may levy sufficient tax for better houses and longer terms. We believe further that after the State opens its doors to the children, they should be compelled to enter, especially the smaller children who are too small to work, and all who are unable to read and write.[5]

He gave more explicit expression to this policy in his first editorial comments. The lead editorial, entitled "Is the School Term Long Enough?," declared that "the average length of schooling for the country child is about three years of four months each." Brooks dismissed as absurd the idea that the state was financially unable to provide better schools and longer terms for rural children and declared that the first remedial step was to amend the constitution to enable the counties to levy taxes sufficient to meet the demands of rural education. In two other editorials he urged the county boards of education to enlarge the powers of the county superintendents and deplored the rapid turnover of teachers, which resulted from appallingly low salaries.[6]

During its first year the *Journal* largely continued the "departmental" arrangement of the initial issue. Editorially, Brooks hammered away on such themes as longer school terms, qualified teachers, and higher salaries. He described the pathetic plight of rural schools, which were kept open less than four months each year and whose qualified teachers "flocked to wealthier counties." He demanded a public high school in each township in order to provide a "training ground to prepare a sufficient number of teachers for the entire pub-

---

ism," *N C E,* XXIII (Sept., 1956), 17, 44; *North Carolina Journal of Education,* I (Sept. 15, 1906). Hereafter cited as *N C J E.*
    5. *N C J E,* I (Sept. 15, 1906), 12.
    6. *Ibid.*

lic schools." In almost every editorial he concluded that the basic problem of public education in North Carolina was "the lack of money," which he attributed to the defects of a Reconstruction constitution and to the decisions of the State Supreme Court in 1870 and 1885. In 1906 the court still held that county officials could not exceed the constitutional tax limitation in providing for the constitutional school term of four months. According to Brooks, it was high time the legislature and the people rectified these "ancient decisions" of the Supreme Court by constitutional amendments increasing the school term and removing the tax limitation for educational purposes.[7]

Immediately prior to the opening of the legislature of 1907, he increased the tempo of his editorial campaign for various reform measures. He insisted that the state possessed adequate wealth to equalize and raise educational opportunities in the several counties and to establish a minimum salary for teachers with superior qualification.[8] For the benefit of legislators, he presented statistics showing that one-fourth of the children in the state did not have advantage of the minimum school term of four months required by the constitution. "Those who have taken an active part in the educational campaign of the past few years," he wrote, "have seen one or two land owners in a district exercise authority over his tenants, whose children ought to be in school, and turn the election against schools, saying . . . that education for these is not a 'necessary expense,' and the children had better work in the fields—yes 130,620 of them."[9] He also implored the legislators to provide adequate facilities for training elementary teachers and heartily endorsed proposals to increase the State Superintendent's salary and enforce school attendance.[10]

In 1907 Brooks threw the support of the *Journal* behind a measure declaring public schools a necessary expense and requiring counties to levy a tax sufficient to maintain at least a four-month term in every school. The defeat of this bill brought him great disappointment, but he urged the teachers and school officials of the

7. *N C J E*, I (Oct. 15, 1906), 8; *N C J E*, I (Nov. 1, 1906), 10; *N C J E*, I (Dec. 1, 1906), 10; Charles L. Coon, "School Support and Our North Carolina Courts," *North Carolina Historical Review*, III (July, 1926) , 403-405, 412-417.

8. *N C J E*, I (Dec. 1, 1906) , 10.

9. *N C J E*, I (Jan. 1, 1907), 12.

10. *N C J E*, I (March 1, 1907), 4.

state to keep such a law before the people until the meeting of the next legislature. Brooks supported Joyner in opposing a bill to elect county boards of education by popular vote. He argued that many people in the state did "not even believe in education at all," and to place the boards of education in the hands of "active politicians" would destroy the educational progress made since 1901. The bill was defeated, largely because the Democrats were as yet unwilling to endanger their power over such local offices. Despite certain disappointments, Brooks concluded that the Legislature of 1907 had taken "no backward steps" and had left the schools "considerably stronger." Later in the same year, the State Supreme Court reversed the Barksdale decision of 1885 and declared that county school officials could exceed the constitutional limitation in levying taxes for the maintenance of the four-month school term.[11]

When Brooks became professor of education in Trinity College in 1907, he retained his position as editor of the teachers' journal. The move to Durham made it possible for him and Seeman to work more closely and conveniently on the publication. By that time, however, it appeared that the magazine would suffer the dismal fate of its predecessors. Brooks declared that subscriptions "came in so slowly that one would think that the teachers of the state had no interest in the publication." So few were the advertising contracts that they were "kept on one page in the ledger."[12] Although Brooks had refused to accept further pay after December, 1906, there was a deficit of $2,000 by the end of the first year of publication. The journal probably would have collapsed had it not been in the hands of such men as Seeman and Brooks, who saw in it something more than a financial investment. Both men had "faith" in the publication. Seeman told Brooks, "We will make it go." In October, 1907, Brooks described the unsound financial condition of the *Journal* to the Association of County Superintendents and insisted that 6,000 subscriptions were necessary to save it. Each superintendent then promised to solicit a certain number of subscriptions from his county. Also, Brooks persuaded Seeman to publish the magazine

11. *N C J E*, I (March 1, 1907), 4; *N C J E*, I (March 15, 1907), 4, 9; *N C J E*, I (April 1, 1907), 8; Coon, "School Support and Our North Carolina Courts," *North Carolina Historical Review*, III (July, 1926), 412-417.
12. Brooks, "Henry E. Seeman," *N C E*, XI (Oct., 1917), 17-18.

monthly instead of bi-weekly and to retain the original price of one dollar. Through these means and increased advertising receipts, the *Journal* reduced its deficit to $500 in 1908.[13]

From 1907 to 1909 Brooks continued to crusade for a progressive educational program through his editorial columns. In May, 1907, he was again writing about the length of the school term and speaking of "four or five months" as the minimum term for rural school children.[14] After the passage of the high school law in the same year, the *Journal* increased the number of articles of interest and value to secondary school teachers and officials. Brooks urged county school officials to take full advantage of the law, but warned against overloading the high school curriculum with textbooks and rote memory work. In this connection he pointed out the necessity for qualified teachers and insisted that the material progress and popular support of public education had surpassed that other essential ingredient to efficient schools—the training of teachers. He was convinced that most teachers were plodding along in "the old ways," adding nothing new to their classroom instruction. He suggested as a partial remedy a more efficient corps of county superintendents, who would personally supervise the work of the teachers and encourage in-service training.[15]

In November, 1908, Brooks answered the attacks of certain church groups who opposed the state high school law on the grounds that it was detrimental to denominational secondary schools. He insisted that state control of education could be traced to Martin Luther and that the problem was not "how far the state shall educate, but how much education can an individual receive." He argued that the separation of church and state necessitated state control of education and that the destruction of state schools was not a part of the church's mission. According to Brooks, the chief claim of the church on education lay in the state's neglect of its duty in the past. "Religious instruction," he concluded, "does not depend upon church control and ownership of the school any more than a religious people depend upon a theocracy.[16] This was a rather strong editorial for a

13. *Ibid.; N C J E*, II (Oct., 1907), 17.
14. *N C J E*, I (May 15, 1907), 9.
15. *N C J E*, II (Feb. 1908), 14-16; *N C J E*, II (March, 1908), 5-7.
16. *N C J E*, III (Nov., 1908), 14-16.

professor in a Methodist college to direct to a leading Methodist journal.[17]

[2]

By the end of the third year of publication, the *North Carolina Journal of Education* had paid off its debt and become self-supporting. Late in 1908 Seeman sold the magazine to W. F. Marshall of Raleigh, a printer and former teacher. It was moved to Raleigh shortly thereafter, and its name was changed to *North Carolina Education* in January, 1909. Brooks remained editor and purchased half interest in the journal in 1910. At the end of the fourth year, he announced that the financial condition of the magazine continued to improve but was yet "unsatisfactory." By 1912, however, the monthly circulation had risen to 1,600 copies. Brooks and Marshall, as editor and publisher respectively, maintained the arrangement of 1910 until August 1, 1919.[18]

One of the principal handicaps to the development of education in North Carolina, as Brooks pointed out, was the large percentage of teachers without normal-school training. In 1908, for example, two-thirds of the teachers in the state lacked such training. A partial remedy for this situation was offered at the meeting of the Association of County Superintendents in August, 1909, by J. A. Bivins, State Supervisor of Teacher Training. He announced the organization of the North Carolina Teachers' Reading Circle, which was designed "to furnish from year to year a carefully selected course of reading adapted to the professional needs of the teacher." The members of the Reading Circle took an annual examination on the books which was prepared by the State Supervisor of Teacher Training and given by the county superintendents. Upon the successful completion of a four-year course in reading, the teacher received a diploma from the State Department of Public Instruction which entitled him to preferential treatment regarding jobs and salaries. The county superin-

17. "Our State Educational Policy," *North Carolina Christian Advocate,* LIII (Oct. 15, 1908), 1.
18. *N C J E,* III (Dec., 1908), 1; Brooks, "Henry E. Seeman," *N C E,* XI (May, 1917), 17-18; Groom, "North Carolina Journals of Education," *N C E,* VIII (May, 1914), 15; *N C E,* V (Sept., 1911), 2; W. F. Marshall to E. C. Brooks, Sept. 19, 1913, Brooks Papers (DUL).

tendents were "advised to renew, free of cost, the first grade certificate to all who are members of the reading circle. . . ."[19]

Brooks attended the meeting of the county superintendents in
1909 and participated in the discussion of the Reading Circle project. In the October issue of *North Carolina Education,* he initiated
the Reading Circle program with a treatment of Hamilton's *Recitation.* He was requested to undertake this work by Joyner and Bivins
because of his success in extension work among Durham County
teachers. Apparently, his direction of the Reading Circle was intended at first to be temporary, but he continued to supervise it for
a decade. Joyner rarely failed to compliment Brooks's conduct of
the project in his biennial reports to the Governor. Since more than
half of the 11,915 teachers in the state participated in the Reading
Circle, Brooks exerted a significant influence in raising the qualification of teachers through his reading courses in *North Carolina
Education.*[20]

In addition to this reading program, the magazine carried a
variety of information valuable to the teacher. Brooks published
articles on the teaching of history which were based upon his work
with the Committee of Eight in revising the elementary-school
courses in history. He frequently included descriptions of efficient
programs and successful innovations in certain school systems. He
had faith in the power of example and publicized "model" school
programs with a view toward arousing other areas to benefit by their
success. Similarly, he seemed to believe that publicity of glaring
defects would elicit a public indignation strong enough to demand
remedial measures. In various ways Brooks's journal stimulated a
professional spirit, an *esprit de corps,* among North Carolina teachers. To determine his influence in this direction is obviously impossible, but the elevation of the professional status of the teacher
was a constant concern and a frequent editorial theme.[21]

In September, 1910, Brooks published his personal observations
on the progress of teacher training during the past decade. After

19. *Report of the Supervisor of Teacher Training, 1908-1910,* pp. 112-114.
20. *Ibid.,* p. 114; *N C E,* IV (Oct., 1909), 16-17; W. T. Laprade, "History of Trinity
College," pp. 23-24; *Report of the President of Trinity College to the Board of Trustees,
1915,* pp. 6-7; *Biennial Report, 1910-1912,* p. 10.
21. *N C E,* IV (Oct., 1909), 8; Knight, *Public School Education in North Carolina,* p.
363.

eight years of summer institute work, he reported: "There is to be found considerable improvement in the professional spirit of teachers and county superintendents. There are, of course, more than one thousand local tax districts. These as a rule draw teachers of superior training, who, mingling with other teachers of the state, have made a better spirit and there is a greater incentive to progress." Despite these improvements, he noted several inexcusable defects. For example, some county superintendents confined their efforts to a "little clerical work"; many teachers did not own the textbooks required by law and did "not know the lessons when they go to class"; and summer institutes still concentrated upon grammar and arithmetic at the expense of literature, geography, and history. "These conditions existed more widely ten years ago," he concluded, "but they exist today and are a barrier to the progress of education."[22]

Between 1909 and 1913 Brooks waged a vigorous campaign for several educational measures with the purpose of gaining support for them among school officials and teachers, who in turn were to arouse the people. One such measure was a legislative provision for agricultural instruction in public schools. Brooks had first published his ideas on the subject in 1902 in the *News and Observer*. By 1909 he was waging an editorial campaign for farm-life schools. He opened the columns of his journal to the editor of the *Progressive Farmer* and to a professor at the state agricultural college; both heartily endorsed the establishment of farm-life schools. Brooks also publicized the work of the Boys' Corn Clubs, a movement initiated in the South by Seeman Knapp in 1908 and financed by the General Education Board. The clubs, enrolling more than three thousand members in North Carolina by 1911, were usually conducted in connection with local schools and were under the direction of State Supervisor I. O. Schaub. The purpose of the clubs was to introduce future farmers to scientific agriculture and to increase soil productivity. Prizes were awarded to boys whose land yielded unusually large quantities of corn. Brooks considered this competition "a significant educational contest" and pointed to the work of the corn clubs as the first step toward bringing scientific agriculture into the public school curriculum. Largely as a result of the agitation for agricultural

22. E. C. Brooks, "Progress in Teaching—Some Notes and Observations," *N C E,* V (Sept., 1910), 6-7.

education by Brooks, the Farmers' Union, and various educational organizations, the legislature provided for ten farm-life schools in 1911; two years later the provisions for the establishment of such schools were extended to every county in the state.[23]

Another educational innovation that Brooks endorsed was the creation of a professional textbook commission. In 1911 he directed an editorial to Governor W. W. Kitchin requesting his support for such a reform. Brooks pointed out that the State Board of Education consistently rejected textbooks recommended by the sub-textbook commission composed of professional school men. At the same time Joyner pleaded with the legislators to amend the law to provide that teachers be represented on the Textbook Commission, which then consisted of members of the State Board of Education. The Legislature of 1911, following the advice of Brooks and Joyner, passed a law which provided that in addition to the seven members of the State Board of Education, six professional school men should be appointed to the Textbook Commission. Since Joyner was already a member, this act gave the school men a majority on the commission.[24]

One of Brooks's favorite editorial topics was "the office of county superintendent," which he considered the fulcrum of the public education system and at the same time one of the weakest links in the whole structure. In his critique of "a good superintendent," he declared that such men "should know how to teach and how to teach well," but above all, they should possess "the saving grace of common sense and should be able to judge good teaching, not so much from the standpoint of so-called theoretical pedagogy as from the effect of the instruction on the child." The superintendent, of course, must be an efficient administrator and business manager, fully acquainted with school law and finance. Brooks believed that the superintendent should "remain long enough in a community to work out something worthwhile," and decried the fact that many county superintendents were political appointees, who devoted only part of their

23. *N C E,* IV (Nov., 1909), 4; *N C E,* IV (Dec., 1909), 8-9; *N C E,* IV (Jan., 1910), 9; *N C E,* IV (Feb., 1910), 21-22; *N C E,* IV (June, 1910), 3, 26; Frederick B. Mumford, *The Land Grant College Movement* (Columbia, Mo., 1940), pp. 133-134; E. C. Brooks, *The Story of Corn,* pp. 259-265; *Biennial Report, 1910-1912,* p. 12; *Biennial Report, 1912-1914,* p. 17; *N C E,* V (May, 1911), 11; *N C E,* VII (Jan., 1913), 3.

24. *N C E,* V (March, 1911), 13; *N C E,* V (Feb., 1911), 4-5; *Biennial Report, 1908-1910,* pp. 18-20; *Biennial Report, 1910-1912,* p. 15.

time to school work. Such men failed to provide that supervision so essential to an efficient school system and offered no assistance to teachers desiring professional improvement. In 1913 Brooks urged the legislature to remedy this situation by requiring all superintendents to possess at least the requirements for a first grade elementary certificate. The General Assembly refused to go as far as he suggested, but it did provide that a superintendent must have taught during the five years immediately prior to his election.[25]

Perhaps Brooks's most vigorous editorial campaign in *North Carolina Education* concerned the six-month school term. In March, 1909, he urged that the state constitution be amended so as to provide for a minimum term of six months.[26] From then on, rarely was there an issue of *North Carolina Education* that did not carry an article or editorial on the six-month term. Brooks intensified his campaign for such legislation in the fall of 1912, an indication that he thought that the next legislature would be receptive to the existing agitation. In November, 1912, he wrote:

It is apparent to all that the public school term in a large number of counties is too short. In fact, a four months term is so short that pupils will forget in the remaining eight months what they have learned in four months. . . . The minimum term should be moved up to six months within the next year and every teacher in North Carolina should become interested enough to make this a live issue in every county. The General Assembly will meet in January. But between now and then teachers and school officers could bring this need home to those who will represent the counties in the next General Assembly.[27]

Brooks later suggested that the legislature provide an additional tax of five cents on each $100 valuation of property in order to increase the school term. The legislature of 1913 followed his advice both in providing a six-month term and a five-cent tax, which yielded $375,-000. The legislators recognized that this amount would hardly insure a six-month term in all schools. Moreover, the constitutional minimum was still four months. In short, Brooks and his cohorts had won only the first round in their fight and had to continue their efforts until 1918, when the people of North Carolina finally ratified a

25. *N C E*, V (June, 1911), 15; *N C E*, V (Sept., 1910), 6-7; *N C E*, VII (May, 1913), 15; *N C E*, VII (Jan., 1913), 3; *N C E*, VII (April, 1913), 5-6.
26. *N C E*, III (March, 1909), 13.
27. *N C E*, VI (Nov., 1912), 19.

constitutional amendment providing a minimum school term of six months.[28]

Brooks exhibited courage in editorials on many occasions. His bold criticisms of the courts and of many accepted educational practices, as well as his rebuttal to the attack on public high schools by a Methodist publication, serve as examples of his fearlessness. Even more significant was his defense in 1909 of Charles L. Coon, Superintendent of the Wilson county and city schools, who had described in an address the unequal division of school taxes between Negroes and whites. Coon concluded that Negro education was not a burden upon white taxpayers. Many North Carolina newspapers were highly critical of Coon's remarks, and some launched a full-scale attack upon him. Brooks's position was that although he had not fully agreed with Coon at the time of the address, he did agree that "the negro school is not a very great burden on the white race." He complimented the Wilson school board for supporting Coon and declared that it was "refreshing to be assured that the members were not swept off their feet by the hysterics of the crowd."[29]

While Brooks was at Columbia University in 1913-1914, he continued to edit *North Carolina Education* with the assistance of S. S. Alderman, executive secretary of the Central Campaign Committee. He still furnished monthly installments of the Reading Circle course. He also published two especially significant articles concerning teacher education and the high school curriculum. In the first article he decried the existing tendency of summer institutes in North Carolina to emphasize "method courses" at the expense of courses providing teachers with "a working knowledge of the school subjects." In his opinion it was absurd to offer instruction "in the general method of conducting a recitation" to teachers without adequate preparation in such subjects as literature, geography, and history. He believed, too, that institute conductors had to apply educational theory to practical situations before their instruction would become worthwhile.[30]

28. *N C E*, VII (Jan., 1913), 3, 5; *N C E*, VII (Feb., 1913), 1-2; Morrison, *A Study of the Equalizing Fund*, pp. 13-14.

29. *N C E*, IV (Nov., 1909), 14. In 1907 Brooks described Coon as "one of the best school men in state" who was often unpopular because of his "plain language." E. C. Brooks to F. A. Woodward, April 20, 1907, Charles L. Coon Papers, University of North Carolina Library, Chapel Hill.

30. E. C. Brooks, "A Word As to Teacher Training," *N C E*, VIII (June, 1914), 6-7.

In the second article, concerning the high school curriculum, he reiterated his demand for a broad, flexible course of study and asserted that the "existing emphasis on the curriculum with its 'points' and 'credits' and pages to be covered, its arbitrary standards, and its logical balance of studies, has gone far to obscure the real meaning of education as a process of choosing and applying those things that will secure the strongest and most profitable reaction in the child." He placed the major responsibility for the rigid high school curriculum, "wrongly conceived and wrongly used," upon the colleges. "No study or group of studies," Brooks concluded, "has any importance for its own sake; its value assists a teacher in bringing a pupil into those relations with his environment that are agreeable, stimulating, and promising for him personally and profitable to society. The curriculum should include any body of knowledge that can be successfully organized to this end."[31]

[3]

When Brooks returned to Durham in 1914, after a year at Columbia University and a summer at Peabody College, war had broken out in Europe. He immediately arranged for the publication of articles to provide teachers with information necessary for a "broader perspective" of the European conflict. In September, 1914, he himself wrote an article on "A European War and the Geography of Europe." His colleague at Trinity College, William T. Laprade of the history department, consented to prepare a series of articles describing the background of the war. Between October, 1914, and May, 1915, Laprade published seven articles in North Carolina Education bearing such titles as "Nationalism in the Balkans and the European War," "Bismarck and the German Empire," and "Policies of Kaiser William II." With the entry of the United States into the war, North Carolina Education participated in the various patriotic and propaganda campaigns conducted in the public schools.[32]

From 1914 to 1919 North Carolina witnessed the passage of much important educational legislation stimulated in part by circumstances

31. E. C. Brooks, "An Example of A Misdirected Educational System," N C E, VIII (March, 1914), 6-7.
32. N C E, IX (Sept., 1914), 6-7. For the Laprade articles, see N C E, IX (Oct., 1914-May, 1915).

produced by the war. By 1916 the public schools had reached a point that demanded significant changes. One proposed reform concerned the method of examining, accrediting, and certificating teachers. According to Superintendent Joyner, the existing method had been "in operation in this State, almost without the crossing of a 't' or the dotting of an 'i,' since 1881." There was no uniformity in the certification of teachers, and each of the one hundred county superintendents could "establish practically his own standard."[33] In 1897 the legislature had created the State Board of Examiners, appointed by the State Board of Education, to prepare and grade examinations of applicants for first grade certificates. With the passage of the high school law ten years later, the Board of Examiners was given charge of certificating teachers in public high schools in rural areas. Thus, teacher certification rested almost solely upon examination.[34] In describing the situation in 1916 Joyner declared:

All teachers in elementary rural public schools are required to be examined and certificated by the county superintendent of the county in which they teach: first grade teachers biennially, second and third grade teachers annually. There is no provision to secure exemption from this endless round of examinations on the same subjects. . . . Previous preparation and successful experience count nothing toward certification. . . . All teachers in all city, town and other public schools operated under special acts of the General Assembly are exempt from examination or certification of any sort by anybody.[35]

In Joyner's opinion this antiquated, chaotic method of teacher certification had to be reformed if the state consolidated the educational progress of the past decade. This reform, he thought, would mean a higher quality of instruction, better trained teachers, and higher salaries for teachers.[36]

Changes in the certification system had the backing of Brooks in *North Carolina Education*. In fact, few measures received such strong editorial support. In January, 1913, he urged the legislature to

33. *Biennial Report, 1914-1916*, p. 24; *Biennial Report, 1912-1914*, pp. 25-26.

34. James E. Hillman, "The Story of Teacher Education and Certification in North Carolina," *The Quarterly Review of Higher Education among Negroes*, XXI (Jan., 1953), 21-22; Gilbert A. Tripp, "James Yadkin Joyner's Contribution to Education in North Carolina as State Superintendent of Public Instruction" (unpublished M. A. Thesis, University of North Carolina), chap. v, pp. 50-71.

35. *Biennial Report, 1914-1916*, p. 71.

36. *Ibid.*, pp. 27-28.

establish "a uniform examination, gradation, and certification system for teachers" with a minimum professional and scholastic requirement "in advance of the present requirement for teachers." Although the legislature ignored the plea, Brooks continued to champion such a provision. By 1914 Joyner was more urgent in his recommendation for the establishment of a "uniform standard of academic qualifications" for teachers by the State Board of Examiners and for a "classification of certificates" that would reward teachers with successful experience and advanced training by reasonable increases in salary. Shortly after this recommendation, the Legislature of 1915 empowered the Board of Examiners, in its discretion, to accept successful experience and academic and professional credit from approved colleges in lieu of examinations. Brooks expressed disappointment with this provision and charged that the legislature had refused to accept Joyner's entire plan, because of its fear of centralization of power in the State Superintendent's office.[37]

At that same time Brooks outlined a plan which would combine the work of the summer institute conductors and examiners under the direct supervision of the State Superintendent. In discussing his plan he wrote:

The law requires that each county hold an institute biennially and the teachers to be certificated biennially. The officers of the institutes are the county superintendents and two institute conductors. It would be a simple matter therefore to have these officers of the institute changed into an examining board with full power to license teachers in the county. The State Department could have supervision over the entire work of this board as it does today. Then, it would hardly be necessary to enforce attendance upon institutes. Furthermore, after a teacher received a first grade certificate, she would not be required to stand examination on the same public school studies two years hence; but a progressive course should be outlined, and it should be part of the work of the institute conductors to outline this course for the approaching year and to examine in the course of the preceding year. In this way the Teachers' Reading Course will be of great advantage to the teachers of the state. This plan could be enforced with but little change in the present law.[38]

37. *N C E*, VII (Jan., 1913), 3; *Biennial Report, 1912-1914*, pp. 26-27; Hillman, "The Story of Teacher Education and Certification in North Carolina," *Quarterly Review of Higher Education among Negroes*, XXI (Jan., 1953), 22; *N C E*, X (Oct., 1915), 12.
38. *N C E*, X (Oct., 1915), 12-13.

Brooks claimed that his plan, which was endorsed by several influential school officials, would incur little additional expense and would avoid the cry of centralization.[39]

He admitted that his plan was "different from that proposed by the State Superintendent."[40] Indeed, Joyner was concerned about the proposal and was willing to modify his own scheme to avoid an open break with Brooks. He argued, however, that Brooks's plan for the institute conductors to become the board of examiners was impractical because of the rapid turnover in institute conductors from year to year. "I should like to talk to you about the plan for the uniform examination and certification of teachers," he wrote Brooks, "before you discuss it further along the line of your last editorial."[41] Joyner's concern about their differences indicated that he considered Brooks's support in *North Carolina Education* of primary importance to the success of the proposed measure.

The objectives of their plans were identical, with differences only in the matter of organization and operation. Both were straightforward men who could discuss their divergent views and appreciate the merits of the other's plan. Moreover, their genuine interest in the progress of public education would not permit them to endanger the success of a needed reform by an open disagreement. The unified endorsement of one plan of certification by all educational forces was a prerequisite for persuading the legislature to enact the measure. Brooks and Joyner continued to iron out their differences from time to time through correspondence and conversation. In the spring of 1916 Brooks still considered "the time ripe for a union of the institute work . . . with the examining work," while Joyner held this combination as a future goal. They discussed the matter when Joyner visited Brooks for several days in the summer of 1916 in order to get his assistance on an address to be delivered at the National Education Association. Finally, a compromise plan incorporating ideas of both men was approved by the Teachers' Assembly. Brooks championed the new plan in *North Carolina Education,* declaring that "the cause of education would be generally improved" by its enactment.[42]

39. *N C E,* X (Nov., 1915), 19.
40. *N C E,* X (Oct., 1915), 12.
41. J. Y. Joyner to E. C. Brooks, Oct. 18, 1915, Brooks Papers (DUL).
42. E. C. Brooks to J. Y. Joyner, April 28, 1916, J. Y. Joyner to E. C. Brooks, June 27, 1916, Brooks Papers (DUL); *N C E,* XI (Feb., 1917), 13.

The work of Joyner, Brooks, and many others on teacher certification came to fruition during the Legislature of 1917. The legislature
abolished the Board of Examiners and created the State Board of
Examiners and Institute Conductors composed of three men and
three women, with the State Superintendent as chairman and the
State Supervisor of Teacher Training as *ex officio* secretary. This
board possessed "entire control of examining, accrediting, and certificating all applicants for teaching positions in the State and was also
put in charge of directing and conducting the teachers' institutes for
a term not less than two weeks biennially in every county."[43] Every
teacher in the state was required to hold a certificate from the board,
except those who were issued second and third grade certificates by
local superintendents. The board certificated teachers on the basis
of professional and academic credit as well as examination.[44]

For Brooks the next important step after the creation of the State
Board of Examiners and Institute Conductors was the appointment
of the "right" people as members. He requested Governor Bickett
to avoid the mistake of appointing persons without an intimate
knowledge of the actual educational conditions in the state. He
feared that such persons would place the academic requirements for
certification too far beyond the reach of the "rank and file of teachers." He suggested that Bickett appoint A. T. Allen, N. W. Walker,
and Edgar Knight as members of the board. Of these, Allen was appointed. Brooks also worked with the board in organizing the certification system and advised the members to work for a "better course
of study," more adequate school libraries, and larger enrollment in
the Reading Circle. On May 12, 1917, he arranged for *North Carolina Education* to become "the official organ of the State Board of
Examiners and Institute Conductors."[45]

In addition to the certification law, the Legislature of 1917
enacted several other measures that Brooks supported in his editorial
columns. In that year the state accepted federal aid for vocational

43. *Biennial Report, 1916-1918,* p. 12.
44. *Ibid.* There was little opposition to the creation of the State Board of Examiners
and Institute Conductors. In 1917 the legislators waged their most vigorous battle over
the perennial question of popular election of county boards of education. See *News
and Observer,* March 4, 1917.
45. E. C. Brooks to T. W. Bickett, April 2, 1917, Brooks Papers (DUL); *N C E,* XII
(Oct., 1917), 4; *N C E,* XI (June, 1917), 15.

education provided by the Smith-Hughes Act, which was passed by Congress while the legislature was in session. For Brooks this was the reward of long years of crusading for the incorporation of agriculture and domestic science into the public school curriculum. The Legislature of 1917 also provided $25,000 for the education of illiterate adults. For several years night or "moonlight" schools for such persons had flourished in various parts of the state. Brooks had publicized the movement through numerous articles, and in his opinion the most beneficial result of these schools was their promise of giving illiterate parents "the mental concepts necessary to reason on educational questions . . . and to think in terms of better schools" for their children.[46]

The General Assembly of 1917 endorsed a constitutional amendment for the six-month school term, which was to be submitted to the voters in November, 1918. Brooks had waged a relentless editorial campaign in behalf of such a measure ever since the establishment of his magazine in 1906. Between the adjournment of the legislature in 1917 and the election more than a year later, he renewed his appeal to the teachers to arouse popular support for the amendment. Joyner, as titular director of the campaign for the six-month term, relied heavily upon Brooks and *North Carolina Education*. In August, 1918, Joyner wrote him: "Give us a strong editorial. You might also print a copy of the planks in the state platforms of the two political parties strongly endorsing the amendment."[47] Brooks wrote articles entitled "Why All Good Citizens Should Work for the Six Months' Amendment" and "Preach a Crusade against Ignorance." Joyner himself published an article in *North Carolina Education* expounding the advantages of the constitutional amendment. In November, 1918, the people of the state passed the amendment for a minimum school term of six months by a vote of 122,062 to 20,095. A week later the First World War ended with the signing of the Armistice. North Carolina was now prepared to imple-

46. *N C E*, IX (Feb., 1915), 11; *N C E*, XI (April, 1917), 5-7; *N C E*, X (Nov., 1915), 4-5; Leon Cook *et al.*, "The Federal Government and Vocational Agriculture in the South," *Secondary Education in the South*, p. 75. See also Fronde Kennedy, "Fighting Adult Illiteracy in North Carolina," *South Atlantic Quarterly* XIX (Jan., 1920), 189-200.

47. J. Y. Joyner to E. C. Brooks, Aug. 18, 1918, S. P. I. Correspondence. See also J. Y. Joyner to E. C. Brooks, Oct. 1, 1918, E. C. Brooks to J. Y. Joyner, Oct. ?, 1918, S. P. I. Correspondence.

ment more fully the educational legislation passed in 1917 and to adjust its school system to the new conditions created by the war.[48]

In the meantime Brooks continued to publish a wide variety of material in *North Carolina Education* that was valuable to teachers and school officials. In addition to the Reading Circle assignments, he provided numerous suggestions on "how to improve the teacher in service," which was a major problem confronting school men. He gave specific hints for more effective classroom procedures, while such regular features of the journal as book reviews and reports of the North Carolina Story-Tellers League afforded teachers other useful information. In 1920 Brooks induced Professor Laprade to write seven articles on "Teaching Citizenship in History Classes," which emphasized the necessity for a broader aim than the accumulation of facts or the promotion of provincial pride. A year later Laprade contributed eight articles to the journal, in which he, a professional historian, discussed such subjects as "The Use of Textbooks in History and Civics" and "Planning the Work of a Course in History." He included lesson plans which the teacher could use as guides for his own class work. Through similar methods Brooks sought to furnish information valuable to school officials. For example, he himself published articles designed for principals and superintendents in *North Carolina Education* in 1917 and 1918 on school law and administration. He also acted as his own "roving correspondent" and reported proceedings of educational meetings in his magazine in order that school men might be informed of developments in the field of education. For Brooks this was an essential factor in the growth of a professional spirit among the educational forces of the state.[49]

[4]

By 1919 Brooks had edited *North Carolina Education* for thirteen years. During that period he had co-operated with the State Superintendent of Public Instruction in all matters affecting public

48. *N C E*, XIII (Sept., 1918), 3-5; *N C E*, XIII (Oct., 1918), 4-5; *N C E*, XIII (Nov., 1918), 4-5; *Biennial Report, 1916-1918*, p. 16.
49. *N C E*, X (Jan., 1916), 4-5; E. C. Brooks to W. F. Marshall, Aug. 3, 1920, S. P. I. Correspondence; *N C E*, XV (Sept., 1920-March, 1921); *N C E*, XVI (Sept., 1921–Feb., 1922); *N C E*, XII (Nov., 1917–Feb., 1918).

schools. Whatever the differences of opinion between Joyner and Brooks, they remained close personal friends and partners in the building of a reputable school system in North Carolina. Brooks rarely missed an opportunity to compliment Joyner's leadership. He supported Joyner in all campaigns for re-election and described him as the "leader of educational thought in North Carolina." When Brooks succeeded Joyner as State Superintendent in January, 1919, he described his "distinguished predecessor" as "one of the finest products of the state," who was leaving office "at the height of his power and popularity."[50]

Upon his elevation to the state superintendency, Brooks feared that he would have to terminate his connection with *North Carolina Education*. Professor M. C. S. Noble of the University expressed a desire to become editor if Brooks relinquished the position. But the Governor and Attorney-General assured him that he would in no way violate "the spirit or letter of the law" by retaining his relation with the magazine while holding a state office. However, on August 1, 1919, Brooks leased his half interest in the publication for $500 to W. F. Marshall, the publisher, and became "contributing editor." For the next four years *North Carolina Education* was in effect the press organ of the State Department of Public Instruction. It, of course, carried a wealth of material of practical value to teachers and also served as a medium of communication between State Superintendent Brooks and the educational forces during a period of rapid change in school legislation which necessitated numerous announcements and explanations. In fact, the volumes of *North Carolina Education* between 1919 and 1923 provide a large part of the history of Brooks's administration as State Superintendent.[51]

For seventeen years Brooks closely adhered to his original editorial policy "to do everything possible to advance the cause of education." He possessed a great deal of pride in the publication, which through his faith and diligence managed to survive longer than any

50. *N C J E*, I (June 1, 1907), 9; *N C E*, XIII (Dec., 1918), 15; *N C E*, XIII (Jan., 1919), 5. For the financial condition of *North Carolina Education* from 1917 to 1919 see Report of the Business Manager of *North Carolina Education*, July 1, 1918, Brooks Papers (DUL); Report of the Business Manager of *North Carolina Education*, July 1, 1919, S. P. I. Correspondence.

51. E. C. Brooks to M. C. S. Noble, Jan. 9, 1919, W. F. Marshall to E. C. Brooks, Aug. 1, 1919, S. P. I. Correspondence.

other educational journal in the state. He reluctantly severed his
connection with the magazine in 1923 upon becoming president of
North Carolina State College of Agriculture and Engineering.[52]

52. After Brooks severed his relation with the magazine, Marshall became the sole
owner and Brooks's successor as State Superintendent A. T. Allen served as contributing editor. In 1924 *North Carolina Education* was purchased by the North
Carolina Education Association and its name changed to *North Carolina Teacher*. Ten
years later, it reverted to the title *North Carolina Education* and celebrated its fiftieth
anniversary in September, 1956. E. C. Brooks to A. T. Allen, Aug. 16, 1923, A. T. Allen
to E. C. Brooks, Aug. 20, 1923, Brooks Papers (DUL); "Two Score Years and Ten,"
N C E, XXIII (Sept., 1956), 17, 44-46.

Five: STATE SUPERINTENDENT OF PUBLIC INSTRUCTION, *1919-1923*

[1]

In the summer of 1918 Joyner informed Governor Bickett of his intention to resign as State Superintendent. During his seventeen years at the helm of the school system, a solid foundation for public education had been carefully constructed. The passage of the constitutional amendment for the six-month school term in November, 1918, was the crowning achievement of his remarkable career. However, this amendment necessitated a major reorganization of the public schools, which Joyner, then fifty-six years old, desired to leave to a younger man, but he refused to specify his choice of a successor. Governor Bickett was well aware of his high regard for Brooks, an opinion shared by the Governor himself.[1] On December 21, 1918, Joyner announced his resignation, which was to take effect on January 1, 1919. Bickett declared that "within ten seconds by his watch" after receiving Joyner's resignation he "was after Dr. Brooks." In fact, he added, "I never thought of anybody else but Dr. Brooks."[2]

The press of the state heartily endorsed his choice. The *State Journal,* expressing the sentiment of numerous newspapers,[3] declared:

Governor Bickett's instantaneous choice of Dr. Brooks will evoke not one criticism. It was inconceivable to the chief executive that any man would have named anybody else. The thing has been done in the Governor's mind since Dr. Joyner informed him that the place of State Superin-

1. T. W. Bickett to J. Y. Joyner, Dec. 21, 1918, *Public Letters and Papers of Thomas Walter Bickett, Governor of North Carolina, 1917-1921,* ed. R. B. House (Raleigh, 1923), p. 369; interview with Mr. A. S. Brower, Oct. 2, 1956.
2. *Durham Herald,* Dec. 22, 1918.
3. See *Durham Herald,* Dec. 24, 1918; *Greensboro Daily News,* Dec. 23, 1918; *News and Observer,* Jan. 2, 1919; W. F. Marshall, "The New Schoolmaster of the Great Commonwealth," *North Carolina Education,* XIII (Jan., 1919), 3-4.

tendent would be vacated during Governor Bickett's term. The new Superintendent should easily hold the office at topnotch. He has what the baseball men call pep and as a public protagonist is hardly to be matched anywhere. No man in the public life of North Carolina presents a theme more interestingly. He is a prince of raconteurs and a public speaker of masterful gifts. Then he is a technician. He knows men best, but men are more interesting than books. He knows books well enough to write them and understands them well enough to relate them to men. He is one of the humanest of all North Carolinians, and he enters the one department that touches more of the humanity than any other office in the Commonwealth.[4]

The *Greensboro Daily News* added that the Trinity College professor was not only "a man of great ability" and personal charm, but possessed the support of Senator F. M. Simmons's "political organization."[5]

Brooks immediately accepted Governor Bickett's offer to become State Superintendent of Public Instruction. He realized that it would be a difficult job, but at forty-seven years of age he was energetic and in good health. He had a diabetic condition, but this as yet had not affected his physical vigor. At noon on January 1, 1919, he took the oath of office before the Chief Justice of the State Supreme Court in the presence of the Governor, relatives, and "a cordial company of friends."[6] Joyner was pleased with the Governor's choice of a "successor so worthy and able." "Of course you know," he assured Brooks, "I am yours to command for the good of the cause at any time . . . and also for the sake of yourself who have been my *long and true friend.*" In Joyner's words, "the hour is ripe, the opportunity is great."[7]

Brooks entered office at an extraordinary moment in the educational history of the state. Drastic reforms and changes were necessary if the public schools were to meet the demands of "the new era" produced in part by the First World War and by the constitutional amendment. Brooks undoubtedly shared Joyner's view that "the

4. *The State Journal* (Raleigh, North Carolina), Jan. 3, 1919.
5. *Greensboro Daily News*, Dec. 23, 1918.
6. Marshall, "The New Schoolmaster," *N C E*, XIII (Jan. 1919), 3-4; interview with Mrs. E. C. Brooks, May 9, 1956. Brooks discovered that he was a diabetic several years prior to becoming State Superintendent, but he suffered no apparent ill-effects until much later. Medical Record of Dr. E. C. Brooks, Hist. No. 5162, 7/12/38, Duke Hospital.
7. *Biennial Report, 1916-1918*, p. 27; J. Y. Joyner to E. C. Brooks, Dec. 24, 1918, S. P. I. Correspondence.

hour is ripe" for achieving the fruition of their labors in behalf of public schools; but he realized, too, that the situation demanded wise and skilful leadership. In many respects educational conditions had greatly improved since he last held a position in the Department of Public Instruction; yet more than 13 per cent of the state's population above ten years of age was still classified as illiterate, and school enrollment had decreased by almost 15,000 pupils between 1916 and 1918. The 15,241 teachers, about a fifth of whom held college diplomas, received an average monthly salary of $46.52. The total expenditure for public education in 1917-1918 was $7,522,372.80, and the total value of school property was $14,303,503.28. More than half of the 8,102 schools in the state employed only one teacher. Negro schools remained in a primitive stage. Their sad plight was only partially relieved by assistance from such philanthropic agencies as the General Education Board and the Rosenwald, Jeanes, and Slater Funds.[8] Moreover, the First World War produced new educational problems in North Carolina, for many qualified teachers left the schoolroom to enter military service and occupations with higher salaries. Brooks, recognizing the gravity of this situation, insisted that the only remedy was to "make the schools more attractive from a financial standpoint."[9] The scarcity of farm labor during the war had also drawn students from the classroom and had thereby caused a sharp decline in average daily attendance. The war had vividly pointed up the problem of illiteracy and the "supreme importance of education" to life in the twentieth century. The acute shortage of competent teachers was a major part of the postwar "crisis in education" that engulfed North Carolina. Implementation of the teacher certification law as well as other school legislation of 1917 had been delayed by the war and the influenza epidemics.[10]

Under these circumstances Brooks assumed the State Superintendency on January 1, 1919. His most pressing task was to secure

8. *Biennial Report, 1916-1918*, pp. 7-10, 279; Tripp, "James Y. Joyner's Contribution to Education," pp. 176-177. See also Elmer D. Johnson, "James Yadkin Joyner, Educational Statesman," *North Carolina Historical Review*, XXXIII (July, 1956), 359-383.
9. *Durham Herald*, April 7, 1918.
10. For the effects of the First World War on public education, see *Biennial Report, 1916-1918*, p. 7; *Report of the State Board of Examiners and Institute Conductors, 1917-18*, p. 82; *N. E. A. Bulletin* (Nov., 1919), pp. 3-12; Lewis, *Philander Claxton*, pp. 220-239; *The National Crisis in Education: An Appeal to the Public*, ed. W. T. Bowden (Bureau of Education Bulletin No. 29, Washington, 1920).

legislation implementing the constitutional amendment for the six-months school term. This he considered the first step toward alleviating the major educational problems of the state. His arrival in Raleigh at the opening of the General Assembly forced him to rush the preparation of this legislation. Joyner had already prepared a law for operating the schools for six months, which had been approved by only thirty-six county superintendents. Undoubtedly, Brooks was fully informed of Joyner's proposal, but he did not commit himself to its support. The proposal called for a state tax of thirty cents on every $100 valuation of property for the creation of a State Public School Fund to be used to pay one-half of the salaries of all county superintendents and other persons concerned solely with the supervision of county schools as well as "three months salary of all teachers of all sorts employed in the public schools of the county, including teachers and superintendents of city and town schools." The remaining salaries would be supplied by a special county tax not to exceed thirty-five cents on the $100 valuation of property and "a corresponding tax on every taxable poll." No county would share in the state fund unless it levied this special tax.[11]

Most city superintendents opposed the Joyner measure on the grounds that it discriminated against their schools. It would pay one-half of the salaries of county superintendents and three months salary of rural teachers whose average school term was 116 days, while it would pay only three months salary of city teachers and superintendents whose term was already 166 days. The leaders of the opposition were Superintendents Charles L. Coon of Wilson and R. H. Latham of Winston-Salem. Coon, who was never reticent, told Brooks that he was unalterably opposed to the Joyner bill and would fight against its enactment.[12] He and Latham quietly planned their strategy and mobilized the city superintendents for a showdown fight. Coon distributed a sheet describing the Joyner measure as an iniquitous attempt to force the wealthier counties to bear the financial burden for public schools. He also drafted a substitute bill that was to be managed in the legislature by Senators James Gray, Jr., of Winston-Salem, and H. G. Connor, Jr., of Wilson. The Coon bill was sup-

11. *Biennial Report, 1916-1918*, pp. 17-19; *The State Journal*, Dec. 20, 1918.
12. *Biennial Report, 1916-1918*, p. 42; Charles Coon to E. C. Brooks, Jan. 15, 1919, S. P. I. Correspondence.

ported by those city superintendents who in reality feared a centralization of power in the State Department of Public Instruction.[13]

In the meantime, Brooks studied the Joyner proposal, requested advice from school officials, and assured the Coon-Latham faction that he desired an equitable plan for financing the six-month school term. He skilfully avoided premature commitments to any proposal, and the opposition was never quite certain of his exact position.[14] Basically he approved of the Joyner bill, but favored several significant revisions. The success of the measure, as he well knew, depended largely upon the way it was managed in the legislature. His personal friend, Victor Bryant of Durham, could be counted upon for powerful support as chairman of the House education committee. The comparable Senate position was occupied by F. C. Harding of Pitt County, whose selection Brooks had endorsed. With allies in these key legislative posts, Brooks revised the Joyner measure, converting it into the "Brooks Bill," and at the same time he began marshaling the support of county superintendents and legislators.[15]

In his revision, Brooks raised the state tax from thirty to thirty-five cents and changed the method of distributing the state funds. The state would pay three months salary of all teachers, one-half of the annual salaries of county superintendents, and one-third of the annual salaries of city superintendents. By the first Monday of November, the county boards of education would submit their budgets for the ensuing year to the State Superintendent, in which "adequate provision" would be made for their portion of the six-month school term. By the first Monday in May, the board was to submit a detailed budget to the county commissioners, showing the amount needed to operate the schools for the following year. After deducting the amount paid by the state, the commissioners would be required to levy a special tax sufficient to cover the remainder of the May budget, but no county would be forced to exceed a rate of thirty-five cents in this tax levy. Brooks drafted the bill with a view toward the con-

13. E. C. Brooks to Charles Coon, Jan. 18, 1919, K. R. Kurtis to Charles Coon, Jan. 8, 1919, R. H. Latham to Charles Coon, Jan. 11, 1919, R. H. Latham to Charles Coon, Jan. 15, 1919, Harry Howell to Harry Harding, Jan. 20, 1919, Charles Coon, "The Joyner Six Months School Bill," H. G. Connor, Jr., to Charles Coon, Jan. 16, 1919, Coon Papers.
14. E. C. Brooks to Frederick Archer, Jan. 8, 1919, E. C. Brooks to Harry Harding, Jan. 16, 1919, S. P. I. Correspondence.
15. E. C. Brooks to O. Max Gardner, Jan. 6, 1919, S. P. I. Correspondence.

solidation of small school districts by making the apportionment of
state funds partially contingent upon the average daily attendance in
schools. His bill also called for $75,000 for teacher training, but this
amount was later reduced to $50,000. The State Board of Examiners
and Institute Conductors was authorized to establish teacher-training
courses in county summer schools and high schools in lieu of the
summer institutes.[16]

In a second bill, called the County Budget Act, Brooks spelled
out the operation of the May and November budgets and specified
the basis for the apportionment of the state school funds. This bill
divided the county school taxes into three separate funds: for teachers' salaries, buildings, and incidentals. In estimating the amount
necessary for the teacher salary fund for 1919-1920, the county
boards of education were to calculate on the basis of the monthly
salaries of teachers in 1918-1919 with minimum increases of from 10
to 25 per cent, depending upon the types of certificates. Included in
this section was a crude salary schedule for teachers, which provided
that the maximum salary for a teacher with a second grade (the
lowest) certificate should be forty-five dollars per month. Brooks
inserted a clause in this bill insuring that no teachers' salaries would
be reduced by the operation of this act.[17]

On January 17, 1919, he discussed his bills with the Legislative
Committee of the Teachers' Assembly. Five days later he appeared
for the first time before the education committees of the General
Assembly and informed the legislators: "The principle that the
strong shall help the weak is too firmly established for any city or
county to claim that each district or each county should be required
to maintain a six-months school without having regard for this fundamental principle."[18] However, on January 24, 1919, a group of city
superintendents convened at the Yarborough Hotel and approved a

16. *News and Observer,* Jan. 22, 1919; *Public Laws and Resolutions, 1919,* pp. 276-
281; *N C E,* XII (March, 1919), 6.
17. *Public Laws and Resolutions of North Carolina, 1919,* pp. 289-290. The salary
schedule for teachers in 1919-1920 was outlined in the following manner:

	Certificates	Monthly salary
1.	Second Grade	$45
2.	Elementary	65
3.	Primary and Grammar Grade	70
4.	High School	75.

See *ibid.,* p. 290.
18. *News and Observer,* Jan. 29, 22, 1919.

resolution stating that "taxes collected locally for school purposes should remain in the locality to be distributed by local officials." These school men were still unsure of Brooks's position until they conferred with him after the meeting at the Yarborough. Brooks listened patiently to their views and resolutions; then divulged his proposed bills, which were, of course, contrary to their "principles."[19]

The real fight was on, and both sides began preparations for the hearings before the joint education committee. Latham set up headquarters in Raleigh, while Coon continued to shower the newspapers with articles denouncing the "centralization feature" of the Brooks Bills. Senator James Gray was their liaison with the legislature. Brooks, however, enjoyed a favorable position, which his opponents feared. Latham declared: "The county superintendents are almost as a unit against us. They have figured out that they are going to get something for nothing and they have spread that stuff among the teachers."[20] He also observed that Brooks had "very shrewdly" diverted attention of the legislators from the salary schedule by placing it in the County Budget Bill rather than in the bill for the six-month school term. But Brooks obviously was not fighting alone; not only was he assisted by the chairmen of the education committees and many county superintendents, but he also had the full support of Governor Bickett. One of his most active supporters was a former student, A. M. Proctor, superintendent of the Roanoke Rapids schools, who charged that Coon and Latham were pawns of reactionary politicians. "You ought to know Mr. Coon well enough," he wrote Latham, "to realize that his leadership of any movement will automatically kill the movement."[21] The *News and Observer* also strongly supported the Brooks Bills, and its publisher, Secretary of the Navy Josephus Daniels, endorsed them in an address to the General Assembly.[22]

On January 30, 1919, Victor Bryant introduced the Brooks Bills in the legislature. Several days later, Coon's measure was sponsored by Senator H. G. Connor and Representative Edgar Pharr. The essential features of this bill were emphasis upon local school control

19. Harry Howell to Charles Coon, Jan. 28, 1919, Coon Papers.
20. R. H. Latham to Charles Coon, Jan. 28, 1919, R. H. Latham to Charles Coon, Feb. 25, 1919, Charles Coon, "Objections to the Bryant Bill," Coon Papers.
21. A. M. Proctor to R. H. Latham, Feb. 10, 1919, S. P. I. Correspondence.
22. *News and Observer*, Feb. 13, 14, 19, 1919.

and the requirement for "pauper" counties to increase their tax levies in order to share in the equalizing fund.[23] On February 11, 1919, the education committees in joint session opened hearings on the various education bills. Brooks began the proceedings with a masterful demonstration of his oratorical and forensic skill. He ridiculed the city superintendents for their fear of centralization and their selfish desire to deny superior educational advantages to children of the "pauper counties." Moving from the rostrum to the floor of the House "in passionate gesticulation," he insisted that these same pauper counties had helped to finance the Carolina Central Railroad, which was the very lifeblood of many cities opposing his bills. He further declared:

They attack the bills as tending toward centralization. There isn't a feature of centralization that isn't already in the law. They attack the proposal to regulate salaries. Well, we have undertaken to make these uniform because we have not been willing to say that one county shall have by reason of paying better salaries, better teachers than other counties; we have opposed the principle of local control of salaries because it would result inevitably in war between teachers and the boards; in a union of teachers organized for the protection from school boards—an anomalous position in the light of the kinship of labor and interests.[24]

He used statistical evidence to point up the sad plight of teachers whose salaries were "not enough to pay their board." Earlier he had told the education committees that the state should provide sufficient funds to equalize the educational opportunities among various counties, because "the child is the ward of the state and not of the county." In concluding his address to the committees on February 11, 1919, Brooks remarked: "The question is not how far the state shall go in education. It must go its limits, so far as its resources permit, and I for one am in favor of a free school that extends from the bottom to the state university."[25] Competent observers agreed that Brooks's defense of his bills assured their success.[26]

The hearing continued with addresses by Coon, Latham, and Connor, who were apparently more concerned with opposing

23. Harry Howell to Harry Harding, Jan. 20, 1919, Coon Papers; *News and Observer,* Feb. 8, 1919.
24. *Raleigh Times,* Feb. 12, 1919.
25. *Ibid.; News and Observer,* Jan. 22, Feb. 12, 1919.
26. *News and Observer,* Feb. 12, 13, 1919.

Brooks's bills than with supporting the Coon measure. Senator Gray, an original member of the Coon-Latham faction, was already disheartened about the prospects for success and was receptive to Brooks's persuasive arguments. In fact, opposition rapidly disintegrated after Brooks's defense of his bills and Victor Bryant's "eloquent" speeches in the House.[27] On February 21, 1919, Latham wrote Coon: "I hardly thought that it was worthwhile to keep up the fight any longer as it was evident that the [Brooks] Bill was going to be put through. It was a Bickett-Joyner-Brooks-Bryant proposition and many of the folks who no doubt really believe the thing is wrong in principle did not wish to go up against that combination."[28] Coon remained "proud" of his stand and still complained about the power given a "few Raleigh bureaucrats" by the Brooks Bills. With only minor changes, however, the Six Months School Act and the County Budget Act were ratified on February 28, and March 4, 1919.[29]

At Brooks's insistence the Legislature of 1919 also enacted measures to implement the vocational education act of 1917 and to promote the establishment of high schools. Under the new legislation, the high school became "a definite part of the public school system," and Brooks as State Superintendent was authorized to formulate and enforce standards and attendance regulations for such schools. Under the new law any school that met the requirements set up by Brooks was entitled to be rated as a high school.[30] While the legislature was in session, another movement attempted to provide free tuition for orphans at the University of North Carolina. Brooks wanted to amend such a bill to include all state and denominational colleges, and he sought to win the support of the state college presidents for it. He argued that since the religious organizations often supported orphans up to the college level, it was only fair to permit them to use state scholarships in denominational schools. Such a measure, he believed, would "go a long way in harmonizing the state

27. *News and Observer,* Feb. 13, 14, 20, 1919; R. H. Latham to Charles Coon, Feb. 4, 1919, R. H. Latham to Charles Coon, Feb. 8, 1919, Coon papers.

28. R. H. Latham to Charles Coon, Feb. 21, 1919, Coon Papers.

29. Charles Coon, "The Bryant School Bill," Feb. 21, 1919, Coon Papers; *Journal of the House of Representatives of North Carolina, 1919,* pp. 261-262; *Journal of the Senate of North Carolina, 1919,* p. 319.

30. *Public Laws and Resolutions, 1919,* pp. 280-281; W. H. Pittman to Mary Barbage, Feb. 28, 1919, W. H. Pittman to J. Y. Irvin, May 27, 1919, E. C. Brooks to L. S. Inscoe, Aug. 16, 1919, S. P. I. Correspondence.

and private institutions."[31] Since officials of the state colleges were cool toward the idea, Brooks dropped the matter for fear of precipitating "an unfortunate discussion."[32]

An act of the legislature in 1919 closely related to the school legislation was the so-called Revaluation Act, providing for a statewide revaluation of all taxable property under the supervision of the State Tax Commission. This law sought to have all property assessed at its true monetary value. Previously, the assessment of property was in the hands of the county commissioners, who generally allowed it to be assessed at 60 per cent of its value. The Revaluation Act was passed largely through the influence of Governor Bickett, an enthusiastic advocate of the "gospel of truthfulness." The total valuation of property in 1919, the last year of the old system, was $1,099,296,290, while the total valuation in 1920 was $3,156,243,202. The revaluation of taxable property was obviously of great importance to public education, since the schools were largely financed by property taxes. The Brooks school laws required all counties to reassess their property by 1920 in order to share in state school funds.[33]

Shortly after the adjournment of the legislature, Brooks set out to enforce the new educational legislation. Under the laws of 1919, he possessed considerable power over local schools—perhaps more power than any previous State Superintendent, because he could force schools to raise their standards through his control of the State Public School Fund. Between April and September, 1919, he explained various phases of the educational "reorganization" at district meetings of the county superintendents. He carefully defined the taxation procedures necessary for a county to follow before sharing in state funds. He found that some school officials feared that the enforcement of the revised compulsory school attendance law would create an acute demand for additional buildings. Brooks, advising "tact and judgment" in securing school attendance, assured them that he had attempted to provide for new buildings through the special

31. E. C. Brooks to Robert Wright, Feb. 14, 1919, E. C. Brooks to J. I. Foust, Feb. 15, 1919, S. P. I. Correspondence.
32. N. W. Walker to E. C. Brooks, Feb. 17, 1919, Harry Chase to E. C. Brooks, Feb. 28, 1919, W. C. Riddick to E. C. Brooks, Feb. 20, 1919, S. P. I. Correspondence.
33. Morrison, *Study of the Equalizing Fund*, pp. 16-17; *N C E*, XIII (March, 1919), 6.

building funds required by the County Budget Act. During the year 1919 he published numerous articles in *North Carolina Education* describing the new school legislation, and much of his official correspondence was devoted to explaining the changes to school officials.[34]

[2]

The most pressing task confronting Brooks after the close of the legislature was the reorganization of facilities for training teachers in service. With a $50,000 appropriation for this purpose, he intended to replace the inadequate two-week institutes with summer schools of at least four weeks' duration. His first step was the reorganization of the State Board of Examiners and Institute Conductors. He particularly wanted to unify the work of the Board under one member and to shift the emphasis of its work from the examination of teachers to the supervision of teacher training. By June, 1919, he had reorganized the Board with A. T. Allen as director. The state was divided into districts, and each member of the Board was assigned to one district for the purpose of supervising the summer teacher-training programs in the counties within his district. The new salary schedule of 1919 provided the main incentive for teachers to attend these county summer schools.[35]

Many teachers, however, refused to take the new school laws seriously. They made no effort to attend summer schools in order to raise their certificates and salaries, because they believed that the teacher shortage would force the Department of Public Instruction to issue emergency certificates to them with salaries equal to those of teachers who had fulfilled summer school requirements. Such teachers obviously did not know their new State Superintendent personally and failed to recognize that his control over the purse strings placed him in a powerful position to force them in line.[36] On August 14, 1919, Brooks declared:

34. E. C. Brooks, "Some Vital Matters Discussed by County Superintendents," *N C E,* XIV (Oct., 1919), 3; E. C. Brooks to L. M. Peele, Aug. 11, 1919, S. P. I. Correspondence. See also *N C E,* XIII-XIV (March-Nov., 1919).

35. E. C. Brooks to N. W. Walker, April 4, 1919, Mrs. T. E. Johnston to E. C. Brooks, June 8, 1919, S. P. I. Correspondence; *N C E,* XIII (June, 1919), 3; *News and Observer,* May 29, 1919.

36. E. C. Brooks to Laura Scott, Sept. 2, 1919, S. P. I. Correspondence.

I have about reached the conclusion that this is the year to draw the line between teachers who desire to improve themselves, thereby improving their teaching, and those who have little professional spirit and pay no attention to the rules and regulations and the law. It seems to me therefore that we should issue *no emergency certificates,* and those who have refused to comply with the requirements of the law, will have to teach on a second grade certificate. We must elevate the profession and we cannot do it if the teachers take advantage of the situation and refuse to make any effort toward professional improvement.[37]

Brooks informed the superintendents of his decision and publicized it in the newspapers. He remained unmoved when teachers who refused to attend summer school threatened "to strike if they were not issued emergency certificates" instead of the second grade certificate with a maximum monthly salary of forty-five dollars.[38]

Brooks, of course, was willing to assist teachers who made some effort to improve their qualifications. In 1919 almost a thousand teachers attending summer schools failed by one or two credits to raise their second grade certificates to elementary certificates with a minimum monthly salary of sixty-five dollars. By the end of the summer schools, Brooks was convinced that he should aid such teachers by issuing "a certificate between the first and second grade certificates—one that will encourage second grade teachers to begin a course of study that will lead to this and having acquired it, to work up to the first grade. Likewise, all first grade teachers who have not complied with the requirements should drop back to it."[39] Shortly afterward, Brooks authorized the issuance of three types of provisional certificates for teachers who had manifested an interest in professional improvement. He also provided provisional certificates for principals and high school teachers. By the end of the school year 1919-1920, a total of 16,322 white and Negro teachers held certificates, while in May, 1919, only one-half that number possessed "any certificate at all." Over one-third of those certificated in 1919-1920 could only qualify for the lowest grade certificate. Despite the increased salaries based on Brooks's certification scheme, the shortage

37. E. C. Brooks to G. M. Guthrie, Aug. 14, 1919, S. P. I. Correspondence.
38. E. C. Brooks to Laura Scott, Sept. 2, 1919, S. P. I. Correspondence; *News and Observer,* Aug. 15, 1919.
39. *News and Observer,* Sept. 19, 1919; E C. Brooks to T. Fletcher Bulla, Sept. 2, 1919, S. P. I. Correspondence.

of teachers prevented the opening of 403 schools during his first year in office.[40]

Brooks came to realize the need for further reorganization of the teacher training program and for a rather radical revision of the certification plan and salary schedule. In planning these changes he called several meetings of the representatives of all colleges in the state offering summer school work, members of the State Board of Examiners and Institute Conductors, and members of the State Educational Commission. At a meeting on January 24, 1920, he outlined his plans and reported that under the law of 1919 the average salary of teachers had increased over 50 per cent. The average salary of rural teachers had increased almost 100 per cent. But Brooks declared that by no means was a living wage paid all teachers and pointed out that the main principle underlying his revised salary schedule was equal salaries for teachers with equal academic and professional qualifications, regardless of the grade they taught.[41]

Brooks's aim was to establish a strictly uniform certification and salary plan for the whole state and to regulate the second grade certificates which county superintendents still "handed out for the asking."[42] In order to execute his plan, Brooks needed the assistance of the collegiate summer schools, which could provide instruction for teachers with high grade certificates. The county summer schools were to be attended by teachers who were not high school graduates and who held second grade or provisional certificates. Throughout the spring of 1920, he perfected arrangements for his new teacher-training program with a view toward placing teachers in a position to reap the benefits of the revised salary schedule that he hoped to push through the special session of the General Assembly in August, 1920.[43]

40. E. C. Brooks, "Provisional Certificates Authorized by the State Board of Examiners," *N C E*, XIV (Oct., 1919), 8-9; E. C. Brooks, *Administration of the Public School System and Teacher Salary Schedule: A Report to the Governor, 1919-1920*, pp. 4-5.

41. E. C. Brooks to Howard Rondthaler, Feb. 20, 1920, S. P. I. Correspondence; *News and Observer*, Jan. 25, 1920; E. C. Brooks, "A New Schedule of Teachers' Salaries," *N C E*, XIV (Feb., 1920), 4.

42. E. C. Brooks to Frank Bachman, May 17, 1920, S. P. I. Correspondence; E. C. Brooks to Harry Chase, Jan. 13, 1920, University of North Carolina Papers, University of North Carolina Library, Chapel Hill.

43. E. C. Brooks, "Plans for Summer School Work Being Completed," *N C E*, XIV (Feb., 1920), 3. For an explanation of the credits toward certification gained through summer school, see E. C. Brooks, "Summer School Program for North Carolina Teachers," *N C E*, XIV (April, 1920), 3-4, and the pamphlet, *Information Relative to the County Summer School, 1920*.

Brooks's certification plan and salary schedule received wide publicity at an educational conference held in Greensboro on May 4-6, 1920. The purpose of this gathering was to discuss "the crisis in education in North Carolina and how to meet it." It was the first of a series of similar conferences called in various states by P. P. Claxton, United States Commissioner of Education. The main discussions focused upon teacher qualifications and salaries, building needs, and the shortage of teachers. Brooks used the opportunity to explain in detail his salary schedule and certification program. Charles Coon's attempt "to trouble the waters" was promptly squelched by Brooks's "remarkable wit," and at the close of the conference the county and city superintendents fully endorsed the various Brooks proposals.[44]

Shortly before the opening of the extraordinary session of the legislature, Brooks submitted a special report to the governor that was described as a state document that would put him "in the company of Archibald Murphey," the father of the public school system in North Carolina.[45] This report stated that in 1919-1920 the state funds for public education amounted to $3,500,000 in comparison to $879,558 in 1918-1919. Brooks explained the teacher training program and reported that 7,000 teachers were in summer school in 1920. There were 4,000 teachers in the collegiate summer schools and 3,000 in the county summer schools. Brooks spelled out his salary schedule and certification plan in detail and wrote: "A state wide certification law was enacted in 1917, but before it could be inaugurated the United States entered the war. So many teachers were drawn from the profession to aid in the war that it was impossible to enforce the rules and supply the teachers for the schools. Therefore the teachers were not properly certificated untill [sic] 1919-1920. . . ." He believed that the experience of that year demonstrated the necessity for a revised salary schedule "to place the emphasis on professional fitness in order that those less qualified teachers may have an incentive to rise in the profession and those already well qualified may be content to remain in the profession and maintain a fair living standard." The total amount of the state school budget for 1920-1921 was already $3,974,600, excluding "the increase due to teachers who

44. *News and Observer*, March 13, May 5, 7, 9, 1920; *N C E*, XIV (April, 1920), 11; *N C E*, XIV (June, 1920), 5; A. F. Sharpe to E. C. Brooks, May 10, 1920, S. P. I. Correspondence.
45. M. C. S. Noble to E. C. Brooks, Aug. 6, 1920, S. P. I. Correspondence.

Table 1: Graduated Salary Schedule for White Teachers

Monthly salary based on length of service

	4 yrs.	3 yrs.	2 yrs.	1 yr.	0
High School, Grammar Grade, and Primary Certificates					
Class A—graduate of a standard A-grade college with 18 semester hours in professional work	$133.33	$120	$110	$105	$100
Class B—completion of three years of standard college or two years of normal school with 12 semester hours in professional work	110	105	100	95	90
Class C—two years of standard college with 6 semester hours in professional work	105	100	95	90	85
Provisional Class C	95	90	85	80	75
Elementary Teachers' Certificates					
Class A—one year of standard college or normal school	95	90	85	80	75
Class B—graduation from standard high school and one unit of summer school work	85	80	75	70	65
Provisional Elementary	75	70	65	60	55
Certificates Below Standard					
Temporary—three years of high school and one unit of county summer school work			$60		
Provisional A—two years of high school			55		
Provisional B—one year of high school			50		
County Second Grade			45		

Table 2: Graduated Salary Schedule for Negro Teachers

Monthly salary based on length of service

	4 yrs.	3 yrs.	2 yrs.	1 yr.	0
High School, Grammar Grade and Primary Certificates					
Class A—graduate of a standard A-grade college with 18 semester hours in professional work	$100	$95	$90	$85	$80
Class B—three years of standard college or two years of normal school with 12 semester hours in professional work	90	85	80	75	70
Class C—two years of a standard college with 6 semester hours of professional work	80	77.50	75	72.50	70
Provisional Class C	75	70	65	60	57.50
Elementary Teachers' Certificates					
Class A—one year of standard college or normal school	75	70	65	60	57.50
Class B—graduation from a standard high school and one unit of summer school work	70	65	60	57.50	55
Provisional elementary	65	60	55	52.50	50
Certificates Below Standard					
Temporary—three years of high school and one unit of county summer school work			$55		
Provisional A—two years of high school			50		
Provisional B—one year of high school			47.50		
County second grade			35.00-45.00		
County third grade			35		

would raise the value of their certificates as a result of attending summer school" in 1920. According to Brooks's calculations, this total increase would be "relatively small," and the new salary schedule could be financed by a 10 per cent increase in the tax rate of 1919-1920. Brooks concluded his report with this challenge: "The teachers have set out with a determination to improve their efficiency. The test therefore has come. Does the State really wish to secure better teachers? If so, it must pay the price."[46]

The legislature convened in special session on August 10, 1920, for the purpose of adjusting the tax rates in accordance with the Revaluation Act. The revaluation of taxable property, of course, took place in the period of postwar inflation.[47] In his message to the General Assembly, Governor Bickett said that he had hoped that the state would not have to take advantage of the 10 per cent tax increase allowed by the Revaluation Act, but the rise of prices had largely shattered such hopes. He added that the "ten per cent increase that would go for the maintenance of the public schools will not be sufficient to pay the increased salaries to which the teachers are so justly entitled."[48] Brooks had already prepared amendments to the school laws providing for special taxes in excess of the limitations fixed by the Revaluation Act. A visit to Durham with Victor Bryant, chairman of the House education committee, had secured Bryant's valuable support for his amendments.[49] "I will bend every effort," Brooks confided to a friend, "to persuade the General Assembly to adopt the salary schedule and to provide funds for it."[50] In his usual convincing manner he described the situation to the legislative committees and insisted that the state could not afford "to go back on" its promises to increase the salaries of teachers who raised their certificates by additional training.[51]

The Brooks Bill, including the salary schedule, met little opposition in the committees. The members, however, were determined to keep the counties within the 10 per cent tax increase, but agreed to

46. Brooks, *A Report to the Governor, 1919-1920*, pp. 4-6, 16.
47. *News and Observer*, Aug. 11, 1920. See also Wager, *County Government in North Carolina*, pp. 108-109, 300-301.
48. *Letters and Papers of Governor Bickett*, p. 58.
49. E. C. Brooks to Victor Bryant, June ?, 1920, E. C. Brooks to Frank Bachman, June 12, 1920, S. P. I. Correspondence.
50. E. C. Brooks to Holland Holton, July 22, 1920, S. P. I. Correspondence.
51. *News and Observer*, Aug. 8, 11, 1920.

establish an equalizing fund sufficient to provide for counties unable to maintain schools for six months after levying the maximum taxes. Brooks drafted his bills with these views in mind, and they were enacted essentially in their original form. Under these measures the state school tax was reduced from thirty-two to thirteen cents, a reduction made possible by the increased property valuation; but no county could participate in the equalizing fund unless it raised by tax levy or in part by borrowing 10 per cent more school funds for 1920-1921 than it had raised in 1919-1920. At the same time no county was required to levy a special tax in excess of fifteen cents on the $100 valuation of property. If this tax, coupled with the county's portion of the State Public School Fund for teachers' salaries, was insufficient to maintain the schools for six months, the county was then entitled to share in the equalizing fund, which was to be drawn from the State Public School Fund in order to cover any remaining deficit for 1920-1921. The amended law gave Brooks the authority to establish a "uniform graduated salary schedule for all teachers, principals, superintendents, and assistant superintendents based upon training, experience, duties, professional fitness, and continued service in the same school system, consistent with the estimated amount to be derived from the state school fund." This graduated schedule was to be the basis for the apportionment of the state funds for teachers and school officials.[52]

Brooks was pleased with the action of the legislators. "They gave me everything I asked for," he wrote, "but not quite in the way I asked for it. But the difference is a minor matter."[53] He was confident that the state tax of thirteen cents together with the county taxes would meet all demands. In fact, he believed that the thirteen cents tax would yield $600,000 more revenue than the thirty-two cents tax of the previous year.[54] His optimism about the new legislation was only surpassed by the confusion of the local school officials, who had barely recovered from the reorganization of 1919. These officials found it difficult to comprehend fully the intimate relation-

52. E. C. Brooks to Charles Coon, Aug. 19, 1920, S. P. I. Correspondence; *Public Laws and Resolutions, Special Session, 1920,* pp. 113-118; Morrison, *Study of the Equalizing Fund,* pp. 17-18.
53. E. C. Brooks to Frank Bachman, Aug. 27, 1920, S. P. I. Correspondence.
54. E. C. Brooks to H. E. Faison, Aug. 27, 1920, S. P. I. Correspondence; *N C E,* XIV (Sept., 1920), p. 3.

ship between salaries and certificates and even more difficult to understand that their genial State Superintendent meant what he said about enforcing a uniform program. In November, 1920, Brooks wrote:

I have no other purpose in all my administrative work other than to advance the teaching profession. The standing of the teachers so far as certification was concerned has been in such confusion that it has been impossible to lay down from the beginning complete rules for the certification of teachers and for fixing salaries. The best we can do is to lay down a few principles and then modify them as the educational conditions demand. . . . Within two or three years I feel certain the whole question of salaries can be definitely worked out and clear cut lines can be drawn. But whenever it appears that injustice is being done, I do not hesitate to modify any ruling that I have made. . . . If I could convince the county superintendents that it is my purpose to leave the running of the schools entirely to them just as soon as we can see through the maze of confusion, I feel there would be a better attitude toward the work of this Department on the part of those who have misunderstood our program.[55]

Following the end of the legislature in 1920, much of Brooks's time was consumed by an almost endless round of correspondence and public addresses explaining the revised school legislation.[56]

The first real test of Brooks's popularity came in the primary and election of 1920. In that year Cameron Morrison became the Democratic gubernatorial candidate after a hard fought contest with Bickett's Lieutenant-Governor, O. Max Gardner. The friends of D. F. Giles of Marion, a member of the State Board of Examiners and Institute Conductors, entered his name for the Democratic nomination for State Superintendent, but Giles withdrew from the race and threw his support to Brooks, who won the nomination without opposition.[57] On November 2, 1920, Brooks was elected "by a majority larger than that received by the heads of his ticket, a tribute to his success in so short a time in leading the state more rapidly toward the provision of adequate means for the education of its youth than it had ever gone in a similar period in its history."[58] He strongly sup-

55. E. C. Brooks to E. P. Bradley, Nov. 11, 1920, S. P. I. Correspondence.
56. See E. C. Brooks to L. E. Edwards, Aug. 27, 1920, E. C. Brooks to J. M. Glenn, Sept. 10, 1920, S. P. I. Correspondence.
57. *News and Observer*, April 28, 30, 1920.
58. Laprade, "History of Trinity College," p. 24. See also *News and Observer*, Nov. 4, 1920.

ported the candidacy of Cameron Morrison for governor, and the two men became fast friends. In fact, Brooks was one of Governor Morrison's closest advisers and missed few opportunities to laud his program for building highways and port facilities. Nor was it unusual for Morrison to summon Brooks to the Executive Mansion to assist him in preparing his public addresses.[59]

Shortly after the election, Brooks began preparations for the next regular session of the General Assembly in January, 1921. His first biennial report revealed that the total amount spent for schools in 1919-1920 was $12,212,258, which was almost twice that spent during the last year of Joyner's administration. The annual salary of rural teachers increased by $140.77, while that of city teachers increased by $151.76. Of the 7,627 teachers who attended summer school, 5,571 received credits raising the value of the certificates. The total enrollment for 1919-1920 was 691,249, an increase of almost 100,000 over the previous year. Although the rural population decreased, the enrollment of rural schools increased by 75,096 pupils. Brooks attributed the rise in school enrollment and attendance "in large measure to the compulsory school attendance law."[60] He recommended $5,170,200 in state funds for public schools. His other recommendations, which were based in part upon the report of the State Educational Commission, called for placing all state normal schools under the Department of Public Instruction and replacing the State Board of Examiners and Institute Conductors with divisions of teacher training and certification within his department. Brooks realized that the divergent views of the members of the Board were detrimental to the success of his uniform program of certification and teacher training.[61]

When the legislature convened in 1921, a number of factors had forced a change in the method of financing the schools. In the general election of 1920 the voters had approved an income tax amendment to the constitution, and the funds from this tax made it possible to relinquish the state property tax of thirteen cents. The property tax

59. Interview with Mr. E. C. Brooks, Jr., July 12, 1956; E. C. Brooks, "The State Should Own Adequate Port Facilities" (An Address), Brooks Papers (DUL).

60. *Biennial Report, 1918-1920*, pp. 9-10.

61. *News and Observer*, Feb. 7, 1921. See also *Public Education in North Carolina: A Report of the State Educational Commission* (Raleigh, 1920), pp. 55-56; interview with Mr. A. S. Brower, Oct. 2, 1956.

was henceforth to be levied by the counties. Brooks's immediate concern, however, was the economic depression, which by this time had settled upon the state. The sharp slump in agricultural prices placed the indebted farmers in a sad plight, while the decline in industrial wages resulted in considerable labor unrest. Under such circumstances it was natural for the legislators to be economy conscious. Since the reduced land values made the tax valuations under the Revaluation Act unjustly high during the depression, the legislature authorized county commissioners in their discretion to make horizontal reductions in property valuations.[62] Brooks immediately perceived the gravity of the situation and its potential dangers for his school program. On January 15, 1921, he wrote a friend: "The present depression is having its effect upon the General Assembly. I am merely marking time until I can see which way to go."[63]

After considerable wrangling, the legislators accepted Brooks's proposal for financing the state's share of the public schools. Under this plan the sum of $1,400,000, derived mainly from the income tax, was appropriated to the State Public School Fund, of which $642,750 was designated for specific purposes. The remainder formed an equalizing fund to be used for two purposes: first, to pay in accordance with the state salary schedule the salaries of county superintendents and assistant superintendents for six months and of city superintendents, supervisors, and principals of standard high schools and elementary schools of ten or more teachers for three months; second, to aid counties unable to pay teachers' salaries for six months after levying a maximum tax of thirty cents on the $100 valuation of property. The legislature also enacted Brooks's recommendation to replace the State Board of Examiners and Institute Conductors with divisions of teacher training and certification and to amend the compulsory school attendance law to include all children between the ages of seven and fourteen. Brooks was pleased with the legislative enactments of 1921 and declared that "the General Assembly was exceedingly good to us."[64]

62. Morrison, *Study of the Equalizing Fund*, pp. 18, 23; *Letters and Papers of Governor Bickett*, pp. 389-391; *Public Papers and Letters of Cameron Morrison, Governor of North Carolina, 1921-1925*, ed. D. L. Corbitt (Raleigh, 1927), pp. 112-117, 160-169, 231-233.

63. E. C. Brooks to N. W. Walker, Jan. 15, 1921, S. P. I. Correspondence.

64. *Public Laws and Resolutions, 1921*, pp. 411-421; *State Centralization in North Carolina*, ed. Paul Betters (Washington, 1932), pp. 31-32; Wager, *County Government*

In the meantime, he continued his efforts to improve the teacher-training program. In 1920 he notified teachers that after July, 1921, Reading Circle work would not be accepted as credit toward raising certificates. Henceforth, certification was to be based largely upon summer-school credits. Brooks, however, attempted to make his certification program flexible enough to avoid injustices to efficient teachers lacking the professional training for a high grade certificate. He fully recognized that at first some worthy teachers would necessarily receive lower salaries. Numerous teachers with many years of experience discovered that they had inferior certificates and descended upon his office demanding explanations. While Brooks and his assistants patiently explained the law, some of the teachers reacted belligerently, and others wept in despair. By the summer of 1921, however, the importance of the state certification program had been sufficiently impressed upon the teachers; that summer 10,911 teachers attended school.[65]

By late 1920 Brooks came to recognize the need for an agency designed to promote co-operation in teacher training between his department and the colleges in the state. First of all, such an agency must determine those schools capable of providing the required instruction, because at the time numerous institutions of doubtful status called themselves colleges. Brooks desired to establish standards for teacher training that would serve as guides in issuing certificates for credits received from these various colleges. For six months he studied the problem and by August, 1921, had decided to call a conference of college representatives "to assist him in establishing a standard of college work."[66] At his request the college presidents and members of the Department of Public Instruction met on October 7, 1921, and organized the North Carolina College Conference. In

---

in North Carolina, pp. 300-301; Morrison, Study of the Equalizing Fund, pp. 18-19; News and Observer, March 16, 1921; E. C. Brooks to Frank Bachman, Jan. 15, 1921, E. C. Brooks to W. Y. Davenport, Jan. 12, 1921, E. C. Brooks to M. E. Haggerty, Jan. 12, 1921, S. P. I. Correspondence.

65. E. C. Brooks to Charles Coon, Sept. 23, 1920, E. C. Brooks to A. S. Webb, May 23, 1923, E. C. Brooks to J. S. Miller, May 24, 1921, S. P. I. Correspondence; News and Observer, June 7, 1921; North Carolina Teachers' Reading Circle for 1921-1922 (Educational Bulletin No. 23); interview with Mr. A. S. Brower, Oct. 2, 1956; A. T. Allen, A Comparative Study of Summer Schools for Teachers in North Carolina in 1922 (Educational Publication No. 63).

66. E. C. Brooks to C. E. Brewer, Dec. 9, 1921, S. P. I. Correspondence; E. C. Brooks to W. P. Few, Aug. 26, 1921, Few Papers; A. T. Allen, Institutions of Higher Learning in North Carolina (Educational Publication, No. 58), p. 2.

his address to this group Brooks insisted that the effectiveness of his uniform program depended upon the standardization of college credits. "I am helpless without your assistance," he concluded, "and you will be in trouble without mine."[67] The conference organized committees to investigate the matter and to make recommendations, and in March, 1922, it accepted a set of "principles for accrediting colleges." Brooks promptly sent a team from his department to inspect and classify colleges in accordance with these principles. The rating of the institutions was completed in time to be used in issuing teachers' certificates to graduates of the class of 1922. Through the North Carolina College Conference, Brooks brought both state and denominational colleges into close co-operation with the Department of Public Instruction.[68]

The establishment of a uniform certification plan and salary schedule won him wide acclaim in educational circles. The major newspapers of the state devoted considerable attention to the significant aspects of his program and lauded what they considered his "remarkable" achievements. All the while, Brooks was gaining recognition far beyond the borders of his native state. In 1920 he was elected to the vice-presidency of the National Education Association, and in 1921 was appointed to its committee on salaries. The next year he was selected as a member of the Educational Finance Inquiry, a group of specialists in public education, taxation, and business, who were to conduct a comprehensive investigation of educational finance in view of postwar economic conditions. Their study, sponsored by the American Council on Education and financed by the Commonwealth Fund, produced a series of publications on the

67. Minutes of the Meeting of College Presidents and Delegates, Oct. 7-8, 1921, S. P. I. Correspondence.

68. The accrediting principles included: (1) admission to college required graduation from a four-year secondary school approved by a recognized agency; (2) college graduation required the completion of 120 semester hours of credit; (3) the size of the college faculty was to be determined by the type of institution and number of students, but all colleges with as many as 100 students should have at least eight department heads; (4) all colleges should possess a minimum annual operating income of $50,000; (5) colleges should have sufficient equipment, lands, and libraries of at least 8,000 volumes; (6) colleges must not maintain preparatory schools; (7) the standing of the college was to be determined in large part by its curriculum, efficiency of instruction, conservatism in granting honorary degrees, and standards of its regular degrees; (8) no college was to be accredited until it had been thoroughly inspected by a committee of the conference. Several of the above principles were not to become effective immediately. See Allen, *Institutions of Higher Learning*, pp. 12-13.

financial problems of education in the various states. The nine members of the group included such prominent educational experts as
George D. Strayer and Ellwood Cubberly. Brooks manifested a great
deal of interest in this work and utilized the findings of the investigations in his reorganization of the North Carolina schools.[69]

One of the most eloquent tributes to his work as State Superintendent appeared in the editorial columns of *The Journal of Education*, published in Boston, Massachusetts. The editor lauded the
rapid progress of public schools in North Carolina and insisted that
Brooks was unsurpassed "on the platform" and "in educational leadership."[70] A comparable tribute to Brooks's efforts was the description
of his educational reforms in the report of the Carnegie Foundation
for the Advancement of Teaching in 1920, which characterized the
first year of his administration as "unique in the history of American
education."[71]

[3]

During 1921 the adequacy of Brooks's method of financing public
schools in North Carolina was seriously jeopardized by the fluctuating tax valuations of property authorized by the legislature of that
year. The reductions in many counties ranged from 10 to 50 per cent
of the tax valuations of the previous year. This, of course, meant a
sharp decline in the county school revenues. The county commissioners, therefore, increasingly turned to the state equalizing fund
for aid in maintaining the six-month school and teachers' salary
schedule. Brooks immediately took steps to avoid the severe strain
upon this fund by forcing counties which had reduced property
valuations to exceed the thirty cent tax rate prescribed by the legislature. He warned the county officials in plain language that the
equalizing fund would not take care of the county school deficits

69. *The Journal of the National Education Association*, X (Feb., 1921), 31; *Journal of the N. E. A.*, X (April, 1921), 85; *Journal of the N. E. A.*, XI (Jan., 1922), 27; E. C. Brooks to W. P. Few, May 22, 1922, E. C. Brooks to George D. Strayer, July 14, 1922, S. P. I. Correspondence; Carter Alexander, *Bibliography of Educational Finance* (New York, 1924).
70. "Notable State Leadership," *The Journal of Education*, XCIV (July 14, 1921), 42.
71. *The Carnegie Foundation for the Advancement of Teaching: The Sixteenth Annual Report of the President and Treasurer* (New York, 1921), p. 85.

resulting from reduced property tax valuations.[72] In a statement to the press he declared: "I didn't write the constitution but I did write the law that provided that before any county participates in the equalizing fund it must provide funds up to a certain amount. Now they have cut the ground out from under the law by reducing property values. It will have to be built back on a rate that will raise the money needed by the schools."[73] He explicitly told the county commissioners that in order to share in the State Public School Fund, a county must levy, if necessary, the maximum rate prescribed by the legislature of 1920 or a rate on the 1921 valuation equivalent to the maximum thirty-cent rate levied on the 1920 valuation.

At the same time Brooks refused to consider proposals for a downward revision of the teacher salary schedule "during these critical times." In July, 1921, he asserted:

I do not believe the State Salary Schedule is too high. It is necessary to hold out reward to those who qualify themselves so that others will seek to become better qualified. The salary schedule is flexible and can easily be adjusted to a county. Many counties that exceeded the State Salary Schedule last year will simply come up to it this year. We have given the teachers a great desire to improve themselves. If we take away the incentive now by reducing the salary schedule, we may find ourselves within a year or two back where we were two years ago.[74]

Brooks stubbornly maintained this attitude and promptly terminated aid from the equalizing fund to any county that reduced teachers' salaries below the state schedule.[75]

In the meantime, teachers had taken advantage of the summer schools to raise their certificates, hence their salaries. The number of teachers holding the highest certificate increased from 2,368 in 1919-1920 to 4,367, a development that Brooks had not anticipated. By the end of the school year 1920-1921, he realized that state funds were inadequate to fulfil the state's obligation toward teachers' salaries. During 1920-1921 not only had the number of "well-trained teachers" increased from 7,491 to 10,141, but the total number of teachers

72. Wager, *County Government in North Carolina*, p. 301; Betters, *State Centralization in North Carolina*, pp. 32-33, 124-125; Morrison, *Study of the Equalizing Fund*, pp. 22-23; E. C. Brooks to E. F. Upchurch, April 25, 1921, E. C. Brooks to A. G. Cox, July 8, 1921, E. C. Brooks to T. T. Murphy, May 25, 1921, S. P. I. Correspondence.
73. *News and Observer*, July 12, 1921.
74. E. C. Brooks to A. G. Cox, July 8, 1921, S. P. I. Correspondence.
75. E. C. Brooks to Ella Thompson, Aug. 10, 1921, S. P. I. Correspondence.

employed in the state had increased by almost 2,000. The result was a deficit of $704,623.59 in the State School Fund. "The deficit therefore is not due to the high salaries paid," Brooks declared, "but to the large increase in well prepared teachers and in the total number of teachers employed." For him the question of the deficit was eclipsed by the importance of the increasing number of qualified teachers in the state. In any case, the deficit in state school funds magnified the controversy caused by decreased county property valuations.[76]

Brooks received valuable assistance from the state courts in his efforts to save his school program from the dangers of reduced tax valuations. When the Nash County commissioners refused to abide by his dictum in levying school taxes, the county board of education instituted mandamus proceedings against them in July, 1921. Judge George W. Connor upheld Brooks's action and ordered the Nash commissioners to levy sufficient taxes to operate the schools for the constitutional term of six months regardless of the legislative tax limitation. This decision undoubtedly induced many counties to provide the necessary taxes without further ado. Nevertheless, certain others continued to resist any additional tax levy; Yadkin County appealed its case to the State Supreme Court, which took action at an opportune moment in December.[77]

Brooks, meanwhile, had conferred with Governor Morrison on means of eradicating the deficit in the State Public School Fund for 1920-1921 and of revising the county tax rates for 1921-1923. They agreed to convene a special session of the General Assembly on December 6, 1921. This would also provide the Governor an opportunity to relieve municipalities suffering from the invalidation of the Municipal Finance Act of 1921. For Brooks, however, this special session of the legislature was to bring the most vociferous opposition to his school program in his entire career as State Superintendent, and was to provide a supreme test for his political tact and finesse. Fortunately, he was strongly supported by Governor Morrison as

76. E. C. Brooks to T. R. Foust, June 16, 1921, E. C. Brooks to Charles Coon, July 13, 1921, S. P. I. Correspondence; *A Comparative Study of Summer Schools for Teachers Held in North Carolina in 1921* (Educational Publication No. 39), pp. 5-7; E. C. Brooks, "Deficit in the State Public School Fund," Brooks Papers (DUL).

77. The Board of Education in Nash County vs. The Board of Commissioners of the County of Nash, July 16, 1921, E. C. Brooks to L. S. Inscoe, July 22, 1921, S. P. I. Correspondence; *News and Observer,* Aug. 12, 1921.

well as by several influential members of the legislature including one of his former students, John G. Dawson of Kinston. Brooks, of course, was cognizant of the opposition, and at a meeting of the county superintendents in November, 1921, he declared that "reactionaries" were fighting his progressive educational program solely because it necessitated higher taxes. Even these superintendents listened to him "without comment, question, or applause."[78]

The smoldering opposition to the state administration of public schools burst into overt criticism and hostility when Brooks appeared before the education committees on December 6, 1921, to explain the deficit in the state school funds. Leading the opposition was T. C. Bowie, the fiery representative from Ashe County, who accused Brooks of extravagance in expending state funds and demanded explanations of the "excessive" expenses of the Department of Public Instruction, including the State Superintendent's salary. He also strongly reprimanded Brooks for ordering the county commissioners to exceed the legislative tax limitation. At this juncture Representative R. O. Everett of Durham suggested that Brooks had "usurped" the power of the State Tax Commission. The author of the legislative tax limitation, R. A. Doughton of Alleghany County, expressed serious doubt that Brooks had ever intended to keep the schools within that limitation. Under this fire of criticism, Brooks firmly stood his ground, defended his actions in terms of the constitutional requirements, and for the enlightenment of some of his most caustic opponents explained that the deficit in state funds was for the year 1920-1921 rather than the current year of 1921-1922 as they supposed.[79] When Bowie described the extravagance of the state salary schedule, Brooks brought out a roster of the teachers' salaries in Bowie's native county of Ashe and asked him to designate those salaries that he would reduce—they were already below the state average. All the while, Brooks impressed upon other legislators the amounts due their counties from the deficit of $704,623. This approach apparently won him considerable support among legislators primarily concerned with the interests of their counties.[80]

78. Minutes of the Council of State, 1889-1924, pp. 399, 454, State Department of Archives and History, Raleigh, North Carolina; *Papers and Letters of Governor Morrison*, pp. 28-29; *News and Observer*, July 15, Nov. 23, 1921.
79. *News and Observer*, Dec. 7, 8, 1921.
80. *Greensboro Daily News*, Dec. 26, 1921; interview with Mr. B. L. Smith, April 28, 1956.

After several days of committee hearings the debate on educational finance was transferred to the floor of the General Assembly, where Bowie and Everett, joined by Senators W. H. S. Burgwyn and L. R. Varsar, led the attack on the Brooks program. But they proved to be no match for Brooks's friends, who persuaded the General Assembly to pay the deficit and validate county tax rates that had exceeded the legislative limitation. In accordance with Brooks's suggestion, the legislators also passed an act requiring other counties to levy a tax of thirty-nine cents on the $100 valuation of property (as currently assessed) for teachers' salaries in 1921-1922 and 1922-1923 in order to share in the state equalizing fund. Brooks believed that one reason for the easy passage of this act was the Supreme Court's decision in the Yadkin County case on December 7, 1921, which he considered "equivalent to asking the legislature to define the tax rate for schools and put an end to litigation." Largely through Bowie's influence $75,000 was transferred from the special appropriations for the Department of Public Instruction to the State Public School Fund, thereby increasing the remainder of that fund to $832,250. The General Assembly also created a commission to investigate and report on legislation "relating to taxation for school purposes."[81]

Brooks emerged victorious from what the *News and Observer* described as "the most serious fight he has had on his hands since he assumed direction of the schools three years ago." The legislature that set out "to clip the flappers of Superintendent Brooks" had actually accepted his plan for straightening out the "tangled disorder" of school finances resulting from changes in property values. One observer was convinced that the "capitulation" of Bowie, Doughton, and Varsar "was a perfect tribute to the diplomacy of Dr. Brooks." On December 30, 1921, Brooks wrote a friend that the departure of the legislators brought him relief, especially since he had received "a good deal of cussing" from them. "After the legislature got through talking about me," he concluded, "it did everything that I asked it to do. I don't mind the cussing."[82]

81. *News and Observer*, Dec. 8-14, 1921; *Public Laws and Resolutions, Special Session, 1921*, pp. 51-56, 70-71; *House Journal, Special Session, 1921*, p. 288; *Senate Journal, Special Session, 1921*, p. 250; E. C. Brooks, "New School Legislation," *N C E*, XIV (Jan., 1922), 2.
82. *News and Observer*, Dec. 7, 1921; *Greensboro Daily News*, Dec., 26, 1921; E. C. Brooks to William K. Boyd, Dec. 30, 1921, S. P. I. Correspondence.

Perhaps Brooks's most notable achievement amid the threats of economy-conscious legislators was the maintenance of his certification program and salary schedule, which were so closely tied to the tax problem. He was thus able to continue the incentive for "the unprecedented progress" in the professional improvement among teachers, in which he took great personal pride. There was considerable justification for his pride in view of the fact that during his administration the number of teachers with standard certificates had doubled, while those holding substandard certificates had decreased by more than 3,000. Moreover, approximately 12,500 were attending summer schools in 1922, and the total number of teachers employed in the state schools had risen by almost 5,000 since Brooks took office. He attributed this "remarkable" growth and improvement of the teaching personnel to his salary schedule and summer school program.[83]

He realized, however, that his educational program still rested upon an unsatisfactory method of distributing state school funds. The special session of the legislature in 1921 had provided only temporary relief, but it had created a commission to investigate the problem of school finance. During 1922 Brooks worked closely with H. G. Connor, Jr., chairman of the commission, in devising a scheme that would divorce the equalizing fund from the revaluation of property. Brooks not only did most of the actual work of the commission, but also wrote its report to the legislature. In fact, he drafted the bills concerning the equalizing fund that were sponsored by Connor in the General Assembly of 1923. Through the enactment of these bills, he attempted to stabilize the method of distributing the equalizing fund by divorcing it from the valuation of taxable property.[84]

In December, 1922, Brooks began paving the way for the easy passage of his measures in the General Assembly of 1923. He enlisted the support of John G. Dawson, who was elected Speaker, and manipulated certain shifts in key committee assignments with the aid of Governor Morrison and Dawson. His measure concerning the

83. *Biennial Report, 1920-1922,* pp. 32-33; E. C. Brooks to J. E. Morgan, Dec. 15, 1922, S. P. I. Correspondence.
84. H. G. Connor to E. C. Brooks, Feb. 23, 1922, E. C. Brooks to H. G. Connor, May 8, 1922, E. C. Brooks to H. G. Connor, Nov. 13, 1922, E. C. Brooks to H. G. Connor, Nov. 21, 1922, S. P. I. Correspondence.

equalizing fund did not arouse much debate, mainly because the
legislators concentrated their attention upon another Brooks proposal, the school code.[85] Although the Legislature of 1923 provided
an equalizing fund of $1,250,000, it did not wholly fulfil Brooks's
desire for a complete severance of the tie between the distribution of
the fund and property valuations. The amount received by each
county was to be apportioned on the following basis:

The State Superintendent . . . shall determine for each county the amount
necessary to pay the salaries of all teachers and principals for the school
year 1921-1922, and for . . . 1922-1923, and the average amount for these
two years. . . . He shall then deduct the gross yield of the legal tax rate
of each county for the six months' school term from the average amount
as determined above, and the difference shall be the amount of the
Equalizing Fund for the salaries of teachers and principals for the years
1923-1924 and 1924-1925. . . . But no county shall receive an amount from
the Equalizing Fund sufficient to raise the average per capita cost for the
state, except as provided in section six: Provided, that in order to receive the amount as specified in this act each county shall raise, together
with the amount it will be entitled to draw from the Equalizing Fund,
an amount which will equal the amount of the salaries of teachers,
principals, and superintendents actually paid not in excess of the adopted
salary schedule for the six months' term for the year 1922-1923.[86]

In addition, each county participating in the Equalizing Fund was
to be paid one-half the salary of its superintendent. Section six of
the act provided that any portion of the Fund not otherwise appropriated was to be distributed to "backward counties," raising the qualifications of their teachers and to counties forced by "economic
reverses" to lower the valuation of property.[87]

During Brooks's administration the idea of state, rather than
local, support of public education gained momentum, a fact that
Brooks noted in his last biennial report. Not until the Great Depression of the 1930's did the state assume the entire obligation of
financing public schools for the six-month term. Although Brooks
left the State Superintendency in 1923, he remained keenly interested
in public school finance and sought to aid in establishing an equit-

85. E. C. Brooks to John G. Dawson, Dec. 2, 1922, John G. Dawson to E. C. Brooks,
Dec. 11, 1922, S. P. I. Correspondence; interview with Mr. John G. Dawson, Sept. 7,
1956.
86. *Public Laws and Resolutions, 1923*, pp. 431-432.
87. *Ibid.*, p. 433.

able plan for distributing the state school funds. He was appointed chairman of the Public School Equalizing Fund Commission, which was created in 1925, and for two years labored to find that equitable plan. In this capacity he again observed that certain counties consciously shifted the financial burden of education upon the state, while clamoring for local school autonomy. When the Equalizing Fund Commission was replaced by another agency in 1927, Brooks terminated his official relations with the public schools. Nevertheless, he remained a strong advocate of an ever expanding school program to meet the needs of North Carolina children.[88]

[4]

For years Brooks had pleaded for greater efficiency in the county administration of public schools, especially through the columns of *North Carolina Education*. This crusade in which he demonstrated such a relentless tenacity of purpose resulted in one of his major contributions as State Superintendent. He considered competent county superintendents absolutely essential to the efficient operation of the schools, but in many instances the office was still considered a political plum at the disposal of local politicians. Many county superintendents devoted only part of their time to the schools and even then were wholly incompetent in educational matters. This situation still flourished when Brooks became head of the school system. He readily perceived that the reorganization and rapid expansion of public schools in the post-World War I period demanded immediate and radical changes in the character of county school administration.[89]

One method that he used to effect the necessary reforms was to expose the gross inefficiency of county school officials and to suggest remedial measures. Through numerous public addresses and articles on the subject, he assumed the role of a muckraker and publicist.

88. *Biennial Report, 1920-1922,* p. 11; Minutes of the Meetings of the Equalizing Fund Commission, 1925, Report of the Equalizing Fund Commission, June 1, 1925, A. W. McLean to E. C. Brooks, April 25, 1925, E. C. Brooks to A. T. Allen, March 29, 1926, Eugene Clyde Brooks Papers, State Department of Archives and History, Raleigh, North Carolina. Hereinafter cited as Brooks Papers (DAH). See also Betters, *State Centralization in North Carolina,* pp. 37-38.
89. Brooks, *Administration of the Public School System, 1919-1920,* pp. 10-11; *Biennial Report, 1918-1920,* p. 13.

He insisted that the growth of schools required the full time of a competent, well-trained county superintendent who was the real educational executive of the county. He deplored the existence of numerous independent educational agents in the county whose work was frequently made ineffective by the lack of wise direction and "unity of purpose." According to Brooks, all such agents should be under the supervision of the county superintendent. "It shall be the policy of the state department of education," he said in 1920, "to magnify the office of county superintendent."[90] Thus, he demanded qualified men as superintendents. Such men should know about schools in general and understand school finance fully; they should have sufficient clerical assistants and trained subordinates so that they might give "their best thought to administration." At the same time, Brooks insisted that county boards of education should promptly remove any superintendent or supervisor who clearly demonstrated incompetence, indifference, or laziness in the execution of his duties.[91]

Brooks himself was always willing to advise officials on ways of improving the administration of local schools. In fact, a large portion of his time was devoted to explaining the educational laws and to settling local controversies. Whenever the General Assembly made significant changes in the school law, he held discussion meetings in various parts of the state in order that county school officials would understand what was expected of them under the law. At these gatherings he rarely failed to emphasize the need for better county administration and to offer pertinent suggestions for improving the administrative personnel. The county officials, of course, sought his advice on all manner of questions ranging from the love affairs of individual teachers to the handling of school funds. Brooks frequently acted as arbiter in local school disputes. For example, in July, 1921, he instructed one of his assistants to hold himself "in readiness to go with me to Charlotte . . . to help settle a difficulty there over the question of consolidation. . . . Together we might go over the territory and see if we can help the people reach an agreement."[92]

90. E. C. Brooks, "How To Secure More Effective Educational Administration," *N C E*, XIV (May, 1920), 3-4. See also E. C. Brooks, "Modern Educational Tendencies" (an address), Brooks Papers (BLS).
91. E. C. Brooks, "Shall We Improve the County Administration of Schools?," *N C E*, XV (Nov., 1920), 5; *News and Observer*, Sept. 20, 1921.
92. E. C. Brooks to S. W. Savage, Jan. 12, 1921, E. C. Brooks to T. T. Hicks, Sept. 22, 1922, E. C. Brooks to L. C. Brogden, July 15, 1921, S. P. I. Correspondence.

One aspect of the county school administration that especially attracted Brooks's attention was the handling of school funds by local officials. County school finances were generally in a chaotic condition. There were grossly inadequate records of receipts and expenditures, negligence and carelessness in disbursing school funds, and indifference to the legal taxation procedures. In 1919 fourteen counties failed to levy the full rate of state taxes because of "carelessness or ignorance of the law." Brooks recognized that his school program would be largely nullified if such financial disorder continued at the local level. The first remedial step was to secure for each county a superintendent who was a qualified school man and a skilful business manager. In order to provide such a corps of superintendents, he sought to arouse public opinion through a publicity campaign exposing the condition of school finances and showing that actually economy could be effected by employing competent school officials. His remedy also provided for the formulation of standards for county school officials by the state and their enforcement by the Department of Public Instruction.[93]

Largely through his influence, the first step in curbing the chaos in county administration and finances was taken by the Legislature of 1919. Under the County Budget Act, passed that year, the distribution of state funds was closely linked to the approval of the county school budgets by the State Superintendent. Since the state paid part of the salaries of teachers and superintendents, Brooks obviously possessed considerable power over county school administration. The method of financing public schools changed several times between 1919 and 1923, but he managed to retain a direct control over superintendents' salaries throughout his administration. During 1919, however, many counties continued to conduct school affairs in the usual slipshod fashion. Brooks impressed this fact upon the special session of the legislature in 1920 in a candid report in which he strongly recommended a "system of county auditing" and an elevation of the standards of county superintendents. The legislators rejected the auditing feature, but did authorize him to formulate a state salary schedule for superintendents "based upon training,

93. Brooks, *Administration of the Public School System, 1919-1920,* pp. 10-12; *N C E,* XV (Oct., 1920), 5.

duties, professional fitness, and continued service in the same school system."[94]

The superintendents, therefore, were included in the certification program which Brooks enforced through his control of state funds used in paying their salaries. His salary schedule of 1920 classified superintendents largely on the basis of the size and type of school systems and the amount of time devoted to school affairs. The maximum salary for a superintendent with a Class-A certificate was $3,500 per annum. In the next year Brooks revised the certification program so that the minimum requirements for a superintendent's certificate included graduation from a standard college, eighteen semester hours of professional credit, and five years of experience as a teacher or principal. The duties of the superintendent, based on the size and type of school system, continued to be a partial basis for the salary schedule.[95] In his report to Governor Morrison in 1922 Brooks wrote:

The most expensive part of the county school system is an inefficient superintendent, and it is tragic to see the children of a county seeking an education while the administration flounders hopelessly in an attempt to spend the people's money wisely. The efficiency of the county superintendent, however, has improved greatly within the past three years. This improvement is one of the most noticeable features of our educational progress. A large majority of the counties have very competent men who are rendering exceptionally fine service.[96]

Indeed, there was a veritable revolution in the qualifications of county superintendents during Brooks's administration.

Despite these improvements, Brooks believed that additional legislation was necessary in order to insure the proper handling of local school funds. He continued to insist upon a system of county auditing that he had first proposed in 1920. During the fall of that year he gathered sufficient evidence to convince the forthcoming General Assembly of the pressing need for such legislation. A group headed by A. S. Brower, one of Brooks's ablest assistants, undertook

94. *Public Laws and Resolutions, 1919*, pp. 276-279; Brooks, *Administration of the Public School System, 1919-1920*, pp. 10-12; *Public Laws and Resolutions, Special Session, 1920*, p. 115.
95. Brooks, *Administration of the Public School System, 1919-1920*, p. 15; *Regulations Governing Certificates for Teachers in North Carolina, 1921* (Educational Publication No. 29), pp. 7-8.
96. *Biennial Report, 1920-1922*, p. 16.

an investigation of school finances in several counties. The report of the investigation, submitted to Brooks in November, 1920, revealed a maze of confusion in collecting and expending county school funds. For example, the Register of Deeds office in Burke County was "almost totally devoid of tax records."[97]

Fortified with such appalling facts, Brooks succeeded in persuading the Legislature of 1921 to enact a system of county auditing. The act provided that the books of the county school fund and the accounts of the county board of education should be audited by August 1 of each year. These records were to contain an itemized statement of the various tax receipts and school expenditures. The auditor was to compare these expenditures with the approved county school budget and to publish his report in a local newspaper. If any county failed to provide for such auditing, the State Superintendent would send an auditor from the State Tax Commission at the expense of the county board of education. Moreover, the State Board of Education had the authority to revoke the certificate of any county superintendent who failed "to keep the records of the county board of education so they can be audited." Through the auditors' reports, Brooks learned whether counties had provided for expenditures in accordance with the budgets previously approved by him. The first audits under the law of 1921 indicated that some counties were still in a "bewildered maze to account for the funds as the law required." Brooks assured the county superintendents in no uncertain terms that he would exercise his full authority to enforce the legal method of managing county school finances. Gradually, he brought the county officials in line with the legal requirements, and by the end of his administration the handling of county school funds had undergone a remarkable reformation.[98]

Obviously, the efficient administration of county schools also depended in large part upon the degree of competence and co-operation manifested by other departments of county government, especially the board of commissioners. Brooks therefore wrote into the school law of 1923 provisions designed to eliminate the friction over school funds that frequently developed between the county board of

97. "Confidential Report to the State Superintendent on Burke, Mitchell, and Caswell Counties," S. P. I. Correspondence.
98. E. C. Brooks to T. L. Sigman, Nov. 15, 1920, S. P. I. Correspondence; *Public Laws and Resolutions, 1921*, pp. 412-415; *News and Observer*, Sept. 2, Nov. 23, 1921.

education and the county commissioners. His amendments completely revised the system of county budgets. Under the amended law
the board of education and the commissioners convened in joint
session each May to prepare the county school budget. Whenever
in doubt about "the reasonableness of the budget," the commissioners could require the board of education to "give cause of the
increase, district by district, and the difference between the total
salaries of the current year . . . and the proposed salaries for the
ensuing school year." After approving the May budget, the commissioners were to levy the necessary taxes and could require the board
of education to publish the budget in a local newspaper. A second
budget, prepared by the board of education by November 15 of each
year, carried a detailed statement of county school finances and
teaching personnel. The November budget revealed the discrepan-
cies between the estimates of the May budget and the actual cost of
school operation under that budget. Brooks used the November
budget in his office "to ascertain whether the teachers are properly
certificated, whether the number of teachers is excessive, and whether
the authorized salary schedule is observed." His approval of the
budget was necessary before a county received its share of the state
equalizing fund.[99]

The amended school law of 1923 changed the legal procedure in
cases of disagreement between the commissioners and board of education over the amount of taxes necessary to maintain the schools
for six months. Previously the board of education alone could appeal
to the courts in the event of such a disagreement. Under the revised
law the clerk of the superior court became a kind of arbiter; if he
failed to settle the difficulty, the commissioners could resort to court
action. This procedure was actually a compromise resulting from
differences of opinion between Brooks and the education committees
of the Legislature of 1923. Another enactment of that year restricted
the power of the county board of education in contracting debts
beyond the county budget. In the past some boards had created large
school debts, then demanded that the commissioners levy sufficient
taxes to cover them. Brooks was "immensely gratified" by the passage
of his amendments in 1923 and believed that they would completely

99. *News and Observer,* Jan. 29, 1923; *The Public School Law of North Carolina:
Codification of 1923,* pp. 43-49.

"eradicate charges of irresponsible administration by county school authorities." Indeed, his campaign for efficient county school administration was considerably strengthened by these enactments. Yet he continued to insist that "good business management" was "the greatest need of the school system."[100]

100. *Public School Law of North Carolina: Codification of 1923,* pp. 18, 49-51; *News and Observer,* Jan. 24, April 19, 1923.

Six: BUILDING NORTH CAROLINA SCHOOLS, *1919-1923*

[1]

The four and a half years that Brooks was State Superintendent marked an era of astonishing growth and expansion in the public schools of North Carolina. He entered office under conditions favorable to educational progress, in large part because during the previous seventeen years his energetic predecessor, J. Y. Joyner, had carefully laid the foundation for a reputable school system. In some instances, Brooks continued the policies inaugurated under Joyner; in others, he pursued an entirely independent course. The difference in the lengths of their terms and in the circumstances under which they labored point up the folly of attempting a comparison of their achievements. Moreover, Brooks and Joyner were so closely allied both in views and actions in the field of public education between 1902 and 1919 that a sharp distinction in their educational policies would be misleading. To be sure, some of the educational movements begun under Joyner came to fruition during Brooks's administration; yet Brooks himself had been a part of these movements for many years through his association with Joyner and through his magazine, *North Carolina Education*. At any rate, it would be difficult indeed to find a single phase of public education which did not feel the influence of Brooks between 1919 and 1923.

Under Brooks the Department of Public Instruction became a powerful force in the educational life of the state. His reorganization of the department in 1921 greatly enhanced its efficiency in dealing with the ever-expanding range of educational activities that came under its supervision. Through the distribution of state funds, Brooks possessed a powerful instrument of control over the local schools—an instrument that he never hesitated to use in forcing schools in line with legal requirements. The charges of "too much centralization in Raleigh" were frequently hurled at his administration, but Brooks remained undeterred by such accusations in his efforts to build a strong school system. In 1921 he informed the county superintendents that "where the state law says that you shall do certain things, there the State Superintendent steps in, and insofar as he is able, will see that the law is observed."[1] His strict adherence to this policy undoubtedly left the State Superintendency a much stronger office than it had been in 1919.

The most formidable task confronting Brooks when he entered office was to secure sufficient financial support for public schools. He recognized that the state must bear a large share of the financial burden in order to provide adequate educational opportunities for all children. His success in persuading the successive legislatures to undertake greater financial responsibility for the schools was in itself a tribute to his political acumen and skilful leadership. To insure the wise expenditure of the greatly increased school funds, Brooks established a system of budgets and audits and raised the standards of county superintendents, thus revolutionizing local school administration. His innovations actually put into operation a state system of schools with the counties, rather than the numerous local districts, as the units of school administration. This idea was embodied in most of the changes in the school system advocated by Brooks, particularly in his schemes for school consolidation, high schools, and pupil transportation.

Brooks himself considered the improvement in the teaching personnel the major achievement of his administration. Certainly, the introduction of an effective program of teacher training and certification coupled with a uniform salary schedule was largely responsible for the revolution in the character of the teaching force that occurred between 1919 and 1923. In Brooks's opinion the school building program was the second most important achievement of his career as State Superintendent. The state loan fund of $10,000,000, created largely through his influence, was a tremendous stimulus to the building of schoolhouses, while his creation of a division of schoolhouse planning insured the most advantageous location of schools

1. *News and Observer,* Nov. 23, 1921.

and the construction of buildings in accordance with current architectural and educational principles. Brooks might possibly have designated the advance in Negro education as the third major accomplishment of his administration, although the educational advantages for Negro children remained strikingly inferior to those for white children. Nevertheless, he laid the foundation for a reputable system of Negro education that gradually materialized under his successors.

[2]

The interruption of the school building program during World War I coupled with the increase in enrollment after 1919 created a great demand for new buildings. According to the survey of the Educational Commission published in 1920, "a majority of the rural schoolhouses—probably three-fourths—are unsatisfactory." Even the buildings constructed after 1914 exhibited many of the defects of the older structures, especially in location, lighting, and ventilation. When Brooks became State Superintendent, he immediately began preparations to remedy this situation. His first step was to insert a clause in the school law of 1919 permitting counties to exceed the tax rate limitation of thirty-five cents in order to provide a maximum building fund of twenty-five per cent of the teacher salary fund. In the same year the State Supreme Court declared that school buildings were a necessary expense in maintaining the constitutional six-month term and could be provided by the county commissioners by taxation without a vote of the people.[2]

From personal observation and work with the State Educational Commission, Brooks recognized that the major defects in schoolhouse construction resulted from inadequate supervision and planning. He desired to insure the erection of school buildings in accordance with the latest architectural and educational principles by possessing the power to force counties to meet certain standards. Using almost every media of communication at his disposal, he strongly advised county officials to take into account "future needs" in building school-

2. *A Report of the State Educational Commission*, pp. 14-19; *Public Laws and Resolutions, 1919*, p. 279; *North Carolina Supreme Court Reports, Fall Term, 1919*, pp. 305-314. The Legislature of 1919 also appropriated $2,000 for the preparation of schoolhouse plans and for the inspection of school buildings. *Public Laws and Resolutions, 1919*, p. 466.

houses and insisted that "a good architect is always less expensive in the long run." But he realized that county boards of education would continue to build schoolhouses as cheaply as possible, with little regard for his advice unless he had the power to enforce it.[3]

In July, 1919, Brooks began to search for means to exert a more direct influence upon the school-construction program. After conferring with the officials of the General Education Board and with Governor Bickett, he secured promise of financial support for a division in the Department of Public Instruction which would prepare plans for school buildings and supervise their construction. In the special session of the legislature in 1920, Brooks got an appropriation for this division. At the same time county boards of education were prohibited from investing any money in new schoolhouses that were not built "in accordance with plans approved by the State Superintendent." He also secured amendments to the State-wide Bond Act whereby local school units could issue bonds for school buildings upon a popular vote of approval to an amount not in excess of 5 per cent of the property valuation in the area involved.[4]

Another provision, written by Brooks, allowed counties to pay all or any part of the costs of school buildings, whereas the old law required local districts to pay at least one-half of the costs. This change promoted his policy of making the county, rather than the local district, the unit of school administration. Brooks lost no time in exerting his new authority over school buildings, and within a month a division of schoolhouse planning had been created in his department with J. J. Blair, former superintendent of the Wilmington schools, as director. During the next four months Blair visited twenty-one towns and rural communities in order to assist in planning and designing new schoolhouses.[5]

Brooks readily perceived the necessity of possessing considerable control over building finances in order to enforce the regulations of

3. *A Report of the State Educational Commission,* pp. 19-22; E. C. Brooks, "A School Building Program Needed," *N C E,* XIV (Sept., 1919), 4; E. C. Brooks to H. G. Harrington, Sept. 24, 1919, S. P. I. Correspondence; *News and Observer,* July 27, Aug. 19, Oct. 10, 1919.

4. Frank Bachman to E. C. Brooks, July 19, 1919, Frank Bachman to E. C. Brooks, July 28, 1919, E. C. Brooks to Frank Bachman, Aug. 17, 1919, E. C. Brooks to Charles L. Coon, May 11, 1920, S. P. I. Correspondence; *Public Laws and Resolutions, Special Session, 1920,* pp. 116-117.

5. *Public Laws and Resolutions, Special Session, 1920,* pp. 116-117; *N C E,* XV (Sept., 1920), 3-4; *N C E,* XV (Oct., 1920), 14; *New School Legislation, 1920-1921* (Educational Publication No. 12), pp. 8-9.

the division of schoolhouse planning. According to his estimates, the demands for new buildings in August, 1920, totaled "over $15,000,-000." Unless his authority were strengthened, he feared that the counties would "waste" much of this money by haphazardly locating schools and by disregarding architectural plans formulated by the division of schoolhouse planning. In other words, he wanted the General Assembly to put teeth in the act of 1920, which gave him supervision of the building program without providing the necessary financial lever. Through his influence the Legislature of 1921 created a special building fund of $5,000,000. The provisions of the act, written by Brooks, clearly incorporated the idea of the county as the unit of educational administration, because counties, not districts, were to receive loans from this fund. Moreover, loans were not available for any proposed schoolhouse of less than five rooms or for any building not approved by the State Superintendent. The counties would repay the loans in twenty annual installments.[6]

Brooks encountered considerable difficulty in selling the state bonds at the specified interest rate to create the special building fund. After prolonged negotiations, he concluded the sale on November 4, 1921, and promised loans to the counties by the beginning of the next year. Meanwhile, the constitutionality of the act establishing the special building fund had been contested, and Brooks had to await a Supreme Court decision before making the loans available. In April, 1922, the court not only upheld the act, but also the right of counties to contract a twenty-year debt for school buildings and to pledge its payment with interest through a county tax levy without the vote of the people. Brooks declared: "Everybody is delighted. Even the Supreme Court is delighted, and this decision helped us more than any decision since 1907 when the old Barksdale decision was reversed. It has strengthened confidence in the Department of Education. . . ."[7] Shortly thereafter, Brooks began distributing the loan fund; and by January, 1923, he had distributed $3,300,000

6. Brooks, *Administration of the Public School System, 1919-1920*, p. 12; *Biennial Report, 1918-1920*, p. 12; *Public Laws and Resolutions*, 1921, pp. 422-426; *News and Observer*, Feb. 7, 1921; E. C. Brooks to G. S. Boren, Jan. 8, 1921, E. C. Brooks to N. W. Walker, March 9, 1921, S. P. I. Correspondence.

7. E. C. Brooks to M. T. Edgerton, May 2, 1921, E. C. Brooks to W. A. Graham, May 23, 1921, E. C. Brooks to W. S. Robeson, Nov. 5, 1921, E. C. Brooks to J. S. Manning, Jan. 19, 1922, E. C. Brooks to J. J. Blair, April 24, 1922, S. P. I. Correspondence; *North Carolina Supreme Court Reports, Spring Term, 1922*, pp. 373-382.

to assist in financing new schoolhouses valued at $9,024,635, approximately the total value of all school property in the state in 1914. He persuaded the Legislature of 1923 to authorize another bond issue of $5,000,000 for schoolhouse construction. During his administration the total value of school property reached $48,874,830 in 1923, three times the value in 1919. This expansion of school facilities was unequaled by any comparable period in the educational history of the state. In many respects Brooks himself was responsible for the unprecedented building program and the construction of "adequate" schoolhouses. His particular interest in rural education was evidenced by the remarkable improvement in rural school buildings which were largely financed with the aid of state loans.[8]

In connection with the building program, Brooks encouraged the consolidation of rural school districts. During his administration the rapid growth in motor vehicle transportation and highway construction greatly mitigated the isolation of rural areas. Such developments reduced the necessity for numerous rural school districts; therefore Brooks undertook a broad program of consolidation which considerably strengthened his policy of making the county rather than the district the unit of school administration. Largely through his influence, the legislature incorporated the "county unit plan" into the regulations for the distribution of the State Public School Fund and the special building funds. The school law of 1919 clearly prohibited the creation of any new school districts. A year later Brooks insisted that North Carolina was "having the greatest interest in the consolidation of districts that the state has ever known." Nevertheless, he recognized the need for some weapon by which to force recalcitrant counties to consolidate small rural districts into larger units in order to establish more efficient schools with adequate faculties and equipment. Late in 1920 he prepared amendments to the school laws which invested him with the power necessary to enforce consolidation.[9]

8. *Biennial Report, 1920-1922*, p. 18; *Public School Law: Codification of 1923*, pp. 71-75; *Biennial Report, 1918-1920*, p. 110; *Biennial Report, 1922-1924*, p. 98; Brooks, "Eugene Clyde Brooks: Autobiographical Sketch," p. 4. See also Mary Sloop and LeGette Blythe, *Miracle in the Hills* (New York, 1953), pp. 134-135.

9. Hobbs, *North Carolina: Economic and Social*, pp. 163-166; *Public Laws and Resolutions, 1919*, pp. 279-280; *Biennial Report, 1918-1920*, p. 13; E. C. Brooks to Abraham Flexner, May 11, 1920, E. C. Brooks to J. M. Manning, Dec. 2, 1920, S. P. I. Correspondence; Daniel J. Whitener, "Education for the People," *North Carolina*

These amendments, passed by the legislature in 1921, provided a considerable stimulus for his county unit plan. As previously noted, the special loan fund for school buildings was restricted for use by counties in constructing larger schools. Brooks was particularly delighted with an enactment giving the county boards of education wider authority in consolidating districts. "The county board of education is given authority," he declared, "to consolidate whenever and wherever in its judgment consolidation is wise and . . . about the only requirement is the wish of the people."[10] Previously elaborate restrictions had protected the autonomy of the local district from the county board of education. But Brooks was convinced that adequate educational opportunities for rural children depended upon "strong central schools," established through the consolidation of small districts. Such schools, according to him, would produce "large community centers" and erase the "clannishness and neighborhood feuds" perpetuated by small, competitive schools. Favorable Supreme Court decisions coupled with the pressure that Brooks exerted upon counties through his control of state school funds greatly promoted the consolidation movement. Despite Joyner's efforts toward consolidation, the number of districts was about the same in 1918 as in 1902, while Brooks under different and more favorable circumstances abolished 756 districts between 1919 and 1923. In the same period schools with four or more teachers more than doubled, and the one-teacher schools decreased from 4,437 to 3,240.[11]

The creation of larger districts and consolidated schools necessitated a more adequate system of pupil transportation. In 1915 only six busses were used in the state for transporting school pupils. Convinced that the success of his consolidation program depended on adequate transportation facilities, Brooks argued that the difference

Historical Review, XXXVI (April, 1959), 192-193; Cecil Brown, The State Highway System of North Carolina: Its Evolution and Present Status (Chapel Hill, 1931), pp. 100-123, 248.

10. E. C. Brooks to I. A. Cain, March 15, 1921, S. P. I. Correspondence. See also Public Laws and Resolutions, 1921, pp. 422-426; E. C. Brooks to M. J. Manning, Dec. 2, 1920, S. P. I. Correspondence.

11. E. C. Brooks to Lee Davis, Oct. 23, 1922, E. C. Brooks to W. J. Adams, Nov. 9, 1922, S. P. I. Correspondence; North Carolina Supreme Court Reports, Fall Term, 1922, pp. 342-355; Biennial Report, 1918-1920, p. 205; Biennial Report, 1922-1924, p. 205; Biennial Report, 1922-1924, p. 110; Tripp, "James Y. Joyner's Contribution to Education" (Master's Thesis), pp. 189-190.

between the cost of instruction in the consolidated school and in several small schools would cover the cost of pupil transportation. Since he considered motor trucks as essential as school buildings, he induced the Legislature of 1920 to permit counties to include the operation expenses of school busses in their budgets and to receive state aid for them on the same basis as teachers' salaries. In the following year he wrote into the law a provision exempting school busses from taxation. Under the impetus of this legislation, the school transportation facilities expanded rapidly during his administration. The 247 busses hauling 7,936 children in 1919 increased to 858 busses hauling 31,544 children in 1923.[12]

An important phase of Brooks's consolidation program concerned the establishment and improvement of rural high schools. In 1917 the Supreme Court had declared that high schools were a vital and necessary part of the school system.[13] Yet at the close of his second year in office, Brooks was deeply concerned about the defects in the system of secondary education and conveyed his concern to the Governor in his biennial report:

It is very difficult to secure accurate information concerning the scope of high school instruction in North Carolina, since so many schools not even prepared to give good instruction in the elementary subjects attempt to give in addition one or more years of high school instruction. The report for 1918-1919 shows 564 schools of all sorts attempting to give such instruction. For 1919-1920 we are able to secure information from 455 schools that seek to give one or more years of high school instruction. . . . A good four year high school, however, cannot be conducted successfully with less than three teachers. There are 214 such schools in the state. The total enrollment in them is 22,140 and the number completing a four year course is 2,536. This is 11 per cent of the total enrollment. In addition to these there are 241 one-teacher and two-teacher high schools seeking to give four year courses. The enrollment in these for 1919-1920 was 8,728, but the number completing the four year courses was only 726. . . .[14]

The report of the State Educational Commission corroborated this

12. L. C. Brogden, *A Larger Type of Rural School an Imperative Need* (Educational Bulletin No. 36), pp. 12-13; E. C. Brooks, *The Consolidation of Schools and the Cost of Transportation* (Educational Publication No. 53), pp. 3-5; *Public Laws and Resolutions, Special Session, 1920*, p. 116; *Public Laws and Resolutions, 1921*, p. 464; *Biennial Report, 1918-1920*, p. 13; *Biennial Report, 1922-1924*, p. 115.
13. *North Carolina Supreme Court Reports, Fall Term, 1917*, pp. 469-477.
14. *Biennial Report, 1918-1920*, p. 11.

description and condemned the prevalent practice of establishing
high schools "at every crossroads."[15]

Brooks insisted upon consolidated high schools large enough to
provide the facilities and instruction for training elementary school
teachers. Indeed, his teacher-training program required the building
of such schools. Prodded by his demands and the Supreme Court
decision, the Legislatures of 1919 and 1920 clearly recognized high
schools as an essential part of the public school system and sought to
encourage their establishment. High school teachers and principals
were included in Brooks's certification program and salary schedule,
and parts of their salaries were paid by the state. In 1920 Brooks induced the legislators to provide special aid for establishing at least
one standard high school in each county. Loans from the building
fund created in 1921 were available for the construction of high
schools. Thus Brooks's control of the various state funds provided
him with a potent instrument for improving secondary education.[16]

Shortly after the enactment of the school law of 1919, Brooks
declared that his department would seek "to organize high schools
wherever we can consolidate and secure students for the same." In
reorganizing the system of high schools, he worked closely with J.
Henry Highsmith, the new state inspector of high schools, and sent
out several members of his department to study the actual conditions
of secondary schools. His aim was to establish efficient high schools
to replace those with one or two teachers attempting to give a four-
year course. His county unit plan envisaged "the building of high
schools so conveniently located that all children of the county may
have good high school advantages without going away from home."
A legislative appropriation of $224,000 in 1921 for various phases
of high school work considerably strengthened this policy and enabled Brooks to undertake seriously a reorganization of secondary
education. One of his first steps was to formulate new "regulations
governing high schools" which could be easily enforced in schools
receiving state funds. The classification of high schools also provided
a partial basis for the apportionment of the equalizing fund in 1922-
1923. The minimum requirements for a "standard high school" were

15. *Report of the State Educational Commission*, pp. 37-39.
16. Brooks, *Administration of the Public School System, 1919-1920*, pp. 12-13; *Public
Laws and Resolutions, 1919*, pp. 289-292; *Public Laws and Resolutions, Special Session,
1920*, p. 115.

an eight-month term, a four-year course of study, three teachers and at least forty-five pupils in average daily attendance. In 1922 Highsmith prepared a course of study for high schools with pertinent suggestions on a variety of subjects.[17]

Brooks realized that all his advice and requirements would have little effect without an adequate plan of inspection. Since Highsmith did not have time "to give the supervision necessary," in 1921 Brooks requested and received the assistance of eleven colleges in providing high school inspection. He persuaded the General Education Board to finance the program. The state was divided into districts each of which was assigned to the education department of a college. The professors of education were to inspect and supervise all public high schools in their respective districts and file reports with the state inspector of high schools. The main purpose of the scheme was to furnish advice to local officials about establishing efficient high schools and to inform Brooks of the degree to which the high school regulations were carried out in the various counties. A county that persisted in disregarding these regulations could almost certainly expect some reduction in its share of state funds.[18]

One aspect of the high school program which particularly interested Brooks was the education of rural children. His original aim was to establish at least one standard high school in every county. He considered the "union school" with eleven grades as the ideal rural school and utilized all means at his disposal to promote the creation of such schools through the consolidation of small school districts.[19] In describing his rural high school policy in 1923, Brooks wrote: "What our country boys and girls need especially is

17. E. C. Brooks to George Sprinkle, Aug. 11, 1919, E. C. Brooks to E. C. Sage, March 6, 1919, E. C. Brooks to Abraham Flexner, Aug. 30, 1919, E. C. Brooks to J. H. Cowles, Dec. 7, 1920, E. C. Brooks to N. W. Walker, March 9, 1921, S. P. I. Correspondence; *Rules and Regulations Governing Public High Schools, 1921-1922* (Educational Publication No. 35); *Standardization and Classification of Public High Schools in North Carolina, 1921-1922* (Educational Publication No. 60), pp. 8-10; E. C. Brooks, "The Relationship of School Organization to School Costs," *N C E*, XVI (March, 1922), 10-12; *Courses of Study for the High Schools of North Carolina* (Educational Publication No. 52).

18. E. C. Brooks to C. E. Brewer, Dec. 9, 1920, E. C. Brooks to Wallace Buttrick, April 16, 1921, E. C. Brooks to Wallace Buttrick, Feb. 10, 1922, S. P. I. Correspondence; *News and Observer*, Oct. 8, 1921.

19. E. C. Brooks, "One Standard High School for Every County," *N C E*, XVI (May, 1922), 5-6; *Biennial Report, 1920-1922*, p. 21; E. C. Brooks to J. F. Landen, Dec. 2, 1922, E. C. Brooks to Lee Driver, October 23, 1922, E. C. Brooks to Clarence Poe, Oct. 19, 1920, S. P. I. Correspondence.

an expansion of their community—to feel the social and intellectual force of a larger number of people. . . . It seems to me to be a crime against youth to bottle up children in little communities when we are supposed to be educating them, and deprive them of that social intercourse that all modern inventions would facilitate, if the schools were not too narrow-visioned to use them."[20]

The rapid growth and improvement of public high schools between 1919 and 1923 indicated the effectiveness of Brooks's program. In 1920 there were no standard high schools in the rural districts of thirty-five counties and no standard high schools whatever in thirty counties; whereas the total number of all types of high schools in the state, both standard and non-standard, was 455. By the end of Brooks's administration in 1923, ninety-five counties possessed four-year standard high schools, and the total number of such schools in the state was 316. There were 5,795 public high school graduates in 1923 in comparison to 2,040 in 1919; and within the same period, the total high school enrollment more than doubled. The Association of Colleges and Preparatory Schools of the Southern States accredited thirteen high schools in North Carolina between 1921 and 1923, bringing the total of such accredited schools to forty-four. Near the end of his administration, Brooks considered "the building of standard high schools in rural districts" among his chief accomplishments as State Superintendent. In reviewing the progress in secondary education under his guidance, he declared that there had been "a tremendous gain, but we should have in the near future one such [standard high] school . . . in every township . . . in the state, if we would make the rural sections strong and vigorous and contribute more largely to the progress of the state."[21]

One of the most significant phases of Brooks's high school program, especially for rural areas, was the rapid development in vocational education. Since 1911 the state had promoted the establishment of farm-life schools, a movement that Brooks heartily endorsed. Then, in 1917, the legislature accepted federal aid for voca-

20. E. C. Brooks, "High Schools for Rural Boys and Girls," *Progressive Farmer,* XXXVIII (June 28, 1923), 646.
21. *Biennial Report, 1918-1920,* p. 11; *Biennial Report, 1920-1922,* pp. 22-23; *Biennial Report, 1922-1924,* pp. 29-30; *Classification and Standardization of Public High Schools, 1922-1923,* pp. 23-24; E. C. Brooks to J. E. Morgan, Dec. 15, 1922, S. P. I. Correspondence.

tional education provided by the Smith-Hughes Act, thereby largely replacing the old farm-life schools. Under the Smith-Hughes Act, the federal government would match state funds for vocational instruction in high schools. The First World War delayed the full implementation of this act in North Carolina, but a department of vocational education had been established at North Carolina State College for training high school teachers. Shortly afterward, a similar department was created at North Carolina Agricultural and Technical College for the training of Negro vocational teachers. In 1918-1919 the total expenditure for vocational education including state and federal funds was $45,864.14 with 551 persons enrolled in all aspects of the program. Brooks insisted that the Federal Board of Vocational Education "should never interfere with the autonomy of states in the plans and management of vocational education," and in 1920 he stated that North Carolina had not been troubled by such interference.[22]

At the beginning of his administration in 1919, the legislature amended and extended the provisions of the vocational education act of 1917. It created a state board for vocational education with Brooks as chairman and three other members representing agriculture, industry, and home economics. T. E. Browne was selected as state director of the program, and within a year there were three state supervisors—one each in charge of agricultural education, trade and industrial education, and home economics education. State College and North Carolina College for Women expanded their facilities for training vocational teachers, and the Department of Public Instruction drew up a certification plan for such teachers. The program of agricultural education included supervised farm projects for school boys, short courses for farmers, and the organization of community fairs. The work in trade and industrial education was largely restricted to evening and extension classes in twenty-two textile centers. The home economics program which began in 1920 included regular high school classes for girls and short courses for farm women. Instruction in vocational subjects for adults as well as school

22. Tripp, "James Y. Joyner's Contribution to Education" (Master's Thesis), pp. 150-151; Cook, "The Federal Government and Vocational Education in the South," *Secondary Education in the South,* p. 93; Financial and Statistical Information for A. T. Allen, Brooks Papers (DUL); E. C. Brooks to W. Carson Ryan, Jr., Aug. 30, 1920, S. P. I. Corrrespondence.

children was an important element in Brooks's plan for making the public high school the rural "community center." Brooks always attempted to provide facilities in high schools for those vocational subjects that corresponded to the predominant occupations of the area surrounding the school. Thus emphasis was placed primarily upon agricultural and home economics courses, since the state was largely rural.[23]

During Brooks's administration the program of vocational education was firmly established and rapidly expanded, largely through the increasing amounts of financial aid. The annual funds increased from $45,364.14 in 1918 to $204,104.99 in 1922. In the same period agriculture was introduced into forty-five schools and home economics in fifty, while the number of classes in trade and industrial subjects increased from five to 180 with an enrollment of 2,103. Under a congressional act in 1920, the state undertook a program "for the vocational rehabilitation of civilians disabled in industry and otherwise." Within two years Brooks counted 100 disabled persons whose special training under this program converted them into "happy, self-supporting citizens." After becoming president of North Carolina State College, Brooks maintained a keen interest in vocational education in public schools and co-operated with his successor, A. T. Allen, in the "development of rural North Carolina, using the rural consolidated school as the center of community life."[24]

[3]

One of Brooks's most spectacular achievements as State Superintendent was the development of public schools for Negroes. Indeed, he was a prominent figure, if not the leader, in the so-called "golden

23. *Public Laws and Resolutions, 1919,* pp. 467-469; *Annual Report of the Federal Board of Vocational Education, 1919,* pp. 110-112; *Annual Report of the Federal Board of Vocational Education, 1920,* pp. 155-157; *Annual Report of the Federal Board of Vocational Education, 1921,* pp. 179-182; *Biennial Report, 1918-1920,* p. 15; *Biennial Report, 1920-1922,* pp. 24-26; E. C. Brooks to Josephus Daniels, May 25, 1921, E. C. Brooks to Martha Brooks, Jan. 6, 1922, T. E. Browne, Report to the State Board of Vocational Education, 1919-1920, S. P. I. Correspondence; Brooks, "High Schools for Rural Boys and Girls," *Progressive Farmer,* XXXVIII (June 23, 1921), 646.

24. *Biennial Report, 1918-1920,* p. 15; *Biennial Report, 1920-1922,* pp. 24-26; Report of the Work of the State Board of Vocational Education, 1922, A. T. Allen to E. C. Brooks, Oct. 30, 1924, S. P. I. Correspondence.

era of Negro education" in North Carolina. His accomplishments are thrown into a more significant light when viewed in terms of the progress of Negro education under his predecessor. One student has declared that the education of Negroes received less of Joyner's time, consideration, and support than any other phase of his school program. Joyner, however, labored under peculiarly unfavorable political circumstances. At the end of his administration "the Negroes had schoolhouses not much improved over those in 1902; their rural school terms were usually no longer than the minimum requirement; and their school equipment still remained crude, meager, and inadequate." Nor was there a single standard Negro high school or farm-life school in the state in 1919. The main encouragement for Negro education came from such outside agencies as the Slater Fund, the General Education Board, the Jeanes Foundation, and the Rosenwald Fund.[25]

Brooks recognized the pressing need for better Negro schools and thoroughly understood the various ramifications of the "problems" of Negro education. He realized too that the solutions could not be left to county and local officials; they had already demonstrated their unwillingness or inability to grapple with the problem. Some other agency, preferably the state, must furnish the stimulus necessary for establishing a system of reputable schools for Negroes. Brooks's tactful approach to the problem was largely responsible for providing that initial stimulus. He co-operated with the Negro leaders in the state, courted the favor of the philanthropic agencies, and utilized diplomacy and skill in presenting the question to the General Assembly. He was by no means a "radical" on the subject of race relations, and would have considered absurd any suggestion to abolish segregation in the public schools. But he possessed a sympathetic attitude toward the Negro and believed that education would enable the race to assume its responsibilities of citizenship. One of his primary aims in developing Negro education was to assist the Negro in becoming "self-supporting" and "feeling his own responsibility in remaking his own race."[26]

25. Dennis Cooke, *The White Superintendent and the Negro Schools in North Carolina* (Nashville, 1930), p. 19; Tripp, "James Y. Joyner's Contribution to Education," pp. 168, 176-178; Harlan, *Separate and Unequal*, pp. 103-134; Ullin W. Leavell, *Philanthropy in Negro Education* (Nashville, 1930), pp. 119-149.

26. Interview with Mrs. E. C. Brooks, May 9, 1956; E. C. Brooks to Julius Rosenwald, Dec. 30, 1921, S. P. I. Correspondence.

In his opinion a frank exchange of ideas between Negro leaders and members of the Department of Public Instruction was a prerequisite for a successful program of Negro education. Brooks inaugurated such exchanges in two meetings in Winston-Salem in February and April, 1919. These conferences apparently assured the Negroes of his sincere desire to improve their educational opportunities and convinced him of the value of such discussions with Negroes. He therefore decided to call a statewide convention of prominent Negroes and set to work organizing this meeting with the aid of N. C. Newbold, state agent of rural Negro elementary schools, and Dr. James E. Shepard, president of the National Training School in Durham (now North Carolina College at Durham) and a leader in the Negro State Teachers Association.[27] Brooks wrote Shepard:

We are planning many improvements in teacher training, high school instruction, erection of schoolhouses, and other educational needs of the colored people. . . . You are acquainted with our summer school work and its far reaching effects. While we are discussing these very important things, it is my judgment that we should discuss ways and means by which we may eliminate much of the distrust that seems to be in evidence here and there in our state. I think it would be wise for you and your committee to be considering some platform that both white and colored people might stand on that would be of mutual interest to all concerned.[28]

On September 26, 1919, Brooks opened a conference composed of Negro leaders and members of his department in the State House of Representatives. He outlined his plans for Negro schools and pleaded for co-operation between the races in putting these plans into operation. Then the thirty-eight Negro leaders discussed the aims of the National Association for the Advancement of Colored People and proposed county meetings of Negroes and whites whenever feasible in order to improve race relations in the state. They also adopted a Declaration of Principles as a guide in creating "an unprecedented era of good feeling" between the races. Brooks considered it a "common ground of safety upon which leaders of both races can stand" in the development of Negro schools. The Declara-

27. E. C. Brooks to Wallace Buttrick, March 5, 1919, E. C. Brooks to S. G. Atkins, Feb. 18, 1919, James E. Shepard to E. C. Brooks, Sept. 16, 1919, S. P. I. Correspondence; N C E, XVIII (May, 1919), 5.
28. E. C. Brooks to James E. Shepard, Sept. 25, 1919, S. P. I. Correspondence.

tion condemned lynching, legal injustices to Negroes, race riots, and "intermingling of the races on terms of social equality." It endorsed Brooks's leadership and declared that "there never was a time in North Carolina when the state was so ready to give educational opportunities to Negroes." Therefore, the Negroes were advised to "quit harping on the injustices done previously by the white man and realize that he is ready to help." Both Brooks and the Negro leaders believed that the conference was influential in dissipating prejudice and in promoting tolerance and confidence between the races. The meeting undoubtedly helped North Carolina to avoid much of the racial violence and tension that characterized the American scene after World War I. So effective did Brooks consider it that he called similar conferences annually throughout his administration.[29]

The primary need for the development of Negro education, according to Brooks, was an adequate supply of competent teachers, especially for elementary schools. This, of course, would require additional teacher-training facilities. In 1919 the state supported three Negro normal schools, located in Winston-Salem, Fayetteville, and Elizabeth City, while ten counties with the aid of the Slater Fund and the General Education Board provided county training schools for Negroes, which were actually industrial schools offering courses in teacher training.

Immediately upon assuming office, Brooks initiated plans for expanding the Negro teacher training program by gaining additional aid from the philanthropic agencies. He apparently concentrated his attention upon the General Education Board and succeeded in winning the confidence and admiration of President Wallace Buttrick and Secretary Abraham Flexner. Throughout his administration he kept these men fully informed of educational developments in the state and of his plans for the future. In his frequent correspondence and conversations with them, Brooks demonstrated an acute insight into the educational needs of North Carolina Negroes and employed tact and honesty in presenting his requests

29. Outline of the Conference, Sept. 26, 1919, E. E. Smith to E. C. Brooks, Oct. 15, 1919, C. C. Spaulding to E. C. Brooks, Oct. 13, 1919, Declaration of Principles (in Brooks's handwriting), E. C. Brooks to S. G. Atkins, July 12, 1920, E. C. Brooks to W. P. Few, Nov. 1, 1922, S. P. I. Correspondence; *A Declaration of Principles by Representative Negroes of North Carolina, September 26, 1919* (Raleigh, n.d.).

for financial assistance from the Board. But his approach was never that of a beggar. In replying to one of Brooks's proposals in 1919, Flexner wrote: "Your proposition—as well as yourself—are, we think, entirely sound. We are delighted to assure you of our co-operation." The cordial relations between Brooks and the officials of the General Education Board were vividly expressed in the Board's increasing financial aid for the training of Negro teachers.[30]

At Brooks's request the General Education Board provided $11,650 for county training schools for Negroes in North Carolina in 1919. This sum coupled with aid from the Slater Fund enabled Brooks to establish nine additional county training schools within one year. At the same time, he attempted to reorganize the three Negro normal schools, which were sadly lacking in equipment, faculty, and buildings. He frankly described the sorry plight of these schools to the General Education Board and enlisted its support in their reorganization. The Board provided $12,500 for improvements at the Slater State Normal and Industrial School at Winston-Salem, and granted Brooks's request for financial aid for summer schools for Negroes. The Anna Jeanes Foundation and the Julius Rosenwald Fund also gave valuable assistance to his program of Negro education through their donations for teachers' salaries and buildings.[31]

In 1917 the legislative appropriation was only $3,300 for the expansion of each of the three Negro normal schools. Brooks, however, persuaded the Legislature of 1919 to appropriate $90,000 for permanent improvements at these institutions and to increase the maintenance fund to $35,000. With a view toward improving "the efficiency of colored teachers," he used a considerable portion of the $50,000 appropriation for teacher training in 1919 for Negroes. In that year eight county summer schools were conducted for Negro teachers. These were joint schools with almost every county sharing in their support. Of the 1,907 teachers enrolled in them, almost 60 per cent

30. Abraham Flexner to Willard B. Gatewood, Jr., Nov. 21, 1956; *The John F. Slater Fund: Proceedings and Reports, 1918*, pp. 15-16; E. C. Brooks to J. S. Manning, April 20, 1922, E. C. Brooks to Wallace Buttrick, March 5, 1919, E. C. Brooks to Abraham Flexner, Aug. 30, 1919, E. C. Brooks to Wallace Buttrick, Dec. 8, 1920, Abraham Flexner to E. C. Brooks, Sept. 1, 1919, S. P. I. Correspondence.

31. E. C. Brooks to E. C. Sage, June 2, 1919, E. C. Sage to E. C. Brooks, March 6, 1919, E. C. Brooks to Abraham Flexner, June 26, 1919, E. C. Brooks to S. G. Atkins, June 28, 1919, S. P. I. Correspondence.

possessed the lowest certificate or no certificate at all, and only 249 teachers claimed any college education. Other Negro teachers re-ceived summer training in colleges and normal schools aided by the state and the General Education Board.[32]

Brooks's certification program and salary schedule, established between 1919 and 1921, included Negro teachers. His jurisdiction over state funds for the payment of salaries of teachers, principals, and superintendents enabled him to enforce the salary schedule for Negroes, which, in turn, provided some incentive for Negro teachers to raise their qualifications through summer school training. Shortly before the meeting of the special session of the legislature in 1920, which authorized a revised salary schedule, Brooks declared: "It is my desire to see that justice is done to Negro teachers, and my pur-pose in pleading for a new salary schedule for Negroes was that they might receive at least the same per cent increase that the white teachers receive." He at first thought that one state salary schedule should include all teachers, both white and Negro. But he later decided to establish separate schedules for the two races and to raise proportionately the salaries of Negro teachers with lower certificates in order to meet the demands of the Negro schools. Actually then, the difference in the salaries of white and Negro teachers with lower grade certificates was very slight, while the salaries of white teachers with higher grade certificates were considerably more than Negroes with similar certificates. This arrangement resulted in a greater salary increase for Negro teachers than for whites, because the former usually lacked the requirements for higher certificates. Brooks did not emphasize this point before the legislators, who authorized him to prepare a revised salary schedule.[33] The Negro leaders, however, immediately realized the boost that the education of their race would receive from Brooks's salary schedule. C. H. Moore, a Rosen-

32. *Report of the Superintendent of the State Colored Normal Schools and the Cherokee Indian Normal School of Robeson County, 1918-1920,* p. 7; *Report of the State Board of Examiners and Institute Conductors, 1919-1920,* p. 9; Brooks, *Administra-tion of the Public School System, 1919-1920,* pp. 9-10; E. C. Brooks to S. G. Atkins, July 12, 1920, E. C. Brooks to E. C. Sage, March 6, 1919, E. C. Sage to E. C. Brooks, March 6, 1919, S. P. I. Correspondence.

33. E. C. Brooks to C. H. Moore, May 11, 1920, E. C. Brooks to Frank Bachman, May 31, 1920, S. P. I. Correspondence; *Teacher Salary Schedule of North Carolina, 1920-1921* (Educational Publication No. 30); Brooks, *Administration of the Public School System, 1919-1920,* pp. 6-7.

wald agent, wrote him: "I feel very proud of the fact that the Negroes of the state have an advocate 'at court' who is a broad and sympathetic friend of the poor and much-discriminated-against colored teachers."[34]

During the regular session of the General Assembly in 1921, Brooks achieved his greatest success in reorganizing Negro education. He persuaded the Budget Commission to approve an unprecedented appropriation of $400,000 for buildings and equipment at the three Negro normal schools in addition to a maintenance fund more than double that of 1919. He then pushed this budget through the economy-conscious legislature. The fund of $400,000 was more than the total building appropriation for Negro normal schools since their establishment. In addition to this amount, Brooks managed to get $10,000 from the General Education Board, $2,000 from the Rosenwald Fund, and $2,500 in contributions from Negroes. Moreover, he gained direct control over the three Negro schools through a legislative act of 1921 placing the state normal schools under the State Board of Education. The financial support provided in that year coupled with another large contribution from the General Education Board in 1922 enabled Brooks to convert these institutions into real normal schools with facilities adequate to prepare Negro teachers for higher grade certificates.[35]

In 1921 Brooks induced the legislature to create a Division of Negro Education in his department with an annual appropriation of $15,000. On March 15, 1921, the Division of Negro Education was organized with N. C. Newbold as director, and by the end of Brooks's administration it contained a staff of nine persons, both white and Negro, a group larger than the entire Department of Public Instruction a decade earlier. Indeed, few of Brooks's accomplishments were a greater source of personal pride than the organization and work of this division, which undertook the supervision and promotion of the education of a large segment of the state's population hitherto grossly neglected. With eight years of experience as state agent for rural Negro schools, Director Newbold was eminently qualified for

34. C. H. Moore to E. C. Brooks, May 10, 1920, S. P. I. Correspondence.
35. E. C. Brooks to Abraham Flexner, Dec. 27, 1920, memorandum to Jackson Davis, Jan. 16, 1922, E. C. Brooks to Abraham Flexner, March 15, 1921, E. C. Brooks to Jackson Davis, April 19, 1921, E. C. Brooks to the General Education Board, April 16, 1923, S. P. I. Correspondence.

his new position, which placed him in charge of all phases of Negro education ranging from the elementary through the normal schools.[36]

The work of building a reputable system of public schools for Negroes was necessarily beset with many problems, but the Division of Negro Education attained immediate success at several crucial points. It exposed those "spurious" institutions posing as teacher-training centers for Negroes, energetically promoted harmonious race relations, and provided competent supervision of work in Negro schools. In discussing the Division of Negro Education in 1922, Brooks wrote:

The creation of the Division of Negro Education, therefore, was very opportune. Its annual cost to the State is negligible. . . . But the fact that the negroes had representation in the government to whom they could look for guidance gave them a new loyalty to the State. Their coopera-tion has been phenomenal. The officials of the State representing this division have secured, through their supervision of the rural schools, donations from negroes amounting to approximately $100,000. As a result of this supervision the negroes complain considerably less. They are more hopeful and they have caught the spirit of cooperation.[37]

One student of Negro education in North Carolina, writing in 1932, declared that "public secondary schools for Negroes developed slowly until the Division of Negro Education was organized in 1921," then their growth became "constant and fairly rapid throughout the state."[38]

In the General Assembly of 1923 Brooks continued his fight for Negro schools, again concentrating upon teacher-training facilities. Through his efforts the legislature provided a bond issue of $500,000 for the Negro normal schools and authorized the purchase of the National Training School in Durham, which would be converted into a normal school. In 1920 Dr. James E. Shepard, president of the Durham institution, had discussed with Brooks the feasibility of a fourth Negro normal school under state control. At that time Brooks insisted that the state "should make the institutions already estab-lished *real* normal schools before attempting to establish another

36. *Public Laws and Resolutions, 1921*, pp. 421-422; *Annual Report of the General Education Board, 1922-1923*, p. 41; E. C. Brooks to Abraham Flexner, March 15, 1921, Abraham Flexner to E. C. Brooks, May 27, 1921, S. P. I. Correspondence.
37. *Biennial Report, 1920-1922*, p. 34.
38. Hollis Long, *Public Secondary Education for Negroes in North Carolina* (New York, 1932), p. 104.

normal school." By 1923 he apparently felt that the time was ripe for undertaking state support of another Negro teacher-training center. At any rate, the Durham institution was transformed into a state normal school in 1923, and was the only state-supported normal school for Negroes whose graduates could receive Class-A Elementary certificates in accordance with the standards of the North Carolina College Conference. Brooks, however, hoped to raise the Slater State Normal School in Winston-Salem to a four-year institution "within the near future."[39]

Despite his energetic efforts, the development of Negro education was necessarily slow and gradual. He was building Negro schools from the ground up, and his financial resources were not large enough for a sudden and complete transformation. Nevertheless, there was considerable progress in almost every phase of Negro education during his administration. The number of Negro public school teachers increased from 3,511 in 1918 to 4,871 in 1923, while the average monthly salary rose from $28.97 to $63.94. The value of Negro school property was more than tripled in the same period, and the average daily attendance increased from 107,181 in 1918 to 161,463 in 1923. Only at the end of Brooks's administration did Negro high schools warrant a place in the report of the state high school inspector, although it was his sixteenth annual report. There were at that time only eight standard public high schools for Negroes with a total enrollment of 1,488 pupils. But the number of county training schools increased from ten in 1918 to twenty-five in 1923 largely through Brooks's success in gaining financial aid from the General Education Board. The Negro schools shared rather generously in the funds for vocational education. In 1922 1,500 Negro men participated in part-time classes in agriculture, and 190 Negro women enrolled in home economics courses.[40]

39. E. C. Brooks to Trevor Arnett, March 2, 1923, E. C. Brooks to James E. Shepard, Dec. 6, 1920, S. P. I. Correspondence; *Institutions of Higher Learning in North Carolina* (Educational Publication No. 58), p. 17; Elizabeth Seay, "A History of North Carolina College for Negroes" (Master's Thesis, Duke University Library), pp. 62-67.

40. Between 1918 and 1923 the number of white teachers increased from 11,730 to 15,665, and their average monthly salaries rose from $46.52 to $107.14. *Biennial Report, 1918-1920*, pp. 80-81, 96-98; *Biennial Report, 1922-1924*, pp. 53, 74-75, 90-91, 96-97; *Annual Report of the Federal Board of Vocational Education, 1922*, pp. 189-190; *Slater Fund: Proceedings and Reports, 1923*, pp. 14-15; *Public Education in North Carolina* (Educational Publication No. 101), pp. 1-16; N. C. Newbold to E. C. Brooks, Nov. 9, 1920, S. P. I. Correspondence.

Perhaps the most extraordinary development in Negro education under Brooks was the improvement in qualifications of teachers. The number of Negro teachers with elementary certificates increased from 674 in 1920 to 1,876 in 1923, and when Brooks left office in 1923 1,550 Negro teachers were enrolled in approved college summer schools and 2,609 in county summer schools. Brooks sincerely believed that the "harmony and prosperity" of both races depended upon providing educational oportunities for Negroes.[41] He built a solid foundation for a progressive program of Negro education, especially through more adequate financial support and better qualified teachers. This forward movement, inaugurating the "golden period in Negro education in North Carolina," gained momentum under his successors.

[4]

Shortly after assuming office in 1919, Brooks inaugurated a rather drastic structural reorganization of the Department of Public Instruction.[42] He had studied this problem two years earlier as a member of the State Educational Commission, a body that continued to exist until 1922. As State Superintendent, he continued to serve the commission in an advisory capacity and co-operated with the General Education Board in making a school survey of the state. In August, 1919, he informed the Board of his plan "to eliminate a certain amount of lost motion and unify our work in the Department of Public Instruction." The organization of the Division of Schoolhouse Planning in 1920 was indicative of his ideas. Brooks wanted to group similar functions together in divisions and define the duties of each division. He apparently impressed his plan upon the State Educa-

41. *Biennial Report, 1918-1920,* pp. 96-98; *Biennial Report, 1922-1924,* pp. 90-91, 96-97.

42. In 1919 the Department of Public Instruction included a conglomeration of officers with overlapping duties. In addition to the State Board of Examiners and Institute Conductors, the Department personnel consisted of eight persons, including two stenographers and a janitor paid by the state, a director of vocational education paid by federal and state funds, and four persons paid by the General Education Board. The Department also contained a Bureau of Community Service that provided films and instruction in citizenship and physical education in rural schools, and a bureau dealing with adult illiteracy and "moonlight schools" under Elizabeth Kelly. See E. C. Brooks to the General Assembly, Jan. 19, 1919, S. P. I. Correspondence.

tional Commission, which included it among its recommendations in 1920.[43]

In the following year, the legislature adopted the main features of the proposed reorganization. It approved the creation of three divisions to deal with Negro education, publication, and physical education, respectively.[44] Two other divisions concerning certification and teacher training replaced the six member Board of Examiners and Institute Conductors. A total of $94,000 was provided for these five divisions. The Legislature of 1921 also placed the state normal schools under the control of the State Board of Education, of which Brooks was secretary. This act gave his department supervision over all Negro normal schools and the two white normal schools at Boone and Cullowhee. Brooks as State Superintendent was already a trustee of the University of North Carolina, North Carolina College for Women, and East Carolina Teachers College. He fully utilized his official connections with the various state Colleges to secure their valuable cooperation in carrying out his public school program.[45]

According to Brooks, the departmentalization of his office promoted efficiency and "lent dignity" to the new positions, although it generally required only a rearrangement of the existing personnel. In order to complete the reorganization, he desired to provide advanced training for the directors of the new divisions. In April, 1921, he wrote Wallace Buttrick of the General Education Board: "We need better trained men and women to give supervision to the educational work of the state. We are moving at a rapid rate and we should secure as quickly as possible the best trained people to give guidance to the progress. I believe our own people who have the

43. *Annual Report of the General Education Board, 1918-1919,* p. 28; *Report of the State Educational Commission,* pp. 109-111; W. H. Pittman to R. A. Nunn, June 16, 1920, E. C. Brooks to W. H. Pittman, Nov. 27, 1920, E. C. Brooks to Abraham Flexner, Aug. 30, 1919, S. P. I. Correspondence.

44. Although Brooks strongly encouraged physical training in public schools, he never created a division of physical education. When the special session of the legislature in 1921 ordered him to reduce expenditures for his department, he apparently decided to forego the creation of such a division rather than endanger other aspects of his program.

45. *New School Legislation, 1920 and 1921* (Educational Publication No. 12), pp. 15-17, 25-28; *North Carolina Manual,* ed. R. D. W. Connor (Raleigh, 1921), p. 63; E. C. Brooks to Frank Bachman, Oct. 4, 1920, E. C. Brooks to J. I. Foust, Nov. 6, 1922, E. C. Brooks to J. I. Foust, Dec. 15, 1922, E. C. Brooks to Harry Chase, Sept. 24, 1920, S. P. I. Correspondence; Minutes of the Board of Trustees of the University of North Carolina, 1919-1923, University Papers.

personality could be trained for this work and give permanency to our supervisory staff that could not be secured by importing men and women from outside the state." The General Education Board granted his request for $15,000, which was used by eight persons employed in the Department of Public Instruction in securing advanced training at Columbia, Harvard, George Peabody, and Hampton Institute.[46]

In his search for greater efficiency, Brooks continued to perfect the organization of his department by rearranging divisions and creating new ones from the existing personnel. In 1922 his department employed forty-seven persons, including secretaries and stenographers, and was composed of nine divisions, namely, certification, teacher training, supervision, school extension, schoolhouse planning, Negro education, finances and statistics, vocational education, and publication. The quarters of the department on the second floor of the State Department Building had become so inadequate that five members were located in rented space at State College. Brooks sought in vain to persuade the State Building Commission to ask the Legislature of 1921 for an appropriation sufficient to supply adequate quarters at one location for his entire department. Two years later he made another futile attempt to induce the legislature to "erect and equip an adequate office building for the State Department of Education."[47]

Among the other proposals that Brooks and the State Educational Commission intended to present to the General Assembly in 1921 was a revisal and codification of the public school laws. Brooks had called for such a school code in 1919 in his *Education for Democracy.* Rapid change in school legislation during his administration had left many local school officials in utter confusion about their powers and duties. The State Educational Commission sought to clarify the legal basis of public education by bringing all school laws together into one body. Brooks "helped to map out the main lines of this proposed code," but was unable to study the details until it was

46. E. C. Brooks to Wallace Buttrick, April 16, 1921, Abraham Flexner to E. C. Brooks, July 1, 1921, E. C. Brooks to N. C. Newbold, Dec. 1, 1921, E. C. Brooks to J. J. Blair, May 1, 1922, S. P. I. Correspondence.

47. *Directory of School Officials of North Carolina, 1922* (Educational Publication No. 57), pp. 4-5; E. C. Brooks to J. A. Salter, Nov. 3, 1920, S. P. I. Correspondence; *News and Observer,* Dec. 23, 1922.

published late in 1920. He then recognized that numerous changes were necessary if the code were to be accepted by the legislature. In certain quarters the code was described as the "Brooks Law" for centralizing control of public schools in Raleigh. The Teachers' Assembly voiced objections to certain amendments to the school laws inserted in the code, especially the popular election of county boards of education. Brooks believed that the lack of time to overcome the opposition of school men was a major obstacle to the enactment of the code in 1921. After consulting the executive committee of the Teachers' Assembly, he wrote Frank Bachman of the General Education Board, who had directed the state educational survey:

It was then decided that it was best under the circumstances not to try to push the code through this General Assembly. . . . The great trouble in the way is the lack of understanding on the part of the school men. . . . Many of them are attacking us openly and accusing us of having some foreign agency [General Education Board] come into the state and tell the General Assembly what to do. . . . The confusion in the minds of the school people since they have read the code is astonishing. They have shot letters to the General Assembly to hold up the code. The members of the General Assembly are strongly advising me not to try to put the whole code through this year.[48]

Brooks refused to recommend the enactment of the code in its existing form, since he believed that it was "too heavily weighted in favor of city schools" and contained serious technical flaws. Moreover, the uneasy state of the legislature as a result of the agricultural depression was hardly favorable to another major innovation. Brooks, acutely aware of the economic situation, predicted quite correctly that the legislature would change the method of financing public schools; and for this reason he desired to postpone the action on the code for two years, at which time the educational reorganization begun in 1919 would have become permanent. He believed that by 1923 it would "be easy . . . to shape up the entire law and prepare a code that will be a good working basis for years to come."[49]

48. E. C. Brooks to Frank Bachman, Jan. 24, 1921, S. P. I. Correspondence. See also E. W. Knight, "The Commission's Report and the Teachers' Assembly," *The High School Journal*, IV (January, 1921), 3-6; *N C E*, XV (Jan., 1921), 3; E. C. Brooks to Galletin Roberts, January 21, 1921, S. P. I. Correspondence; *Asheville Citizen* (Asheville, North Carolina), Jan. 20, 1921.

49. E. C. Brooks to T. R. Foust, Jan. 17, 1921, E. C. Brooks to Frank Bachman, Feb. 4, 1921, E. C. Brooks to N. W. Walker, Jan. 15, 1921, T. R. Foust to E. C. Brooks, Jan. 15, 1921, E. C. Brooks to M. E. Haggerty, April 12, 1921, S. P. I. Correspondence.

A newspaper cartoon critical of the school code.

Brooks personally undertook the rewriting of the code in order to eliminate those features that created a furor in 1921. He was assisted by the State Educational Commission and by the commission created by the special session of the legislature in 1921 to recommend changes in the school taxation laws. After several months of rather intensive labor, he published the code in pamphlet form in the summer of 1922 and discussed it at the meeting of the Teachers' Assembly in November. When the legislature convened in 1923, the revised school code was apparently endorsed by a majority of the school men of the state.[50]

In the codified school laws introduced in the legislature on January 23, 1923, Brooks had inserted several new measures and deleted those sections of laws that had become obsolete. The *News and Observer* predicted that "trouble is brewing" for the Brooks school code, while H. G. Connor, Jr., chairman of the House education committee, anticipated serious opposition to its enactment. He urged Brooks to explain "certain matters" to the committees on education "to the end that the mental attitude of some of the members may be changed." He especially wanted Brooks to refute the legislators' notions that his department "fixed" the salaries of all teachers; that certification was unjust to older teachers "long in service" but without college training; that the method of handling the salaries of county superintendents was extravagant; and that nearly all power over public schools was centralized in the State Superintendent's office.[51]

The opening of the committee hearings on January 31, 1923, found the galleries and lobbies of the House "filled to capacity." As soon as Brooks appeared, several legislators initiated an inquisitorial session in which they charged him with an "unwarranted usurpation of power in control of the public school system." In describing Brooks's defense of his administration and program the *News and Observer* reported: "For two hours and a half he defended himself in brilliant oratory, parried with his critics giving thrust for thrust, gave a comprehensive outline of his proposed school code, and concluded with a half hour of rapid answers to questions shot at him." At one point he turned upon his opponents and angrily declared: "If this is autocracy, then make the most of it." Some of the legislators undoubtedly gained their first clear understanding of the school laws upon reading Brooks's code; others realized for the first time the amount of power that the state had over public schools. When Brooks finished his initial outline of the proposed code, Representative Lindsay Warren of Beaufort County exclaimed: "This proposed law is centralization run riot." Nevertheless, Brooks had won the support of the education committees, including W. H. S. Burgwyn, his implacable foe in 1921.[52]

After conferring with the education committees for almost three weeks, Brooks compromised on sections of the code which were opposed by legislators fearing too much centralization of power in his department. The revised provisions, concerning the teacher salary schedule, which many legislators believed to be "fixed and inflexibly binding upon county boards of education," allowed cities and counties to establish their own salary schedules. Actually, this revisal made little difference, because the state salary schedule remained an important determinant in distributing the equalizing fund. The last cry of centralization was quieted when the section requiring all school officials "to obey instructions of the State Superintendent and accept his construction of the law" was deleted from the code. Three other provisions changed by the education committees concerned the powers of the county in contracting school debts, issuing bonds, and initiating legal proceedings to secure taxes sufficient to run the schools for six months.[53]

The close co-operation between Brooks and the education committees in altering parts of the code headed off the "bitter fight that seemed inevitable on the floor of the legislature." The code, which clearly recognized "a state system of schools based on the county as the unit of organization," was enacted into law and became effective on April 15, 1923. For more than three decades, the so-called Brooks school code with its numerous amendments and revisals remained the basic school law of North Carolina.[54]

52. News and Observer, Feb. 1, 2, 7, 22, 1923.
53. News and Observer, Jan. 24, Feb. 7, 25, 1923; Public School Law: Codification of 1923, pp. 19, 123-124.
54. News and Observer, Feb. 7, 22, 1923; Charlotte Observer, March 4, 1923; Brower, "Eugene Clyde Brooks" (an address), pp. 6-7.

Seven: COUNTY GOVERNMENT
REFORMER, *1921-1931*

[1]

While Brooks was campaigning for greater efficiency in county school administration as editor of *North Carolina Education* and as State Superintendent, he was urging with equal vigor certain reforms in county government that were not chiefly concerned with public education. As early as 1910, for example, he proposed standard systems of county bookkeeping and "fixed salaries" for county officials entirely independent of the collection of fees.[1] The suggestions of such drastic reforms were apparently disregarded with cool indifference by officials, who, suspicious of any change, manifested a general satisfaction with the existing methods of conducting county affairs. For the time being, therefore, Brooks concentrated his attention upon the educational departments of county government.

As State Superintendent he was largely responsible for a revolution in the character of county school administration. He eradicated much of the lethargy among county school officials by enforcing a system of budgets and audits as well as by raising the standards of county superintendents. While transforming the county school administration, he recognized anew the pressing need for a general reform of local government, particularly in the conduct of financial affairs. His probes into the handling of school funds revealed extraordinary disorder and negligence in the management of county finances in general. Brooks contended that the proper administration of the reorganized school system demanded efficiency in all departments of county government. Thus, his agitation for the general

1. *N C E*, V (Nov., 1910), 11.

reform of county government was at first closely tied to the state educational program and was frequently included in his campaign for the improvement in county school administration.[2]

Through his authority under the County Budget Act of 1919, Brooks collected much data concerning county government and finances. The investigation that he initiated in 1920 under A. S. Brower uncovered further evidences of appalling mismanagement by county officials. Brower reported that "the outstanding fact discovered by this investigation is the lack of an adequate system of records in the county." At the same time Professor E. C. Branson, founder of the department of rural social-economics in the University of North Carolina, pleaded for county government reform on the basis of a vast quantity of information that he had collected since 1914. For years Branson and his students had called attention to the "antiquated and wasteful practices" in county government. Their activities in behalf of county government reform were greatly augmented by the establishment of the Institute for Research in Social Science at the University in 1924. Within three years investigators under Branson's direction had completed "intensive courthouse studies" of forty-three of the one hundred counties in North Carolina. Brooks and Branson, who were personal friends, became closely allied in the agitation for county government reform. Brooks not only had considerable influence in the higher political echelon, but he was also a highly respected and popular figure in the state. Moreover, his eloquence enabled him to present his themes with simplicity and clarity. In fact, President Chase of the University believed that Brooks "held a large audience almost better than any man in the state." Brooks, in effect, became the vocal leader of the movement for county government reform.[3]

In 1921 he began in earnest his public speaking campaign in be-

2. Charles M. Johnson, "County Government Reform in North Carolina (An Address Presented to the National Association of State Auditors, Treasurers, and Comptrollers, August 9, 1927), GP-516, Governors' Papers (McLean); Stewart Robertson, "County Government Legislation Begins Operation in the State," *News and Observer*, May 22, 1927.

3. Brower, "Confidential Report to the State Superintendent on Burke, Mitchell, and Caswell Counties," S. P. I. Correspondence; Wager, *County Government in North Carolina*, p. vii; Hobbs, *North Carolina: Economic and Social*, pp. ix-x; Reed Kitchin, "Story of the North Carolina Club," *North Carolina Club Year Book, 1924-1925*. See also *North Carolina Club Year Book, 1917-1918*, which is devoted to county government. Harry Chase to David Hill, Sept. 7, 1921, University Papers.

half of county government reform. He delivered addresses to numerous groups with a view toward gaining support for the movement. He sincerely believed that the "first step" in improving county administration was "to arouse the public conscience through publicity that will cause the people to demand better government." His confidence in the people to implement reforms whenever defects were sufficiently exposed was reminiscent of the views of the muckrakers of the Progressive Era. His expressions were always those of an optimist who refused to believe that the "world is degenerating." Neither inefficiency of local government in North Carolina nor the Teapot Dome scandals on the national level could shatter his optimism for the future and his faith that the people would right these wrongs. In 1925 he declared that "the best shall prevail, and therein lies hope, and I remain an optimist." Such views underlay most of his public utterances on county government, regardless of the prevalence and seriousness of the defects that he exposed.[4]

In an address to the first Regional Conference on Town and County Administration at Chapel Hill in September, 1921, Brooks outlined six major shortcomings in the existing conduct of county affairs. First, many county officials, being ignorant of the cost of government and the bonded indebtedness of the several departments, did not know "what tax rates to levy to meet the full legitimate expenses of the county." Second, the large number of delinquent taxpayers forced an increase in tax rates. Third, the fines, penalties, and forfeitures of counties were "not always properly accounted for and applied in accordance with law." Fourth, the failure to segregate funds according to legal requirements resulted in excessive funds for certain departments of county government, while others had to borrow money for current expenses. Fifth, the special local taxes in many counties were "improperly levied, collected, and disbursed." In addition to grossly inadequate records, Brooks found "positive evidence" that in some areas the more powerful interests escaped local taxes altogether. For example, in one district the Postal Telegraph Company, the Pullman Car Company, the Southern Bell Telephone Company, and the Western Union Telegraph Company,

4. E. C. Brooks, "County Government and Public Education," *N C E*, XVI (Oct., 1921), 3-4; *News and Observer*, March 13, 1924; E. C. Brooks, "The Need of Cooperation between Ministers and Teachers" (an address, June, 1925), Brooks Papers (BLS).

which were liable to taxation, neither paid "a cent of taxes" nor
were even listed on the tax books. Finally, Brooks declared that most
counties lacked "unity of management to fix responsibility and insure efficiency." His proposals for remedial measures included a
vigorous campaign to arouse public opinion; strong state supervision
to insure the proper management of county affairs; and a program of
instruction in local government in public schools and colleges. He
especially emphasized the need for state supervision of county finances through a uniform auditing system under the direction of
the State Auditor. He insisted that whenever county officials demonstrated incompetence or failed to meet a "given standard of efficiency," they should be removed immediately and replaced by temporary appointees until the people could elect their successors.[5]

Brooks reiterated similar themes in speeches in almost every part
of the state and never hesitated to relate specific, though anonymous,
examples of inefficient county administration. He pointed out that a
bonding house called upon officials of one county for interest long
overdue on its bonds only to find that they were wholly ignorant
of the existence of such bonds. In another county the sheriff overpaid
his account by more than $1,000 and was entirely unaware of his
error. The press of the state in general heartily endorsed Brooks's
activities in behalf of better local government. The *News and Observer* declared that he was "making way for the fight that is to
come for a closer scrutiny and a more accurate check by the people
of the State upon their public officials holding county offices."[6]

In 1922 Brooks continued his speaking campaign regarding
county government. He addressed almost every teachers' summer
school in the state in an effort to awaken the teachers to the need of
immediate action.[7] In his speech at the University on June 30, 1922,
he stressed the importance of establishing "workable standards" for
county officials which would be enforced by the state. He used as an
example his own department and asserted:

5. E. C. Brooks, "County Government and Public Education," *Attainable Standards
In Municipal Programs: A Partial Report of the First National Conference on Town
and County Administration*, Prepared by Howard Odum (*University of North Carolina Extension Bulletin*, Chapel Hill, 1921), pp. 116-119.
6. *News and Observer*, Aug. 31, Sept. 2, 20, 1921; E. C. Brooks, "County Government Reform," *The Bond Buyer*, LXXV (Nov. 12, 1927), 4.
7. *News and Observer*, July 2, 4, 1922; E. C. Brooks, "County Government and
Education," Brooks Papers (BLS).

When a county fails to observe the certification law, the State Department of Education checks its teachers' salaries and corrects its errors. When they fail to obey the law governing school attendance, the State checks their budgets. As a result of this power to compel counties to obey the law, the State Department last year reduced the amount of their budget over $500,000. The State Department may make certain suggestions and authorize certain standards, but county officials are not compelled to follow them *unless* they wish to draw state money—and state money is paid out in accordance with the law.[8]

Brooks then suggested that the General Assembly establish and enforce similar standards for all county administration.

The State Association of County Commissioners invited him to address its annual meeting on August 16, 1922. His speech on "County Government and State Progress" demonstrated that his ideas on local government reform had become more specific and refined. Brooks told this influential group that 10 to 15 per cent of the taxes in many counties remained uncollected each year and that counties were "living on bond issues to pay current expenses rather than levy the constitutional limit in taxes." He pointed up the confusion about legislative and executive functions of certain county departments, especially the board of commissioners, which possessed both functions. But since the board met only twelve days in each year, it could hardly be expected to perform its executive functions. Therefore, Brooks suggested a "continuous executive" comparable to a county manager and a system of "traveling auditors under the jurisdiction of the State Auditor," who would conduct institutes for county officials. He believed that the power of example would be a potent force in reforming county administration; thus he held up Pitt County to the Association of County Commissioners as an example of a county with a highly efficient government. The Pitt County officials had accomplished their exemplary administration with the assistance of Brooks, who desired to make Pitt a "workable standard" for other counties.[9]

Brooks undoubtedly discussed his views with Governor Morrison, whom he advised on a variety of matters. At any rate, on March 24,

8. E. C. Brooks, "County Government and the Public School System," June 30, 1922, Brooks Papers (BLS).
9. E. C. Brooks, "County Government and State Progress, Aug. 16, 1922," Brooks Papers (BLS).

1922, the Governor appointed a commission consisting of Josephus Daniels, E. C. Branson, O. Max Gardner, and several others to study and recommend changes in county government laws. Morrison declared that the existing county government was "a patchwork affair wholly dependent for efficiency upon the character of county officials." His commission apparently had no appreciable influence upon the General Assembly in 1923, for the question of county government reform was almost wholly disregarded by the legislators. The *Progressive Farmer* strongly rebuked the legislature for its failure to attend to county government in view of the "startling revelations" produced by "Dr. Brooks and Dr. Branson."[10]

[2]

Brooks continued his agitation for local government reform after becoming president of North Carolina State College in June, 1923. The following year, Angus W. McLean, who was elected governor, pledged himself to the improvement of the administrative structure of state government, especially through the centralization of fiscal control. McLean, who in 1922 had served on Governor Morrison's county government commission, was also interested in a general overhauling of county government. The new governor, then, held views closely akin to those of Brooks; and so an intimate friendship developed between the two men. In fact, Brooks was often considered McLean's "right hand man." Certainly, they formed an effective team in the movement for county government reform, which by 1925 was attracting wide attention in the state.[11]

In the Legislature of 1925 the question of county government was largely eclipsed by several measures on state administrative reorganization strongly backed by Governor McLean. Brooks, how-

10. Statement by Governor Cameron Morrison, March 24, 1922, A. D. Watts to Cameron Morrison, March 27, 1922, Governors' Papers (Morrison); *Progressive Farmer,* XXXVIII (March 17, 1923), 294.
11. E. C. Brooks, "Five Great Enterprises That the State Should Support with Emphasis," Brooks Papers (BLS); *News and Observer,* March 13, 1924, Jan. 9, 1925; *Public Papers and Letters of Angus Wilton McLean, Governor of North Carolina, 1925-1929,* ed. D. L. Corbitt (Raleigh, 1931), pp. 4, 6-8; Paul Wager, "Business Efficiency in County Government," *North Carolina Club Year Book, 1924-1925,* pp. 34-35; interview with Mr. A. S. Brower, Oct. 2, 1956; E. C. Brooks to A. W. McLean, Sept. 26, 1928, E. C. Brooks to A. W. McLean, Jan. 22, 1922, Angus Wilton McLean Papers, Duke University Library, Durham, North Carolina.

ever, sought to focus the legislators' attention upon needed reforms in county government by publishing a lengthy article on the subject in the *News and Observer* on January 18, 1925, in which he insisted that defects in local administration were not caused by the state constitution, but by "the attitude of our political leaders." The politicians had "not considered that from the standpoint of public welfare, the supervision of local government and the protection of the people from ignorant and other incompetent officials should take equal rank with the supervision of roads, schools, health etc." His article described in detail the government of Pitt County, which he still considered the "best governed county in the state." According to Brooks, most counties were organized around a system of fees for officials who rendered "individual services," such as the issuance of marriage licenses, recording of deeds, and surveys of land. He insisted that many defects of county government resulted from the failure of its organization to keep abreast with its increasing functions for "the general welfare." The counties were attempting to execute modern programs in education, highways, and health with the same methods and machinery employed during Reconstruction. But Brooks maintained that constitutional amendments were unnecessary; he still believed that the establishment of exemplary government in a few counties coupled with adequate state supervision would lead to reforms in the others.[12]

Brooks was convinced that any delay in correcting defects in county administration of public funds would be costly. On January 23, 1925, he wrote Branson:

I think that this legislature should act. I do not believe that a committee appointed to investigate for the next two years will be of much help. What we need to do now is to start a plan whereby counties can go forward under that gentle pressure that the State alone can give. I have enough information in my office to make the most optimistic man morbidly pessimistic. . . . We need now to study the good points of government and what can be put into practice.[13]

Branson was inclined to favor a legislative commission to study county government and recommend changes to the General Assem-

12. *News and Observer*, Jan. 18, 1925; *Report on a Survey of the Organization and Administration of State Government in North Carolina*, prepared by the Brookings Institution (Washington, 1930), pp. 21, 26-32.

13. E. C. Brooks to E. C. Branson, Jan. 23, 1925, Brooks Papers (DAH).

bly of 1927. He urged Governor McLean to appoint Brooks and A.
C. McIntosh, professor of law in the University of North Carolina,
as members of the commission if it were created. Branson believed
that "best of all public men in the state," Brooks knew "the facts,"
while McIntosh was an expert on the "state and public-level laws on
county government."[14]

The Legislature of 1925 "seriously considered" the question of
county government reform, although its chief concern was a reorganization of the state fiscal administration. Senator W. L. Foushee of
Durham drafted a bill providing for a commission on county and
state government with an appropriation of $25,000 for the purpose
of recommending changes that would promote economy and eliminate duplication. For some reason this bill was never introduced
in the legislature, although Branson strongly endorsed it. However,
Senator A. F. Sams of Winston-Salem introduced a bill on county
government which was undoubtedly more acceptable to Brooks than
the Foushee proposal and might well have been drafted by him. This
measure called for the creation of a county government commission of seven members and a county examiner who would act as a
field agent. The purpose of the commission was to provide advice
and "minimum standards" of good government for county commissioners and to recommend reforms to the next legislature. The bill
authorized all counties to employ auditors and tax supervisors and
specified penalties for officials who failed to follow legal requirements in executing their duties, especially in the handling of public
funds. The Sams Bill was killed by the Senate committee on counties,
cities and towns. To the great disappointment of Brooks the Legislature of 1925 adjourned without providing any reform in county
government.[15]

Brooks did not give up the fight with this setback. He at once
began working with Governor McLean in an effort to insure favorable action by the General Assembly in 1927. They decided to

14. E. C. Branson to Angus W. McLean, Jan. 19, 1925, E. C. Branson to E. C.
Brooks, Jan. 19, 1925, Brooks Papers (DAH).
15. News and Observer, Jan. 19, 1925; Brooks, "County Government Reform in
North Carolina," The Bond Buyer, LXXV (Nov., 12, 1927), 2; E. C. Branson to Angus
W. McLean, Jan. 19, 1925, Brooks Papers (DAH); A Bill Entitled An Act to Improve
County Government, S. B. 772, Session 1925, Brooks Papers (DUL); Senate Journal,
1925, p. 445.

launch their drive at the annual meeting of the State Association of County Commissioners at Blowing Rock on August 13, 1925. In an address to this group, McLean expressed a desire to place county government upon a sound financial basis and suggested that a commission to study conditions and recommend reforms might be valuable. The Association, already disturbed by the growing agitation about county fiscal administration, requested the Governor to appoint such a commission. McLean readily granted the request and on September 14, 1925, appointed Brooks to the commission, along with eleven other prominent persons, including Professor McIntosh and Frank P. Spruill, president of the Association of County Commissioners. Later two influential representatives from women's organizations were added to the membership of the group. At the first meeting of the commission, Brooks was elected chairman and McIntosh secretary. Five subcommittees were set up to study county business methods, managerial forms of government, county reports to state departments, county organizations and standards, and county government laws. Since the commission was not authorzied by the legislature, there was no appropriation to finance its activities.[16]

Brooks was mainly responsible for organizing and initiating the work of the commission. He served on the committees on county business methods and county organization and standards. Each committee was "given wide latitude" in pursuing its investigations, but Brooks had no intention of permitting the commission to present a superficial report. Each committee was expected to undertake a thorough study of the existing conditions of a particular phase of county government—a study that would result in concrete suggestions for remedial action. Professor Branson assured Brooks that the Institute for Research in Social Science and his completed surveys of six counties were at the command of the commission. Moreover, the Institute would study any county suggested by the members of the commission and approved by the board of commissioners of the

16. E. C. Brooks to A. W. McLean, June 17, 1925, E. C. Brooks to A. W. McLean, Sept. 17, 1925, Governors' Papers (McLean); A. W. McLean to E. C. Brooks, Sept. 14, 1925, Brooks Papers (DAH); *Greensboro Daily News*, Aug. 15, 1925; *News and Observer*, Aug. 13, 1925; Resolutions Passed by the State Association of County Commissioners, Aug. 13, 1925, Governors' Papers (McLean); "Committee of the County Government Commission, 1926, Brooks Papers (DAH); *Papers and Letters of Governor McLean*, pp. 114, 892-893.

county in question. Indeed, Branson and his students provided invaluable assistance to the County Government Commission.[17]

Brooks soon realized that the commission must use discretion in publicizing its findings, for the alienation of county officials would impede the progress of its initial work. On one occasion he wrote McIntosh: "After reading the report on Edgecombe County I can see very well why it would not be advisable to distribute among the members [of the commission] generally the criticism of certain officials." But Brooks believed that the defects of county government should continue to receive full publicity in order to keep the question before the people. In April, 1926, he suggested that county government reform become a plank in the state Democratic party platform. He sought also to keep in the good graces of the county officials and to win support for the work of the commission among such influential organizations as the Association of Superior Court Clerks, North Carolina Press Association, and Retail Merchants Association.[18]

After seven months of study the County Government Commission convened in Chapel Hill on April 15, 1926, to formulate its report. Each subcommittee recommended changes in specific areas of county administration, and the commission incorporated these recommendations along with a general statement on county government into its report which asserted:

The Commission finds that where the greatest reform is needed is in fiscal management. Progress in this respect has not kept pace with the improvement in the machinery for rendering service either to the individual or to society as a whole; and further improvement in the machinery for serving the public awaits the improvement so badly needed in fiscal management. Therefore, the report of the commission deals in the main with defects in fiscal management and suggestions for its improvement.[19]

17. E. C. Brooks to A. C. McIntosh, Oct. 21, 1925, E. C. Brooks to A. C. McIntosh, Oct. 27, 1925, E. C. Brooks to Members of the County Government Commission, Oct. 29, 1925, E. C. Branson to E. C. Brooks, Sept. 26, 1925, Brooks Papers (DUL).

18. E. C. Brooks to A. C. McIntosh, Nov. 25, 1925, E. C. Byerly to E. C. Brooks, Oct. 29, 1925, E. C. Byerly to E. C. Brooks, Dec. 27, 1925, Brooks Papers (DUL); E. C. Brooks to A. W. McLean, April 21, 1926, John G. Dawson to E. C. Brooks, April 24, 1926, Brooks Papers (DAH); A. W. McLean to Frank P. Spruill, Aug. 31, 1925, Governors' Papers (McLean).

19. "Report of the Commission on County Government," *Papers and Letters of Governor McLean,* p. 115. See also *News and Observer,* April 16, 1926.

Brooks presented the complete report to the Association of County Commissioners at Morehead City in August, 1926. The recommendations were grouped under seven headings: (1) maintaining unity in county fiscal management; (2) preserving the taxables of a county; (3) collecting the revenue fairly and justly; (4) safeguarding the revenue through proper accounting; (5) safeguarding the expenditures through budget control and a central purchasing agent; (6) protecting the physical property of the county; (7) providing for the proper administration of justice.[20]

The commission strongly recommended centralizing fiscal control in the board of county commissioners, which would appoint all administrative officers concerned with financial matters. Such officers included a business manager with general supervision of all county finances and a supervisor of taxables whose main function was the keeping of adequate tax records and the inspection of taxable property. A collector of revenue, also appointed by the commissioners, would be required to deposit all funds "as he collects them." Only in small counties would the sheriff remain tax collector, and even then he would be "held to strict accountability by the commissioners." In order to safeguard the expenditure of funds, each county was to create an adequate system of budgets and a central purchasing department under one official. "No agency of the county should borrow money except the board of county commissioners." Moreover, every department of county government was to maintain a "continuous audit" under the direction of the county auditor, and county credit was to be protected "by providing for prompt payment of all interest, principal of notes or bonds, and by meeting promptly every obligation of the county." The commission also suggested that some officer be appointed custodian of all physical property owned by the county to inspect and report on its condition and needs. All officials appointed by the board of commissioners, including the business manager, supervisor of taxables, collector of revenue, auditor, and purchasing agent, were to be paid fixed salaries. In some instances, the duties of two of these offices, such as those of the auditor and supervisor of taxables, could be performed by one person; but any county with an annual expenditure of $1,000,000 or more should

20. "Report of the Commission on County Government," *Papers and Letters of Governor McLean*, p. 115.

employ separate officials for each office. In order to insure continuity of business management, the board of commissioners should be elected for a term longer than two years, and never should all members retire within a given year. Finally, the commission recommended that the legislature "should by a general act make it possible for any county to adopt and maintain an improved form of local government." It should create a state department of finance and accounting to aid counties in adjusting to the reforms and should establish "a code on county government law."[21]

The Association of County Commissioners enthusiastically endorsed the commission's report, which Brooks submitted to the Governor in September, 1926. Frank P. Spruill, president of the Association, wrote Brooks:

I think you are due a large share of the credit for having a report of this kind approved by the State Association of County Commissioners and to my mind it is a masterpiece. I am glad the Association stamped its approval on this report, as it will go a long way towards getting the proposition before the General Assembly.[22]

Following an address by Brooks, the North Carolina Bar Association also endorsed the report and appointed a committee to co-operate with the County Government Commission.

However, the commission's recommendations by no means escaped criticism. For obvious reasons the sheriffs objected to the proposals for a separate tax collector in counties with a certain annual expenditure. Other county officials believed that a central purchasing agent would be an unnecessary expense and that each department should continue to buy its own supplies. Brooks explained that each department could still purchase its supplies provided "all requisitions" passed through "one central office in order that the county might know what is being paid for supplies." There was also some opposition to the commission's report on the grounds that it concentrated too much power in the hands of the board of commissioners. Undoubtedly too, some local officials were hostile to the idea of fixed salaries rather than an elaborate system of fees. These various

21. *Ibid.*, pp. 116-126. The County Government Commission made no recommendations on the administration of justice, but referred the question to the North Carolina Bar Association.
22. Frank Spruill to E. C. Brooks, Aug. 8, 1926, Brooks Papers (DAH).

criticisms probably accounted for the Governor's desire to minimize the report during the political campaigns in 1926 in order to avoid any "unfortunate" discussions.[23]

Brooks worked closely with Governor McLean in preparing legislative bills to implement the commission's recommendations. In fact, Brooks and McIntosh wrote the county government bills that McLean submitted to the General Assembly on February 15, 1927, accompanied by a special message.[24] Shortly after the legislature had convened, D. W. Newsom of Durham, a member of the County Government Commission, wrote Brooks:

You have done a single piece of statesmanlike work. You had a big job, and you have taken to it your usual vision, patience and unflagging zeal. I know of no field of labor and thought that needed the heart and mind of an unselfish champion more than the reorganization of county administrative affairs. You saw the need and you have brought to it a high order of leadership. No man can see how far reaching will be your faithful and painstaking endeavors. The state and the individual counties owe you a debt of everlasting gratitude.[25]

Brooks himself believed that "the idea" of local government reform had achieved wide popular support through the work of the commission. Nevertheless, the legislators opposed several important sections of the bills, especially those transferring the collection of taxes from the sheriff to a new officer called the collector of revenue. Another point of disagreement was whether counties already operating under a budget system would be affected by the budget provisions of the county government bills. The opposition collapsed when a clause exempting such counties from the budget provisions was inserted in the bills. The five county government bills, enacted by an overwhelming majority, largely embodied the basic reforms suggested by the commission.[26]

23. E. C. Brooks to A. W. McLean, Sept. 20, 1926, E. C. Brooks, "County Government Reform," E. C. Brooks to E. C. Bridges, Aug. 16, 1926, Frank Spruill to E. C. Brooks, Aug. 18, 1926, E. C. Brooks to Leonard Tufts, Aug. 16, 1926, E. C. Brooks to E. C. Branson, Oct. 23, 1926, Brooks Papers (DAH).

24. Edwin Bridges to E. C. Brooks, Jan. 11, 1927, E. C. Brooks to E. M. Lyda, Feb. 14, 1927, E. C. Brooks to Sam White, Feb. 23, 1927, Brooks Papers (DUL); *News and Observer*, Feb. 16, 1927.

25. D. W. Newsom to E. C. Brooks, Jan. 9, 1927, Brooks Papers (DUL).

26. E. C. Brooks to Edwin Lyda, Feb. 14, 1927, E. C. Brooks to Sam T. White, Feb. 23, 1927, Brooks Papers (DUL); *News and Observer*, Feb. 26, 1927; *House Journal, 1927*, pp. 686, 753; *Senate Journal, 1927*, pp. 431, 640.

The County Fiscal Control Act directed county commissioners to appoint a qualified person as county accountant; established a budget system for counties; concentrated fiscal administration in the hands of the commissioners; and provided for a strict separation of the various funds. The budget had to be filed for public inspection at least twenty days before the passage of the appropriation resolution by the commissioners. The purpose of this measure was to create "a uniform system for all counties . . . by which the fiscal affairs . . . may be regulated to the end that accumulated deficits may be made up and future deficits prevented . . . and to the end that every county . . . may balance its budget and carry out its functions without incurring deficits."

A second major enactment of 1927, the County Finance Act, concerned the issuance of bonds and notes and the property taxation necessary for their payment. It described specifically the purposes for which bonds could be issued and taxes levied, and fixed rigid limitations on debts incurred by counties. Generally, loans contracted to fulfil appropriations for the current year in anticipation of the collection of taxes could not exceed 80 per cent of the uncollected revenue. The commissioners were required to allow a certain period of time to elapse between the introduction of a motion to issue bonds and the actual order for their issuance. After publication of the bond order, a referendum could be called upon the petition of 15 per cent of the voters in the preceding gubernatorial election. This procedure applied to the issuance of all bonds, even those for "necessary expenses." The County Finance Act prescribed in detail the election regulations on bond issues in order to eliminate the prevalent practices that resulted in minority action and extravagance. It also required that bond funds "be used only for the purpose" for which the bond was issued, and provided severe penalties for county officials violating this regulation. Those commissioners who failed to levy the necessary taxes for the prompt payment of interest and principal of bonds were subject to stiff fines and possible imprisonment.

A third major act in 1927 authorized two plans of county government, the commissioner and the manager plan. The provisions for a county manager, however, did not invest that official with the broad powers usually associated with city managers. This act described the structural organization, the powers and duties of county officials, and the relationships of officials to one another under both plans of county government.[27]

The General Assembly of 1927 rewrote the existing law on tax collection, which had been largely ignored by county officials. The new act specified time limitations for these officials to collect, deposit, and settle for all county taxes. Their failure to comply was punishable by fines and imprisonment. The legislature also amended certain statutes dealing with tax deeds and foreclosure of certificates of sale, which "had fallen into disuse." The amendments provided for the sale of the personal property of the taxpayer for payment of his taxes before resorting to his real estate. They also sought to enforce foreclosure proceedings for delinquent taxes within a specified period of time.

Finally, the legislature created the County Government Advisory Commission "to advise and assist county officials in the proper administration of the county government." The commission was composed of five members appointed by the governor for a maximum period of four years. Three members had to be selected from county commissioners then in office. Among its chief duties the commission was to recommend changes in county government laws to the next legislature. The executive secretary of the body and his assistants were to visit counties to advise local officials on various phases of fiscal management. The secretary was to receive a fixed salary, whereas the members were to serve without compensation "except their actual expenses." An appropriation of $15,000 was provided to cover all expenses of the commission.[28]

[3]

On March 12, 1927, Governor McLean appointed Brooks chairman of the County Government Advisory Commission for a term

27. *County Government Law Applicable to North Carolina Counties,* issued by the Secretary of State (Raleigh, 1927), pp. 3-29. See also Brooks, "County Government Reform in North Carolina," *The Bond Buyer,* LXXV (Nov. 12, 1927), 2-4; Paul Wager, "North Carolina to Have Better Government," *National Municipal Review,* XVI (Aug., 1927), 519-525; Wager, *County Government in North Carolina,* pp. 161-176; *News and Observer,* Feb. 16, 17, 20, 1927; E. C. Brooks to A. W. McLean, March 11, 1927, Governors' Papers (McLean).

28. *County Government Law Applicable to North Carolina Counties,* pp. 30-38.

of four years. The other members were A. C. McIntosh of Chapel
Hill, J. E. Woodland of Morehead City, D. W. Newsom of Durham,
and E. M. Lyda of Asheville, all of whom had served on the County
Government Commission. Professor Branson "declined" membership and was "abundantly satisfied to have Brooks as chairman . . .
because he is better fitted for the diplomacies of practical politics."
Although Branson was "willing for Brooks to receive the popular
acclaim and credit," he was not reticent to point out his own efforts
for county government reform "for twelve years." Brooks cared little
for the "popular acclaim and credit," and certainly never used his
position to build up a political following among county officials
that would have been useful in a future contest for public office. To
be sure, his work in county government did keep his name in the
limelight, and occasionally he was mentioned as a candidate for
governor; but there is no evidence that he seriously considered this
possibility. His energetic efforts to improve county fiscal administration apparently sprang from a genuine desire to see the people reap
the greatest possible benefit from their taxes and avoid the conse-
quences of costly blunders committed by inept officials.[29]

At Brooks's request an organizational meeting of the County
Government Advisory Commission was held in the Governor's office
on March 14, 1927. The task of making the commission an effective
instrument for reforming county fiscal affairs under the new laws
actually fell to Brooks, who employed accountants and stenographers
to aid in the preparation of county budgets. He appointed A. S.
Brower as temporary secretary of the commission. In April, 1927,
Charles M. Johnson, deputy State Auditor, became the permanent
executive secretary. From his office in the Revenue Building as well
as through visits to various counties, he executed the policies of the
commission and directly assisted the county officials.[30]

The first job of the commission was to prepare budgets required
by the new laws. Brooks enlisted the aid of the Budget Bureau officers, several county auditors, and Herbert Wilson of the Brookings

29. A. W. McLean to E. C. Brooks, March 12, 1927, E. C. Branson to Archibald
Henderson, June 1, 1927, Brooks Papers (DUL); *Papers and Letters of Governor Mc-
Lean*, p. 863; interviews with Mr. A. S. Brower, Oct. 2, 1956, Mr. Jones Fuller, Dec. 2,
1956, Mr. E. C. Brooks, Jr., July 12, 1956.
30. Minutes of the County Government Advisory Commission, March 14, April 20,
1927, Brooks Papers (DUL); *News and Observer*, April 19, 1927.

Institution in drawing up uniform budget blanks for all counties. At the same time the Commission inaugurated its chief function of advising county officials by issuing letters and bulletins explaining the establishment of budget systems. On April 20, 1927, the Association of County Commissioners convened in special session to hear Brooks and several other members of the County Government Commission explain "a simple plan for preparing budgets." One of the main points in this "question and answer fest" concerned the relationship of the county accountant to the public school fund. Brooks insisted that the accountant had "no authority to disapprove any claim submitted by the county board of education" that was "within the law." According to him, the accountant was "merely a ministerial officer," who must endorse all public funds required by law. Brooks discussed at length the purpose of the county government acts and attempted to answer all questions raised by the county commissioners. "It is the sole purpose of these acts," he concluded, "that accumulated deficits be made up and that every county in North Carolina balance its budget."[31]

From March through May, 1927, Brooks personally attended to many inquiries from county officials seeking to adjust their fiscal affairs to the new legal requirements. In some counties the officers had no clear conception of a budget and its operation. The County Government Advisory Commission sought to enlighten them by sending the executive secretary and his assistants into their counties and by issuing explanatory pamphlets. When the permanent secretary assumed office, Brooks turned over to him the work of dealing directly with specific counties. Recognizing the need for additional publicity of the Commission's work, Brooks outlined three "practical" types of publicity, namely, weekly letters to county newspapers for keeping "the people informed as to the operation and success of the County Government Acts"; special articles to Sunday papers; and published estimates of the value of the new legislation. This publicity program was inaugurated with the aid of Professor Stewart

31. Minutes of the County Government Advisory Commission, March 23, April 6, 1927, E. C. Brooks to Sam T. White, March 17, 1927, "To the Board of County Commissioners, March 18, 1927," E. C. Brooks to County Commissioners and County Accountants, April 13, 1927, E. C. Brooks to F. A. Edmundson, April 21, 1927, Brooks Papers (DUL); *News and Observer*, March 24, April 21, 1927.

Robertson of State College, with the first "exclusive to weeklies" issued on May 28, 1927.[32]

As president of State College, Brooks desired that the institution "become definitely identified with the reorganization of county government." With the approval of the Commission, he organized a County Government Institute at the college. This was a short course designed to aid county officials in questions of public finance. The Institute opened on July 19, 1927, with instruction provided by members of the commission, the executive secretary, and professors at State College. The instructors set up a miniature county in order to provide "a clearer working knowledge of the administration of county fiscal affairs and a better understanding of relationships between officials operating under the new requirements." According to Secretary Johnson, the Institute was "highly successful" and the attendance "quite large." Brooks, too, considered it valuable and immediately began preparations for a similar course during the following summer.[33]

Amid his executive duties at the college, Brooks always found time for his numerous activities as chairman of the County Government Advisory Commission. He rarely failed to note in his many public addresses the progress and continuing defects in county fiscal administration under the laws of 1927. Although the legislation was "being well received," county officials were slow to introduce innovations in their conduct of financial affairs because of their own ignorance of accounting procedures and the disorder of previous records. Brooks also maintained close contact with Governor McLean and the officers of the Association of County Commissioners, and apparently impressed upon them the dangerous financial policies of most counties, especially their proclivity to incur extraordinary debts. At any rate, on October 31, 1927, the Governor permitted him to employ four additional accountants "to aid counties fulfill their obligations under the county government acts." Two days later, the

32. E. C. Brooks to J. E. Woodland, May 6, 1927, E. C. Brooks to Stewart Robertson, May 26, 1927, "County Government Information," May 28, 1927, Brooks Papers (DUL).
33. Minutes of the Faculty Council of North Carolina State College of Agriculture and Engineering, March 26, April 12, 1927, Archives of the North Carolina State College of Agriculture and Engineering, Raleigh; "County Government Information," June, 1927, "County Government Institute," E. C. Brooks to J. E. Woodland, Aug. 17, 1927, Brooks Papers (DUL); Johnson, "County Government Reform in North Carolina," Governors' Papers (McLean); News and Observer, July 17, 1927.

reform movement in county fiscal administration was bolstered by a State Supreme Court decision upholding the County Finance Act.[34]

During 1928 the County Government Advisory Commission intensified its efforts to reorganize county fiscal affairs. The executive secretary, his assistants, and the four additional accountants visited counties to assist officials in the installation of new bookkeeping and budget systems. The commission, of course, continued its information service and publicity program. Brooks and Secretary Johnson drew up a code of business ethics for county officials designed "to raise the standard of government and place it in harmony with the spirit of the age." But Brooks's participation in the commission activities was very limited until the fall of 1928. During an illness in the winter, he was hospitalized in the Battle Creek Sanitarium for several weeks. After his recovery he made a six-week tour of Europe in the summer of 1928. Throughout this period, however, he remained in close touch with the activities of the County Government Advisory Commission. On February 10, 1928, Secretary Johnson wrote him: "We are getting along fine and I think the people and the county officials are showing more interest than ever before."[35]

Early in June, 1928, the revised law concerning the sale of property for delinquent taxes created quite a commotion in certain sections of the state. Under the act the property for which taxes were due in October, 1927, and remained unpaid in the following May, was to be sold on the first Monday in June, 1928. Superior Court Judge Henry A. Grady described the act as an "outrage to the people of eastern North Carolina" and enjoined the sale of property for delinquent taxes in four eastern counties. He urged the Governor to support the "repeal of this iniquitous law." Referring to Brooks, he declared: "I understand that this law was carefully prepared and engineered through the General Assembly by a certain well-known educator who pays practically no taxes at all and who evidently has little regard for the welfare of the great masses of people." Brooks

34. *News and Observer*, May 18, Aug. 12, 1927; "County Government Information," June, 1927, E. C. Brooks to J. E. Woodland, May 6, 1927, E. C. Brooks to J. E. Woodland, Aug. 17, 1927, E. C. Brooks to Charles Johnson, Oct. 31, 1927, "Recommendations to the Governor," Oct. 24, 1927, Brooks Papers (DUL); *North Carolina Supreme Court Reports, Fall Term, 1927*, pp. 358-363.

35. "Business Code for County Officials, 1928," Charles M. Johnson to E. C. Brooks, Feb. 10, 1928, Brooks Papers (DUL); *News and Observer*, Aug. 27, 1928; Minutes of the Faculty Council of State College, March 6, 1928.

simply did not consider Grady's diatribe worthy of a reply. The
News and Observer lavishly praised Brooks's work in county government reform, but added that "the workings of the law show that
amendments are needed."[36]

Governor McLean informed Judge Grady that his injunctions
were legally untenable and grossly unfair to the majority of taxpayers in the four counties. Frank P. Spruill, a prominent figure in
the Association of County Commissioners, heartily endorsed the
Governor's position and insisted that the terms of the foreclosure
process in the new law were "by far an advantage over the old law
to the taxpayer." On June 20, 1928, Governor McLean called a joint
meeting of the Tax Commission and the County Government Advisory Commission to discuss the validity of Judge Grady's charges.
All those attending the meeting apparently supported the full enforcement of the county government laws. This show of determination by state officials coupled with the favorable decision of the State
Supreme Court on the County Finance Act undoubtedly dampened
the desire of any other Superior Court judge to follow the example
of Judge Grady, who came to realize that his action had no sound
legal basis.[37]

Late in December, 1928, the County Government Advisory Commission reported to the Governor on the condition of county fiscal
administration after one year under the laws of 1927. The report,
highly critical of "the lax methods in collecting taxes," declared that
the provision for the daily deposit of taxes was largely ignored. Of
the one hundred counties, only forty-nine operated within their
budgets, while only thirty-three complied with the legal provisions
for safeguarding expenditures. The evidence collected by the commission showed that the county government laws of 1927 had "not
effected a remedy" in fiscal administration, mainly because only
twenty counties "substantially" complied with these laws. Therefore,
the commission recommended an increase in its power sufficient to
force counties in line. Brooks added that the "mass of local legislation" in every General Assembly was a "major block to better county

36. *News and Observer*, April 22, June 8, 9, 11, 1928; *County Government Laws
Applicable to North Carolina Counties*, pp. 32-34.
37. *Greensboro Daily News*, June 11, 1928; *News and Observer*, June 21, 1928;
A. W. McLean to J. A. Taylor, June 23, 1928, Frank P. Spruill to A. W. McLean, June
21, 1928, *Papers and Letters of Governor McLean*, pp. 716-720.

government." He was obviously referring to changes in county government and fiscal affairs that were made at the whim of legislators through local bills generally enacted by "courtesy" in the General Assembly.[38]

In his inaugural address to the legislature in 1929, Governor O. Max Gardner recommended that the "county government laws be strengthened where necessary and that they be made to apply to all alike." The long-standing friendship between the new governor and Brooks presaged a bright future for county government reform. However, there were rumblings of discontent about the County Government Advisory Commission among certain legislators, who were jealous of any state interference whatsoever in local affairs. A bill to abolish the commission was sponsored by Representative D. S. Poole of Hyde County and undoubtedly had considerable backing among his colleagues. Poole defended his measure on the grounds of "economy," a convenient disguise, and insisted furthermore that the commission had "completed its work." The officials of the Association of County Commissioners immediately descended upon the legislature to oppose the Poole Bill and to urge Governor Gardner to support an annual appropriation of $31,000 for the commission. The Poole measure met its death at the hands of a House committee.[39]

At the same time, Gardner was seriously considering a proposal to consolidate the State Board of Assessment, the County Government Advisory Commission, and the State Board of Equalization into one body. Brooks vigorously opposed this plan and pointed out that the "County Government Advisory Commission has functions that in no sense duplicate the functions of the others." He suggested the establishment of a permanent Tax Commission to absorb all duties of the Board of Assessment and the Board of Equalization concerned directly with taxation. The remaining functions of the latter body would be transferred to the State Board of Education. This plan fulfilled Gardner's desire to eliminate duplications and introduce economy in the state administrative organization. In the

38. *News and Observer,* Dec. 22, 1928, Jan. 8, 1929; Betters, *State Centralization in North Carolina,* pp. 90-93.

39. *Public Papers and Letters of Oliver Max Gardner, Governor of North Carolina, 1929-1933,* ed. D. L. Corbitt (Raleigh, 1937), p. 13; *News and Observer,* Jan. 16, 18, 1929; *House Journal, 1929,* p. 122.

final analysis, Gardner acquiesced in that portion of Brooks's proposal to retain the County Government Advisory Commission as a separate entity.[40]

The General Assembly of 1929 enacted amendments to the county government laws that only slightly increased the commission's power over county fiscal administration. The commission, with an annual appropriation of $21,500, was empowered to approve auditing firms that were soliciting county business and to determine the scope of the audits. In an attempt to standardize accounting practices in all counties, the amendments provided that no system of bookkeeping could be installed in any county without the approval of the County Government Advisory Commission. The General Assembly sought to prevent the reckless issuance of bonds by counties through an act requiring the State Sinking Fund Commission to approve all bond issues by local government units before they could be sold, unless the proposed indebtedness had received popular approval. A third act of 1929 provided that any county commissioner who failed to vote for raising sufficient revenue for operating expenses of the county as required by the County Fiscal Control Act was to be guilty of a misdemeanor punishable by fine or imprisonment. A similar provision applied to any county accountant who certified an expenditure without "a sufficient unencumbered balance." Probably as a result of the agitation climaxed by Judge Grady's injunctions, the legislature reduced the penalty on delinquent taxes from 20 per cent for the first year to 12 per cent for the first year and 8 per cent thereafter. According to Secretary Johnson, Brooks and the County Government Advisory Commission were responsible for most of the legislation on county government in 1929.[41]

During the two years following the passage of this legislation, the Great Depression hit North Carolina with full force. Only then did the counties with their accumulated debts of $157,244,247 realize the error of their ways. For more than a decade Brooks had warned county officials of the inherent dangers of their fiscal poli-

40. E. C. Brooks to O. Max Gardner, Jan. 24, 1929, Brooks Papers (DUL); *News and Observer*, Jan. 18, 1929.
41. *Public Laws and Resolutions, 1929*, pp. 164, 241-242, 376-377, 257-258; Betters, *State Centralization in North Carolina*, pp. 92-94; *Report of the County Government Advisory Commission, 1930*, p. 7.

cies. As the economic depression settled upon the state, he and the County Government Advisory Commission not only exerted their full authority under the acts of 1927 and 1929 to curtail excessive use of credit by counties, but they also attempted to hold them within their budgets. However, the commission still remained advisory in character and actually was powerless to enforce "sound" financial policies. But the increased appropriations and "inspectional powers" granted by the Legislature of 1929 enabled the body to expand its advisory services. Through its supervision the counties reduced their auditing expenses by $89,897 in 1929-1930. Oddly enough, the activities of the commission, all of which were designed to improve county fiscal administration, came in for severe criticisms from certain individuals suffering acute attacks of economy as the state plunged deeper into the depression. For example, Senator J. T. Alderman of Vance County described the commission as "a bunch of men drawing big salaries in Raleigh calling themselves a 'county government bureau' who assume to be greater than the legislature. It seems that all they are there for is to draw big salaries and tell county commissioners how to run their counties."[42]

Brooks, already accustomed to similar attacks, refused to permit such statements to interfere with his efforts to aid counties weather the economic storm. He publicly deplored the prevalent idea that an "office is for the man who holds it"—an idea held by many county officials. In August, 1930, he was again the principal speaker at the annual meeting of the Association of County Commissioners, and his address emphasized the need for counties to balance their budgets, publish their expenditures, and raise the ethical standards of their officials. Through his influence the association adopted resolutions requesting the legislature to increase the appropriations and enlarge the duties of the County Government Advisory Commission. Brooks recognized the drastic need for direct state supervision of local finances in order for the heavily indebted counties to withstand the impact of the depression.[43]

The report of the County Government Advisory Commission in November, 1930, vividly pointed up this need. It first outlined the

42. *Report of the Tax Commission, 1930*, p. 237; *Report of the County Government Advisory Commission, 1930*, pp. 5-7; *News and Observer*, July 26, 1929.
43. *News and Observer*, Feb. 11, Aug. 14, 1930; "Resolutions Adopted by the State Association of County Commissioners, August 14, 1930," Brooks Papers (DAH).

work of the commission in establishing bookkeeping systems in counties and in advising officials "in the performance and exercise" of their duties. There was, of course, no way to evaluate their work in terms of dollars and cents, although such an evaluation at that particular time would have enhanced the prestige of the commission. It was all too obvious, however, that county fiscal administration retained many of those glaring defects exposed by Brooks and Branson ten years earlier. Many counties paid lip service to the legal requirements by employing county accountants who lacked even "the rudiments of bookkeeping" and by establishing budgets which were later disregarded. In some cases expenditures not only exceeded budget appropriations, but even revenues. Accumulated deficits were temporarily covered up and tax rates kept low by issuing funding bonds. The indiscriminate selection of depositories resulted in "tremendous losses," with the failure of numerous banks after the Crash of 1929. The report stated that members of the commission had noted mistakes and irregularities which later proved costly to the taxpayer, "but they were compelled to stand by helplessly and watch the results." The most serious defects were in the methods of tax-collecting officials, especially by the sheriffs, whose practices frequently produced "gross irregularities." The commission frankly reported that "defalcations in public office are occurring with consistent regularity . . . with the resultant loss of thousands of dollars to the taxpayers and to surety companies." Among the recommendations of the commission was a plea for an increase in its own powers of "inspection and supervision" and a request for stronger state supervision of local finances with the commission as the agency of state control. Both the Tax Commission and the Association of County Commissioners strongly endorsed these proposals.[44]

By the time the General Assembly convened in January, 1931, the depression had thrown the indebted counties into acute distress. They could "no longer pay their own way." To meet the emergency, Governor Gardner undertook a broad program of reform embracing schools, roads, and local government finance, which involved a centralization of power in the state government. The Legislature of 1931 enacted sweeping changes in state governmental operations

44. *Report of the County Government Advisory Commission, 1930,* pp. 7-18; *Report of the Tax Commission, 1930,* pp. 12, 60-61.

in its turbulent session of 141 days. The Local Government Act, designed largely to apply brakes to the uncontrolled issuance of bonds by county commissioners, has been described as "the most far-reaching legislation enacted by any state to that date." This law was based upon the recommendations of a Brookings Institution survey team and the report of the County Government Advisory Commission. Both emphasized the need for state supervision of local finances. The Local Government Act created a Local Government Commission of nine members to assume all the powers and duties of the County Government Advisory Commission and those functions of the State Sinking Fund Commission related to local financial affairs. This new body was invested with broad powers of control and supervision necessary to curb the reckless fiscal practices of local government units, including both counties and municipalities.[45]

With the abolition of the County Government Advisory Commission in 1931, Brooks terminated his official relations with the movement for county government reform. For more than a decade he had waged a relentless campaign in behalf of the cause. If Branson initiated the movement, Brooks was largely responsible for bringing about actual reforms. He gave unstintedly of his time and energy, oratorical abilities, and skill in practical politics. The two county government commissions of which he was the most prominent and active member rendered invaluable services to the cause of county government reform that could not be calculated in monetary terms. A major hindrance to the successful reorganization of county finances between 1925 and 1931 lay in the inadequate authority invested in these commissions. Throughout this period Brooks reiterated time and again his Cassandra-like warnings to counties that issued one bond after another, while tax rates were kept low, budgets disregarded, and legitimate taxes uncollected. His experience as State Superintendent of Public Instruction had impressed upon him the necessity for a certain amount of state supervision of county financial affairs. Only through a calamitous economic depression did the state

45. *Papers and Letters of Governor Gardner,* pp. xxviii, 55-56; *Report on a Survey of the Organization and Administration of County Government in North Carolina* (Washington, 1930); Betters, *State Centralization in North Carolina,* pp. 106-115; Robert Rankin, *Government and Administration in North Carolina* (New York, 1955), pp. 383-389.

undertake that direct supervision of local government finances which Brooks had persistently advocated since 1921. Probably at his own request, he was not appointed to the Local Government Commission in 1931. By that date he was burdened with the formidable task of guiding State College safely through the economic crisis and the impending consolidation of the University of North Carolina.

Eight: A SPONSOR OF THE GREAT SMOKY MOUNTAINS NATIONAL PARK, *1924-1933*

[1]

Throughout his public career Brooks was closely identified with movements for economic and social improvements in North Carolina. Such activities were essential parts of his educational work, since for him education encompassed "all forces" influencing man's development and progress. Among these forces were the conservation of natural resources and adequate recreational facilities, which he considered necessary for the "general welfare." The idea of a national park in the Great Smoky Mountains, a lofty ridge in the Appalachians along the North Carolina-Tennessee border, fired his imagination for reasons other than his own fondness for the scenic beauty of these peaks. In his opinion a park in this area would protect forests and headwaters of streams, attract a profitable tourist trade, and preserve botanical specimens unexcelled in North America. The establishment of a national park, as Brooks clearly recognized, would involve considerable time, large financial resources, and delicate negotiations. Nevertheless, he threw himself into a campaign for such a venture in the midst of his activities as president of State College and as leader of the crusade for county government reform.[1]

The movement for a national park in the Appalachian Mountains of North Carolina actually began late in the nineteenth century. The first organized effort to procure such a park was initiated by citizens of Asheville, a town already enjoying the status of a mountain resort. Under the leadership of Dr. C. P. Ambler, in

1. Brooks, "The Education of A North Carolinian," p. 1; Brooks, "Our Educational Institutions," Brooks, "Five Great Enterprises That the State Should Support with Emphasis," Brooks, "How To Preserve Our Prosperity," Brooks Papers (BLS).

November, 1899, the Asheville Board of Trade organized the Appalachian National Park Association, which included prominent public figures from nearly all Southern states. For six years the association waged a vigorous publicity campaign and won the support of many notable political figures, including President Theodore Roosevelt, who at the time was dramatizing the conservation issue.

The association, however, soon realized the futility of seeking federal funds for a national park; thus it concentrated upon securing a forest reserve and changed its name to the Appalachian National Forest Reserve Association. Despite the widespread support of the movement, the opposition was strong enough to prevent the establishment of forest reserves in the southern Appalachians for twelve years. Among the major obstacles were the lumber interests, the sectional stigma of the movement, and the hostility of David Henderson and Joseph Cannon, successive speakers of the House of Representatives. Finally, after Speaker Cannon's power had been curbed and the association had transferred its functions to the American Forestry Association to avoid the sectional stigma, the national forest reserves were established in the Carolina mountains by the Weeks Law of 1911.[2]

The idea of a national park in this area had by no means been forsaken. Interest in the project was kept alive by the publication in 1913 of Horace Kephart's *Our Southern Highlanders* and Margaret Morley's *The Carolina Mountains*, two first-hand accounts of the southern Appalachians. Both authors enthusiastically described the natural beauty of the Great Smoky Mountains, "the greatest mass of highland east of the Rockies." They emphasized the need for the protection of wildlife and forests in the Great Smokies and suggested that the area would provide "a glorious pleasure ground in the eastern part of our continent."[3]

The "mysterious realm" of the Great Smoky Mountains de-

2. Minutes of the Appalachian National Park Association, 1899-1905, C. P. Ambler, "The Activities of the Appalachian National Park Association and the Appalachian National Forest Reserve Association," Appalachian National Park Association Papers, State Department of Archives and History, Raleigh, North Carolina; Charles Washburn, *The Life of John W. Weeks* (New York, 1928), pp. 74-81.

3. Horace Kephart, *Our Southern Highlanders* (New York, 1913), pp. 15-16, 57, 69; Margaret Morley, *The Carolina Mountains* (Boston, 1913), pp. 24-35, 239-247. See also *The Wachovia*, XXIV (Oct., 1931), 4; Laura Thornborough, *The Great Smoky Mountains* (New York, 1937), p. 10; Elizabeth S. Bowman, *Land of High Horizons* (Kingsport, 1938), pp. 124-125.

scribed by these writers was penetrated by a considerable number of logging railroads during and after World War I. This era also witnessed an increasing number of automobiles and highways in North Carolina, and motorists began skirting the Great Smokies, viewing from afar the majestic peaks covered with forests, laurel, and rhododendron. Realtors attempted to capitalize on the future growth of tourist travel and in 1925 initiated a land boom in the area that might have resulted in disaster had it not been short-circuited by the timely collapse of the Florida real-estate fiasco. This revived interest in the Great Smokies as "a glorious pleasure ground" coincided with the emergence of a nation-wide interest in national parks. In April, 1917, the National Park Service was established in the Department of the Interior. The organization of the National Parks Association two years later provided an added impetus to the park movement. Amid this atmosphere state officials and congressmen from North Carolina and Tennessee renewed the fight for a national park in the Great Smoky Mountains.[4]

[2]

In 1923 several bills were introduced in Congress to provide for the creation of national parks in various sections of the southern Appalachians. Congress, however, adjourned without enacting them. In February, 1924, Secretary of the Interior Hubert Work, cognizant of the existing agitation, appointed a committee of five prominent proponents of conservation to study lands east of the Mississippi River with a view toward determining areas that could meet the requirements for a national park. He also informed the several states of his "desire to establish a great National Park east of the Mississippi River." The report of his committee, which was presented to Congress on December 13, 1924, mentioned the Great Smokies as a possible site for such a park.[5]

4. *Great Smoky Mountains National Park,* issued by the National Park Service, 1956; W. C. Allen, *Annals of Haywood County, North Carolina* (n.p., 1935), pp. 203-205; Brown, *State Highway System of North Carolina,* pp. 249-250; *Our National Resources and Their Conservation,* ed. A. E. Parkins and J. R. Whitaker (New York, 1936), pp. 8-9; Harlean James, *Romance of the National Parks* (New York, 1941), pp. 65-91.

5. *Report of the North Carolina Park Commission, 1931,* p. 3; *Congressional Record,* 66th Congress, 1st session, LXV, 270; 67th Congress, 1st session, LXVI, 601-602.

In the meantime, the North Carolina legislature had convened in special session in the summer of 1924 to consider Governor Morrison's program for harbor and port facilities. Brooks, Speaker John G. Dawson, and three legislators from the mountain counties, Mark Squires, Plato Ebbs, and Harry Nettles, were eager to follow up Secretary Work's interest in establishing a national park in the east. Through their influence the legislature created a "special commission for the purpose of presenting the claims of North Carolina for a national park" and appropriated $2,500 for expenses in addition to travel allowances. The commission was composed of eleven members, five of them chosen by the Speaker of the House and three by the President of the Senate. In a separate resolution the presidents of State College and the University and the Speaker of the House were appointed to the commission.[6]

The real reason for this resolution was to insure the selection of Brooks and Dawson, who had manifested special interest in the park project. Dawson was not only largely responsible for creating the commission; he was also an influential figure in state politics and a resident of the eastern section of the state. The "proper" geographical distribution of the commission's membership was considered an important factor in winning statewide support for the park, which was generally looked upon as of potential value only to the western area. Several legislators, including Dawson, felt that Brooks ought to be placed on the commission for two main reasons: he was keenly interested in the park, and he possessed the *savoir-faire* necessary for the successful conduct of complex and tedious negotiations. Moreover, the park advocates in the legislature realized that the purchase of park lands would necessitate financial assistance from private sources, such as the Rockefellers. They believed that Brooks would be a valuable asset in securing a donation from the Rockefellers because of his reputation with the directors of the General Education Board. But the appointment of the president of State College (Brooks) raised the possibility of criticism by the more rabid friends

6. John G. Dawson to J. C. B. Ehringhaus, July 19, 1933, Governors' Papers (Ehringhaus); interview with Mr. John G. Dawson, Sept. 7, 1956; memorandum by Mr. Harry Nettles, Sept. 17, 1956; Minutes of the Special Commission for the Purpose of Presenting the Claims of North Carolina for a National Park, Oct. 8, 1924, John G. Dawson to E. C. Brooks, Aug. 23, 1924, Brooks Papers (DUL); *House Journal, Extra Session, 1924*, pp. 192, 219, 224; *Senate Journal, Extra Session, 1924*, p. 211; *Report of the North Carolina Park Commission, 1931*, p. 3.

of the University; so President Harry Chase was also appointed to the park commission, though he resigned within two years.[7]

The organizational meeting of the park commission was held in Raleigh on October 8, 1924. State Senator Mark Squires of Lenoir was elected chairman and Brooks secretary. Obviously, the most pressing task of the group was to persuade the federal officials of the desirability of a national park in the Great Smoky Mountains. A committee of five, including Brooks, Squires, and Dawson, was selected to plead the cause of the park in Washington, employ "publicity agents," and prepare reports for the Department of the Interior. Brooks was convinced that "all North Carolina" should agree on one park site and "press it to the utmost" rather than risk everything by seeking "too much."[8]

In January, 1925, the matter of a national park in the southern Appalachians was championed in Congress by several Southern delegations and by Representative H. W. Temple of Pennsylvania, chairman of the survey committee set up by Secretary Work in 1924. The proponents of a national park in the Shenandoah region in Virginia seemed determined to achieve their aim regardless of claims presented by neighboring states. A permanent lobby in Washington was assisting Virginia congressmen push the Shenandoah project.[9]

The North Carolina Park Commission immediately sensed the danger of Virginia's activities to its own cause. On January 19, 1925, Brooks and other members of the commission met in Senator F. M. Simmons' office along with several North Carolina congressmen to plan their strategy. They agreed that Congress should be requested to authorize an official investigation of the proposed park sites in the southern Appalachians to determine those that would meet federal requirements. On the next day, Brooks and Representative Charles Abernethy of North Carolina, a member of the House Committee on Public Lands, conferred with Secretary Work, who agreed to co-operate and consider park areas in the North Carolina mountains other than the Great Smokies. Various conferences between representatives of North Carolina, Tennessee, and Virginia resulted in an

---

7. Interview with Mr. John G. Dawson, Sept. 7, 1956.
8. Minutes of the Special Commission, Oct. 8, Nov. 19, 1924, Mark Squires to E. C. Brooks, Nov. 13, 1924, John G. Dawson to E. C. Brooks, Dec. 20, 1924, Brooks Papers (DUL).
9. *News and Observer*, Jan. 20, 21, 1925.

agreement to place the Shenandoah and Great Smoky sites on "equal footing" in their campaigns for national parks. Congressman Temple revised his bill in accordance with this agreement. The Temple Bill, enacted on February 16, 1925, provided that the Secretary of the Interior should determine the boundaries and areas of the proposed national parks of the Shenandoah and Great Smoky regions; receive offers of land and money donations for these projects; and report his findings to Congress. The secretary was authorized to appoint a commission of five members to undertake the investigation. Brooks and Dawson were convinced that "prospects for acquiring the park are brighter than they have ever been."[10]

While the Secretary investigated the park sites, the North Carolina Park Commission intensified its campaign to win public support for the project within the state. However, one member, A. M. Kistler of Morganton, informed Brooks that "the people of the western part of the state, as a general rule, do not want the park in the Great Smokies." At the same time Mark Squires, a very energetic but emotional man, reported that the commission was "being played for a bunch of suckers" by the federal survey group. Brooks sought to temper Squire's outbursts and to maintain harmony within the commission. In fact, he assumed the role of peacemaker more than once in his efforts to secure a national park. In August, 1925, he conferred again with Secretary Work about the "independent course" being pursued by Virginia despite the previous agreement to co-operate in the establishment of two parks. Brooks plainly told the Virginia delegation that its activities threatened to defeat the whole park program for the southern Appalachians and suggested that representatives from the three interested states hold a meeting in order to iron out difficulties and renew their agreement. At such a meeting held in Richmond on September 9, 1925, he made an eloquent plea for co-operation among the proponents of the two parks. After a full discussion, the delegates agreed to "pool their interests and work for

10. Mark Squires to F. M. Simmons, Jan. 8, 1925, Joseph H. Pratt to F. M. Simmons, Jan. 20, 1925, Furnifold M. Simmons Papers, Duke University Library, Durham, North Carolina; *News and Observer,* Jan. 20, 21, 29, 30, 1925; Press Memorandum by Senator Simmons, Jan. 28, 1925, E. C. Brooks to A. M. Kistler, Jan. 12, 1925, Charles L. Abernethy to E. C. Brooks, Jan. 30, 1925, E. C. Brooks to Charles L. Abernethy, March 3, 1925, Wingrove Bathon to Mark Squires, Jan. 28, 1925, John G. Dawson to E. C. Brooks, Jan. 27, 1925, Brooks Papers (DUL); *House Reports,* 68th Congress, 2nd session, I, No. 1320, 1-6.

two national parks." To promote co-operation they organized the Appalachian National Parks Association, composed of representatives from North Carolina, Tennessee, and Virginia.[11]

In the meantime the North Carolina Park Commission was planning its campaign to collect private subscriptions and donations to purchase lands in the Great Smoky Mountains. In 1925 the understanding was that the park site would be purchased without financial assistance from the federal and state governments. On September 2, 1925, the North Carolina park commission created a "holding committee," called Great Smoky Mountains, Incorporated, for the purpose of raising money. The publicity work was reorganized under F. Roger Miller of the Asheville Chamber of Commerce and Horace Kephart, author of *Our Southern Highlanders*. Later the park commissions of North Carolina and Tennessee employed a New York firm to conduct a fund-raising campaign with a goal of $1,000,000 by March, 1926. Brooks suggested that for campaign purposes the state be divided into districts with a prominent man from each district as manager. This plan was endorsed and apparently used with considerable success. The publicity bureau under Roger Miller, all the while, was distributing literature on the Great Smokies and sponsoring essay contests in the public schools.[12]

By January, 1926, however, only $500,000 had actually been secured by North Carolina and Tennessee for the purchase of park lands. Squires informed Governor McLean that the opposition of the lumber and pulp interests to the movement had "seriously embarrassed the campaign in Asheville," and complained that western North Carolina was bearing the financial burden with almost no assistance from the eastern counties. By April, 1926, the park commis-

11. A. M. Kistler to E. C. Brooks, July 6, 1925, Mark Squires to E. C. Brooks, July 1, 1925, E. C. Brooks to Mark Squires, Aug. 25, 1925, Joint Meeting of the N. C. Park Commission, the Great Smoky Mountains Conservation Association, and the Shenandoah Park Association, Sept. 9, 1925, E. C. Brooks to H. J. Benchoff, Sept. 29, 1925, Brooks Papers (DUL); interview with Mr. E. C. Brooks, Jr., July 12, 1956.

12. *Report of the N. C. Park Commission, 1931*, p. 4; Minutes of the North Carolina Park Commission, Sept. 2, Oct. 21, 1925, Mark Squires to E. C. Brooks, Dec. 1, 1925, Minutes of the Meeting of Great Smoky Mountains, Inc., Dec. 15, 1925, E. C. Brooks to Roger Miller, Oct. 27, 1925, E. C. Brooks to Plato Ebbs, Oct. 31, 1925, E. C. Brooks to Mark Squires, Dec. 19, 1925, Brooks Papers (DUL). See also Horace Kephart, "The Great Smoky Mountains National Park," *The High School Journal*, VIII (Oct.-Nov., 1925), 59-65; Horace Kephart, "The Last of the Eastern Wilderness," *The World's Work*, LI (April, 1926), 617-636; Horace Kephart, "The Last of the Eastern Wilderness," *Tarheel Banker*, VII (June, 1929), 43-50.

sion reported $450,000 in private subscriptions for its part of the $1,000,000 goal, "assuming that Asheville will complete the Buncombe County quota." Of the amount subscribed only $50,000 came from areas east of the mountains, an indication that the commission had not aroused the state-wide support of the park that it desired. In April, 1926, however, the State Democratic Convention included the establishment of a Great Smoky national park in its platform. At the same time, the need for state funds for the purchase of park lands was becoming increasingly apparent and was being considered by the advocates of the project.[13]

On April 14, 1926, the Secretary of the Interior designated the appropriate boundaries for national parks in the Great Smokies and the Shenandoah region on the basis of the report of the special commission created in the previous year. Representative Temple, chairman of that commission, introduced a bill in Congress for the establishment of national parks in these two areas. In describing his bill before the House Committee on Public Lands, he declared that "the parks are to be acquired without cost to the United States Government, and to be accepted by the Secretary of the Interior, when they are turned over to the United States in fee simple." The Great Smoky Mountains claims were ably presented to the committee by Mark Squires, Charles Abernethy, and Zebulon Weaver of North Carolina and by David Chapman of Tennessee, the so-called "father of the Great Smoky Mountains National Park." They emphasized that the park would not only protect the the headwaters of major rivers, but would provide recreational facilities near the eastern centers of population. At the time the only national park east of the Mississippi River was located in Maine. The delegates managed to secure important changes in the Temple Bill, which reduced the minimum area of land necessary before the federal government would assume limited administration of the park from 300,000 to 150,000 acres. However, "no general development" of the Great Smokies was to be undertaken by the National Park Service until "a major portion" of the area specified by the Secretary of the Interior had been accepted by the federal government. The Temple

13. Mark Squires to A. W. McLean, Jan. 5, 1926, Governors' Papers (McLean); Minutes of the N. C. Park Commission, Oct. 21, 1925, Brooks Papers (DUL); *News and Observer*, April 6, 30, 1926.

Bill with the committee amendments was enacted by Congress and signed by President Coolidge on May 22, 1926.[14]

Following the passage of the act, the North Carolina Park Commission was confronted with the formidable job of securing the necessary lands for the Great Smoky Mountains National Park. The efforts of Brooks and others to raise funds for the purchase of park lands through private subscriptions had produced a wealth of promises, but little actual cash. They became convinced that a state appropriation was necessary in view of the large amount of land that would have to be acquired from hostile lumber and pulp companies. Both Brooks and Squires were keenly aware of the opposition of the lumber interests to the park movement and clearly perceived the commission's need for additional powers and state financial support to overcome this obstacle. In November, 1926, Brooks, Squires, and Plato Ebbs began preparing their strategy for the forthcoming legislature. They drafted a bill increasing the powers of the park commission and providing a state appropriation of $2,000,000 for the purchase of park lands. The bill was managed in the legislature by Squires and Ebbs, while Brooks urged the commission's publicity director to initiate a campaign to arouse the interest of legislators from all sections of the state. "I believe," he wrote, "perhaps the best campaign would be through such literature as will convey to our people the advantage of the establishment of such a park. I think if we could set up some kind of financial as well as recreational advantage we would have a most convincing argument."[15]

By the opening of the legislature in January, 1927, prospects for a state appropriation for a national park appeared to be favorable. But at this juncture, Squires, who was physically ill and nervous, "conceived a bitter dislike" for Governor McLean and openly criticized him. There seemed to be some danger that Squires's behavior would endanger the passage of the park bill, but Brooks immediately

14. *Congressional Record,* 69th Congress, 1st session, LXVII, 7806, 9450-9459, 9581, 9886; *News and Observer,* April 10, 15, May 12, 1926; *Hearings Before the Public Lands Committee of the House of Representatives,* 69th Congress, 1st session, May 11, 1926, pp. 5-6.

15. Great Smoky Mountains, Inc.: Statement of Receipts and Disbursements, Oct. 22, 1925—July 31, 1926, E. C. Brooks to Mark Squires, Sept. 14, 1926, Mark Squires to E. C. Brooks, Sept. 14, 1926, E. C. Brooks to Roger Miller, Nov. 27, 1926, Brooks Papers (DUL); *Hearings Before the Committee on Public Lands,* May 11, 1926, p. 17; *The Technician* (N. C. State College newspaper), March 7, 1930.

got in touch with the Governor and "smoothed things over." Following this episode, Brooks and Squires arranged a dinner for a delegation of park advocates including Representative Temple and A. B. Cammerer, assistant director of the National Park Service, who were in Raleigh to aid in the passage of the park bill. Thirty key members of the legislature attended the dinner at which Temple and Cammerer expounded the advantages of a national park to the state. By early February, 1927, the park commission apparently had marshaled all forces necessary for the passage of the bill except the support of Governor McLean, who still remained silent. Senator Simmons had already publicly endorsed the $2,000,000 appropriation. Finally, on February 16, 1927, McLean broke his prolonged silence on the park bill with a statement strongly favoring its passage. Several days earlier, the Secretary of the Interior, having determined the approximate size of the park, notified him that North Carolina's part would consist of 225,500 acres.[16]

The park bill passed the legislature without serious opposition, although the Champion Fibre Company, a large landholder in the park area, had its spokesman on hand to fight the measure. The act provided for a "body politic and corporate under the name of 'North Carolina Park Commission' " composed of the eleven members of the existing commission. The Great Smoky Mountains, Incorporated, the holding company, was dissolved, and its powers and funds were transferred to the new park commission. The act authorized a state bond issue of $2,000,000 for the purchase of park lands and vested the commission "with the power of eminent domain to acquire . . . and to condemn for park purposes land and other property." An important amendment to the original bill stipulated three prerequisites for the expenditure of bond funds by the commission. First, the Secretary of the Interior must have specifically designated the area to be acquired in North Carolina and Tennessee. Second, Tennessee must have made adequate financial provision for the purchase of its portion of the designated area. Third, the North Carolina Park

16. J. D. Murphy to E. C. Brooks, Jan. 19, 1927, E. C. Brooks to J. D. Murphy, Jan. 24, 1927, E. C. Brooks to Charles Webb, Feb. 4, 1927, Brooks Papers (DUL); News and Observer, Jan. 27, Feb. 3, 12, 17, 1927; Hubert Work to A. W. McLean, Feb. 8, 1927, Governors' Papers (McLean). The amount of land in the North Carolina side of the park changed several times between 1927 and 1931, ranging from 214,000 acres to a high of 232,085.48 acres.

Commission must have sufficient financial resources, including the $2,000,000 appropriation to purchase that part of the park within North Carolina.[17]

At the first meeting of the North Carolina Park Commission on March 18, 1927, Squires and Brooks were re-elected to their positions as chairman and secretary, and Plato Ebbs became treasurer. The commission soon realized, however, that the purchase of all park lands in the Great Smokies would require approximately $10,000,000. According to its estimates, North Carolina would need $4,816,000 to secure its portion of the land. But the state bond issue of $2,000,000 and the private subscriptions of $463,000 provided about one-half of the amount necessary for the park commission under the law of 1927 to proceed with the purchase of lands. While the commission was devising means to raise sufficient funds, Brooks expressed his desire to resign as secretary. On August 18, 1927, he wrote Ebbs: "After the surveys are made, it will be necessary to start condemnation proceedings and your office in Asheville should not be handicapped by having to refer every bill and all its details to Raleigh." Ebbs and Squires, both of whom greatly admired Brooks and valued his judgment, persuaded him to remain as secretary, because in their opinion his "services" were essential to the realization of the park.[18]

In 1927 John D. Rockefeller, Jr., was approached with a request to include the Great Smoky Mountains National Park among his philanthropies. A. B. Cammerer of the National Park Service was apparently the first person to arouse Rockefeller's interest in the park. Later, Squires visited the Rockefeller offices in New York, and Brooks may have accompanied him. In any case, on February 28, 1928, Rockefeller appropriated $5,000,000 from the Laura Spelman Rockefeller Memorial to promote the establishment of a national park in the Great Smokies. The gift was to be available as soon as

17. Interview with Mr. Jones Fuller, Dec. 2, 1956; *News and Observer*, Feb. 10, 1927; *An Act To Provide for the Acquisition of Parks and Recreational Facilities in the Great Smoky Mountains of North Carolina*, Feb. 25, 1927, pp. 3-17.

18. Minutes of the N. C. Park Commission, March 18, 1927, E. C. Brooks to Plato Ebbs, Aug. 18, 1927, Mark Squires to E. C. Brooks, Aug. 22, 1927, Brooks Papers (DUL); Memorandum by Mr. Verne Rhoades, Nov. 20, 1956; *Report of the N. C. Park Commission, 1931*, pp. 4-5; *Annual Report of the Secretary of the Interior, June 30, 1927*, p. 131.

North Carolina and Tennessee provided funds from their bond issues.[19]

This financial assistance enabled the North Carolina Park Commission to begin the actual work of creating a national park. The commission organized an executive staff in the spring of 1928 and selected Verne Rhoades of Asheville as executive secretary. Rhoades set up an office in Asheville and employed "a staff of surveyors, foresters, and men acquainted with land values." In describing his activities Rhoades later stated: "I had charge of the entire program of acquisition of land within the purchase area of the North Carolina side of the Great Smoky Mountains. This work embraced boundary surveys, title examinations, timber valuations, farm land valuations, ascertaining timber stands by actual cruise, employment of necessary personnel, preparation of reports covering each ownership and the presentation of these reports to the Commission for consideration." Brooks as secretary of the commission worked closely with Rhoades and was well informed on all activities in both the field and the office.[20]

On April 16, 1928, the commission directed Rhoades to proceed with the condemnation of land within the park area. Brooks, like other members of the commission, disliked the condemnation approach for acquiring park lands, especially when it involved small farm owners. He sincerely sympathized with families forced to move off lands that had been theirs for generations. His recognition of the emotional, physical, and economic effects upon such families was shared by other members of the commission. The commission therefore employed its powers of condemnation against small farmers only as a last resort. To some residents the park was "uninvited and unwelcome"; to others it provided an opportunity to purchase farms in areas with better schools and roads. On the other hand, several large lumber and pulp companies demonstrated a spirit of defiance. They accelerated their timber-cutting activities in the park area, then held out for prices which the commission could not justify

19. Memorandum by Mr. Verne Rhoades, Nov. 20, 1956; interview with Mr. John G. Dawson, Sept. 7, 1956; Testimony Re: N. C. Park Commission, 1933, Governors' Papers (Ehringhaus); *Report of the N. C. Park Commission, 1931*, p. 5; Raymond Fosdick, *John D. Rockefeller, Jr.: A Portrait* (New York, 1956), p. 320; Beardsley Ruml to A. W. McLean, Nov. 1, 1928, Governors' Papers (McLean).

20. Memorandum by Mr. Verne Rhoades, Nov. 20, 1956. See also *Report of the N. C. Park Commission, 1931*, p. 5.

by its surveys. Brooks played an important role in the delicate, sometimes exasperating, negotiations with representatives of the lumber interests.[21]

Frequently the park commission was forced to institute condemnation proceedings against the lumber companies' lands. Its first serious legal battle was with the Suncrest Lumber Company, which owned 32,853.53 acres within the proposed park site. The company continued to cut timber in this area and consistently rejected the commission's bids on its property. In the summer of 1928 when the commission condemned the Suncrest lands, the company tested the constitutionality of the park act of 1927, and the courts upheld its validity. Finally, in September, 1932, the Suncrest lands were purchased for $600,000. Brooks played a vital role throughout the negotiations with Suncrest officials. His patient and diplomatic approach to disputed points of values and boundaries contributed greatly to the satisfactory settlement of one of the most difficult problems confronting the commission.[22]

In July, 1929, the commission had completed the surveys and timber estimates of the park area and had appraised every tract of land except the small farms located on Cataloochee Creek in Haywood County. It had halted all timber-cutting in the park area and had acquired 54,495.13 acres at a cost of $442,576 (approximately $8.12 per acre) from ninety-six individual owners. The litigation involving the commission had become so extensive by July, 1929, that Squires was employed at a salary of $7,500 as an additional attorney. Brooks frequently assisted Squires in negotiations with land owners in an effort to reach a settlement out of court. Brooks was also deeply concerned about the protection of park lands until they were turned over to the federal government. In the spring of 1930

21. Memorandum by Mr. Verne Rhoades, Nov. 20, 1956; memorandum by Mr. Harry Nettles, Sept. 17, 1956; interview with Mr. John G. Dawson, Sept. 7, 1956; Robert H. Woody, "Cataloochee Homecoming," *South Atlantic Quarterly*, XLIX (Jan., 1950), 8; Irving Melbo, *Our Country's National Parks* (New York, 1941), I, 139; Minutes of the N. C. Park Commission, April 16, 1928, Brooks Papers (DUL).

22. Minutes of the N. C. Park Commission, April 16, Aug. 31, 1928, Report of the Executive Secretary of the N. C. Park Commission, Oct. 1, 1931, Mark Squires to Members of the Park Commission, April 22, 1932, Brooks Papers (DUL); Report of the Activities of N. C. Park Commission, June 30, 1931, Governors' Papers (Gardner); *North Carolina Supreme Court Reports, Fall Term, 1930*, pp. 199-202; *Biennial Report of the Attorney General of North Carolina, 1928-1930*, pp. 119-121; *News and Observer*, Aug. 16, 1932; *The Asheville Citizen*, Oct. 1, 1932.

he secured additional funds from the Budget Bureau for the State Department of Conservation and Development to use in fire prevention in the Great Smokies.[23]

Brooks desired that whenever possible State College should render practical assistance to state projects and was especially interested in having the institution aid in the development of the park. At his request B. W. Wells, professor of botany at the college, prepared a pamphlet entitled *The Remarkable Flora of the Great Smoky Mountains*. Brooks secured summer work in the park surveys for several engineering students in 1928, and the following year the chairman of the civil engineering department at the college suggested that the surveying of a portion of the proposed park site be assumed by his classes. The campus newspaper, *The Technician*, claimed that the park was actually the handiwork of State College, since Brooks and three of its trustees had not only secured the passage of the park bill in 1927, but were original members of the park commission.[24]

[3]

On February 6, 1930, the governors of North Carolina and Tennessee delivered to the Secretary of the Interior deeds to 158,876.5 acres of land in the Great Smokies. The area then assumed "limited park status" under the congressional act of 1926. On August 28, 1930, Secretary of the Interior Ray L. Wilbur notified Governor Gardner that "the park is established and the United States through the National Park Service has assumed its administration and protection." He had already installed a "protective force" and planned to transfer a trained park superintendent there within a few months.[25]

23. Report of the Activities of the N. C. Park Commission, June 30, 1929, Governors' Papers (Gardner); Minutes of the N. C. Park Commission, July 11, 1929, E. C. Brooks to Mark Squires, May 1, 1930, Brooks Papers (DUL).
24. B. W. Wells, *The Remarkable Flora of the Great Smoky Mountains* (Asheville, n.d.); E. C. Brooks to Mark Squires, May 13, 1927, E. C. Brooks to Verne Rhoades, March 26, 1928, Brooks Papers (DUL); *The Technician*, March 7, 1930; Report of the Department of Civil Engineering, 1929-1930, State College Papers, Archives of the North Carolina State College of Agriculture and Engineering, Raleigh.
25. Minutes of the N. C. Park Commission, Feb. 6, 1930, Brooks Papers (DUL); *Annual Report of the Secretary of the Interior, June 30, 1930*, p. 83; *Report of the N. C. Park Commission, 1931*, p. 71; *News and Observer*, Feb. 6, 1930; Ray L. Wilbur to O. Max Gardner, Aug. 28, 1930, Governors' Papers (Gardner).

The work of the North Carolina Park Commission was by no means completed with the transfer of this minimum area to the federal government. In fact, the next three years proved to be the most difficult of its entire existence. The economic depression that settled upon the state in 1930 seriously affected the work of the commission. In the following year the legislature was quite naturally concerned about questions of public finance. The activities and expenditure of the park commission provided a convenient target for economy-conscious legislators who had never possessed any real interest in the park project. They at first considered introducing a bill to abolish the commission, but for some reason gave up the idea. At the same time Governor Gardner received letters from citizens in the western section of the state variously describing the activities of the park commission as "a racket," "confiscatory," and "a squandering of money." The legislature finally enacted a bill whereby the terms of the members of the existing commission were to expire on January 1, 1933, and their successors were to be chosen by the Governor. The act also required the State Auditor "as soon as practical" to audit all books and accounts of the commission. This action by the General Assembly in 1931 seems to have been evidence of its lack of faith in the commission's handling of park funds.[26]

While the commission was under fire by the legislature, Brooks was negotiating the purchase of lands in the park area owned by the Champion Fibre Company. He and Squires, vested with full power to act for the commission, joined a Tennessee delegation and representatives of the company for the purpose of reaching an agreement about the sale of these lands. Horace Albright, Director of the National Park Service, acted as referee during the discussions. Brooks, who was in charge of the whole procedure, rapidly led the negotiations to a satisfactory conclusion. Reuben Robertson, president of the Champion Fibre Company, later wrote him: "While we are fully aware . . . that we accepted a price for our property far below its real value, still we feel that the negotiations as conducted by you were carried on on the highest possible plane and with consummate

26. E. Grover Roberson to O. Max Gardner, March 9, 1931, Edwin Gaskill, "A Fight For North Carolina Integrity or to Save the Face of a Few State Agents, Jan. 15, 1931," L. Woody to O. Max Gardner, March 12, 1931, Mrs. Ralph Lee to O. Max Gardner, March 8, 1931, Governors' Papers (Gardner); *Public Laws and Resolutions, 1931* pp. 286-287.

skill by you." The Champion Fibre Company lands were purchased for $3,000,000, of which North Carolina paid $2,000,000 and Tennessee $1,000,000.[27]

During the next two years Brooks was a key figure in the negotiations for the purchase of two other major tracts within the park area. As mentioned before, his contact with the officials of the Suncrest Lumber Company led to the purchase of its 32,853.53 acres in September, 1932. Despite his "consummate skill" in negotiations, Brooks was unable to bring about an agreement between the park commission and the Ravensford Lumber Company, which owned 32,709.57 acres within the park boundaries. The commission, believing that the price set by the company was too high, condemned the property and thereby precipitated a legal battle that continued even after Brooks left the commission. By 1933, however, the Ravensford property was the last major tract to be secured on the North Carolina side of the Great Smokies.[28]

On January 1, 1933, the commission reported that it had transferred deeds of 138,463 acres to the National Park Service. By that time the official area of the park within North Carolina had been increased to 228,960 acres, which of course would necessitate additional expenditures. This official area included 357 "different and distinct tracts of land." The report described the activities of the park commission as follows:

In handling the acquirement of this area, it has been necessary to make numbers of surveys of individual tracts and locate disputed lines and lappages; and in order to comply with the requirements of the Federal Government, abstracts of titles in a very complete and complicated form were essential. It has been necessary to employ timber cruisers and various kinds of experts in order to determine values within the area. Further, the commission has had to acquire mineral interests of an indefinite value and meet the argument of land owners as to consequential damages. Land has been acquired by condemnation, options, and outright

27. Minutes of the N. C. Park Commission, Dec. 14, 1929, Feb. 16, 1931, "A Statement of the Negotiations in Washington, D. C., April 27, 1931, To Secure the Property of the Champion Fibre Company Lying within the Area of the Proposed Great Smoky Mountain National Park," Reuben Robertson to E. C. Brooks, May 7, 1931, Minutes of the N. C. Park Commission, May 7, 1931, Brooks Papers (DUL).
28. Report of the N. C. Park Commission, 1931, p. 5; Mark Squires to Members of the Park Commission, April 22, 1932, Brooks Papers (DUL); A. Hall Johnston to J. C. B. Ehringhaus, Aug. 23, 1933, Governors' Papers (Ehringhaus); News and Observer, Feb. 3, 1934.

purchases. In all condemnation proceedings, where the Park Commission took an appeal from the commissioners' award, the jury awarded greater sums for lands condemned. The appeals made by the commission have followed only the appeals of land owners and were made on behalf of the commission to protect its supposed interests.[29]

One of the park commission's depositories, the Central Bank and Trust Company of Asheville, had failed on November 30, 1930, amid the tightening economic depression. The commission, however, had guaranteed its deposits of $326,016.70 with surety bonds and other securities. The immediate payment of one bond and the sale of securities reduced the amount due from the bank to $122,716.35. The companies holding other surety bonds refused to pay, whereupon the commission initiated legal proceedings against them. The commission report concluded that in order to complete the purchase of park lands either the state or some other agency would have to provide an additional appropriation.[30]

The defensive tone of the commission report indicated that Brooks and Squires, who wrote it, were aware of the mounting opposition to the expenditure of park funds. At any rate, the Legislature of 1933, convening just as the depression plunged the state to the bottom of the economic abyss, voiced loud and bitter criticism against the park commission. The legislators suggested that members were guilty of gross extravagance and porkbarreling. The leaders of this opposition, Senator W. O. Burgin and Representative Hubert Olive, concentrated their attack on the loss of park funds in the defunct Asheville bank and the "enormous" ($7,500) legal fees paid to Squires. Burgin introduced a bill that would abolish the park commission and transfer its functions to the Department of Conservation and Development. Brooks prevented the passage of this bill through his personal influence with key legislators.[31]

Burgin, however, continued to proclaim that "something rotten" was involved in the park project, while Senator John Sprunt Hill demanded that the commission give "an accounting" of its activities.

---

29. *Report of the N. C. Park Commission, 1933,* p. 3.
30. *Ibid.,* pp. 6-8, 10.
31. Harry Rotha to J. C. B. Ehringhaus, March 9, 1933, John G. Dawson to J. C. B. Ehringhaus, April 1, 1933, Governors' Papers (Ehringhaus); E. C. Brooks to A. B. Cammerer, Feb. 2, 1933, Brooks Papers (DUL); *News and Observer,* Feb. 2, April 1, 1933.

The newly-elected United States Senator from North Carolina, Robert R. Reynolds of Asheville, had already requested Governor Gardner to withhold the reappointment of Squires to the park commission. J. C. B. Ehringhaus, who succeeded Gardner as governor in January, 1933, was instructed by the General Assembly to undertake an investigation of the financial transactions of the commission.[32] On April 1, 1933, John G. Dawson, a member of the park commission and a prominent figure in state Democratic politics, wrote the Governor: "It would be impossible for me to say how embarrassing to me this continued talk in the General Assembly of wrong doing has been. I have taken more pride in my efforts in connection with the establishment of Great Smoky Mountains National Park than I have ever taken in anything in all my life."[33] Harry Nettles, another active sponsor of the park movement, later declared that "petty politics" replaced the commission of which he was a member. He presumably referred to the stand taken by Senator Reynolds. In accordance with the desire of the legislature, Governor Ehringhaus appointed an entirely new park commission of five members. In view of "all the argument" in the General Assembly, the members of the old commission heartily approved the Governor's action.[34]

Brooks not only was grieved by the quarrel over the commission, but was convinced that the attitude of the legislators had been grossly unfair to the men actually responsible for the establishment of the park. "We made the park a certainty," he wrote Squires, "and practically completed all the details necessary." Squires, of course, fully agreed with this view. Brooks declared that "Moses was permitted to stand on a high elevation and see the Promised Land, but another was permitted to lead the people." "I am led to believe," he concluded, "that Moses still has more credit than Joshua." Apparently Brooks harbored no bitterness toward the new commission and

32. *News and Observer,* Feb. 2, 1933; Robert R. Reynolds to O. Max Gardner, Dec. 3, 1932, Governors' Papers (Gardner); *House Journal, 1933,* pp. 53, 114, 443, 457; *Senate Journal, 1933,* pp. 579, 636; Edward Moses to J. C. B. Ehringhaus, March 30, 1933, Governors' Papers (Ehringhaus).

33. John G. Dawson to J. C. B. Ehringhaus, April 1, 1933, Governors' Papers (Ehringhaus).

34. Memorandum by Mr. Harry Nettles, Sept. 17, 1956; *Addresses, Letters and Papers of John Christoph Bulcher Ehringhaus, 1933-1937,* ed. D. L. Corbitt (Raleigh, 1950), p. 447; John G. Dawson to J. C. B. Ehringhaus, July 19, 1933, Governors' Papers (Ehringhaus).

assured its chairman of his wholehearted co-operation in the completion of the park.[35]

In November, 1934, the Attorney General reported that the investigation of the financial dealings of the park commission had "never been held." If a formal investigation was never conducted, certainly a large quantity of testimony on the subject was presented to the Governor sometime late in 1933. In the recorded testimony of A. B. Cammerer of the National Park Service was the statement: "There has been no dissipation of funds; it has been a real magnificent project and carried through very well." Plato Ebbs, the treasurer, testified that the park commission had spent "around four million dollars" and that its legal expenses had necessarily been "enormous." The executive secretary, Verne Rhoades, pointed out that the commission spent an average of seventy-seven cents per acre in comparison to eighty-four cents by the United States Forest Service. He concluded that "the commission has worked as hard as any public agency I ever saw and they have done it with interested minds." In effect, the testimony indicated that the commission had demonstrated remarkable efficiency in its work and that the charges of financial mismanagement were based upon rumors fostered by petty politics and economy-conscious legislators in need of a convenient scapegoat.[36]

For some reason Brooks was not quoted in the testimony presented to the Governor, but he had reason to be pleased with it. For almost a decade he had unselfishly promoted the establishment of the Great Smoky Mountains National Park. One of his colleagues on the park commission throughout this period later described him as "the master mind and master key" in the development of the park. Brooks continued to manifest a deep interest in the park after 1933 and considered writing a history of the park movement in North Carolina, an undertaking prevented by his continued ill health. The park was completed through aid from the federal government and was formally dedicated by President Franklin D. Roosevelt on September 2, 1940. Brooks must have experienced a certain pride as he

35. E. C. Brooks to Mark Squires, Sept. 15, 1933, Mark Squires to E. C. Brooks, Aug. 10, 1933, E. C. Brooks to W. W. Neal, Sept. 25, 1933, Brooks Papers (DUL).
36. *Biennial Report of the Attorney General, 1932-1934*, p. 99; Testimony Re: N. C. Park Commission, 1933, Governors' Papers (Ehringhaus).

witnessed the number of visitors to the park increase from 150,000 in 1931 to 1,204,017 in 1947, making "the last of the eastern wilder- nesses" the most popular national park in America.[37]

37. Interview with Mr. John G. Dawson, Sept. 7, 1956; Mark Squires to E. C. Brooks, Nov. 24, 1936, Brooks Papers (DUL); *Travel Statistics of the Great Smoky Mountains National Park,* issued by the Park Superintendent; *The Asheville Citizen-Times,* March 26, 1950.

Nine: PRESIDENT OF NORTH CAROLINA STATE COLLEGE, 1923-1934

[1]

In 1916 Brooks was seriously considered for the presidency of North Carolina College of Agriculture and Mechanic Arts, but the trustees selected a man from its own faculty, W. C. Riddick, professor of engineering. The Riddick administration from 1916 to 1923 has been characterized as a "trying" period "filled with heroism, sadness, readjustments, and growing pains." In 1917 the legislature changed the name of the institution to North Carolina State College of Agriculture and Engineering, a possible indication of an attempt to lift it to a higher professional status. After World War I, however, the curriculum and administrative organization were still inadequate to meet the increasing demands placed upon the college. Thus, President Riddick initiated a general reorganization program in the fall of 1922, and at his request the United States Bureau of Education sent its specialist in higher education, Dr. George Zook, to study the institution. In May, 1923, his findings and recommendations, known as the Zook Report, were accepted by the college trustees.[1]

In the meantime, Riddick had indicated his desire to resign the presidency and return to his favorite field of work as dean of the new school of engineering proposed in the Zook Report. Regardless of expressions to the contrary, the trustees welcomed Riddick's voluntary resignation. In fact, on several previous occasions strong opposition to his administration had been voiced by those who

1. See David Lockmiller, *History of North Carolina State College of Agriculture and Engineering of the University of North Carolina, 1889-1939* (Raleigh, 1939), pp. 125-151.

charged that he was emphasizing engineering at the expense of agriculture. Coupled with this lingering dissatisfaction was the realization by the trustees in 1923 that the success of the reorganization program depended upon an energetic executive with "broad educational views." They therefore accepted Riddick's resignation. Their search for a man qualified to lead the college through its "renaissance" resulted in the unanimous election of Brooks to the presidency of State College.[2]

The trustees had first approached Brooks regarding the matter late in April, 1923. Governor Cameron Morrison, *ex-officio* chairman of the board, insisted that Brooks alone could convert State College into a strong technological school directly beneficial to the people of North Carolina. Clarence Poe, another influential trustee, agreed with the governor. Poe had come to know Brooks intimately through their association in the Watauga Club, a small group first organized in 1884 by Walter Hines Page and one of the major forces behind the establishment of State College five years later. In addition to Brooks, two other members of the club were considered as possible candidates for the college presidency. They were Dr. B. W. Kilgore, director of the Agricultural Experiment Station and a well-known farm leader, and Dr. Carl C. Taylor, a professor of rural sociology at State College. The trustees, however, preferred Brooks, a native North Carolinian, who was considered a "statesman in education" with a "broad view of education" essential to the direction of the college. Riddick, too, joined the chorus advocating Brooks as his successor and purportedly refused to step down unless he agreed to accept the position.[3]

Brooks reached his decision only after a careful appraisal of all relevant factors. He was fifty-one years old and had occupied the State Superintendency for four and a half years. His job, however rewarding, placed many demands upon his physical strength, and the

2. Minutes of the Board of Trustees of North Carolina State College of Agriculture and Engineering, May 21, June 9, 1923. Office of the Business Manager, North Carolina State College, Raleigh. Hereinafter cited as Minutes of the Trustees. *News and Observer,* April 15, 17, 18, 1919, Jan. 30, Feb. 1, 1921, May 29, 1923; Lockmiller, *History of State College,* p. 139; interviews with Mrs. E. C. Brooks, June 19, 1956, and Mr. Clarence Poe, July 6, 1956.

3. *News and Observer,* May 23, 1923; interviews with Mrs. E. C. Brooks, May 9, 1956, Mr. E. C. Brooks, Jr., July 12, 1956, and Mr. Clarence Poe, July 6, 1956; *Progressive Farmer,* XXXVIII (June 9, 1923), 603; Clarence Poe to E. C. Brooks, Jan. 14, 1921, S. P. I. Correspondence.

extra official duties of the office, especially speechmaking, had reached staggering proportions. Moreover, he believed that schools of technology and vocational schools, such as State College, were the "up and coming" institutions of higher learning. State College, he reasoned, would offer him a fertile field for additional contributions to the educational life of North Carolina. He was convinced that the college should "take the lead" in promoting "the art of living well at home," the basic idea behind his efforts to establish rural community high schools. In addition to these considerations, Brooks took into account the question of his personal finances in reaching his decision about the college presidency. His income consisted of an annual salary of $5,000 after 1921, together with royalties from his books and varying amounts of honoraria for public addresses. But his expenses considerably increased while he was State Superintendent. Among his major expenditures were those for the college education of his three children, the purchase of a home in Raleigh, and the numerous donations expected of state officials by civic and charity organizations.[4]

After considering these and other factors, Brooks agreed to go to State College if he received the same salary as the president of the University of North Carolina. On May 21, 1923, the college trustees met his terms by raising the annual salary of their president to $8,500, "the same as the president of the University," and providing a yearly allowance of $1,500 for renting a home. From both a personal and professional standpoint, Brooks found the State College offer too attractive to reject. Thus, he resigned as State Superintendent of Public Instruction in order to assume direction of a loosely organized and comparatively young college.[5]

On June 9, 1923, Brooks appeared in person before the trustees to accept the college presidency. In outlining what his objectives would be, he proposed that State College not only blaze trails in

4. E. C. Brooks to Edgar Knight, July 11, 1921, E. C. Brooks to P. H. Gwynn, March 29, 1923, E. C. Brooks to R. L. Davis, Oct. 26, 1922, S. P. I. Correspondence; interviews with Mrs. E. C. Brooks, May 9, 1956, June 19, 1956, and Mr. A. S. Brower, Oct. 2, 1956; News and Observer, Jan. 12, 1921; Henry London to E. C. Brooks, June 27, 1923, E. C. Brooks, "Address to the Board of Trustees of N. C. State College," June 9, 1923, Brooks Papers (DUL).

5. Minutes of the Board of Trustees, May 21, 1923; interview with Mr. E. C. Brooks, Jr., July 12, 1956; E. C. Brooks to Cameron Morrison, June 11, 1923, Papers and Letters of Governor Morrison, p. 302; News and Observer, May 29, 1923; Durham Herald, May 29, 1923; Greensboro Daily News, May 29, 1923.

scientific research, but also seek solutions to social and economic problems confronting North Carolina. He insisted that "human relationships are our most valuable possessions" and that instruction in the social sciences should have a prominent place in every technological school. The college president, he felt, should strive to perfect "an efficient organization divided into self-governing but cooperating units, the affairs of which are directed by capable leaders trained to work in harmony with the ideals of the institution and each given the widest possible freedom for the development of his own initiative." In conclusion he assured the trustees:

I am not resigning from the State Superintendency . . . in order to find an easier berth in the shades of a great educational institution. . . . I believe I have accomplished my best work as State Superintendent and there is another task closely related to my work in the past which I wish to perform before the mellowing touch of advancing age reverses my perspective, and the task, I believe, can be accomplished better at North Carolina State College . . . than any other institution within the State.[6]

This speech "greatly delighted" the trustees and assured them that they had chosen the right man to carry through their reorganization program.

The inauguration of Brooks as the fifth president of State College took place a year later on May 26, 1924, during the graduation exercises. At his request the representatives from various educational institutions did not follow the custom of wearing academic costume, and he himself wore a frock coat and gray trousers. In addition to Governor Morrison, who presided at the inaugural ceremony, the speakers included O. Max Gardner, William P. Few, and Harry W. Chase. Brooks's successor as State Superintendent, A. T. Allen, brought greetings from twenty thousand public school teachers, whom Brooks had "made respectable by providing a decent salary schedule." Governor Morrison, more lavish in his praise, declared that Brooks was "as eloquent as Aycock, as gracious as Alderman, as hard a fighter as Tillman, and a better politician than Simmons."[7]

Brooks's inaugural address, entitled "The Relation of Education to Public Welfare," embodied his conception of the college's

6. Brooks, "Address to the Board of Trustees of N. C. State College," June 9, 1923, Brooks Papers (DUL). See also Minutes of the Trustees, June 9, 1923.
7. News and Observer, May 25, 27, 1924.

role in a period troubled by the activities of the Ku Klux Klan and the clash of science and religion on the question of biological evolution. According to him, the fundamental aim of any college should be the creation of "enthusiasm for truth as applied to social well-being." The college should prepare students for specific professions; promote research in social, economic, and political fields; and formulate a "fair standard" for measuring the "value of local government." Brooks pointed out the dangers of any education that lacked a broad foundation in the social sciences. Strictly technical training would produce mutually unsympathetic groups of specialists without any common ground for co-operating to promote the general welfare. Brooks insisted that technical education "should be based on the same liberal culture that all receive in order that the technically trained may be like-minded in the relation to social progress."[8]

[2]

Brooks had been at the helm of State College for a year prior to his official inauguration in 1924. When he actually assumed the office in 1923, the college plant consisted of a group of unimpressive buildings scattered over a campus of uneven terrain along the railroad tracks in West Raleigh. The total enrollment was 1,210 students, and the faculty was composed of 95 professors, about half of whom held the rank of instructor. The administrative organization of the college was unwieldy and unco-ordinated, while the curriculum consisted largely of technical courses in agriculture and engineering, with little instruction in the social sciences. The school was unable to meet the accreditation requirements of the Association of Colleges and Secondary Schools of the Southern States. In fact, the idea of State College as a mere "trade school" was still prevalent, and in some quarters its students were considered "roughnecks," lacking manners and social graces. Such attitudes seemed to affect the morale of the students themselves, who were well aware of the college's antiquated buildings and trade-school curriculum, and who bemoaned the paucity of important positions in industry and politics

8. E. C. Brooks, "The Relation of Education to Public Welfare," May 26, 1924, Brooks Papers (DUL). See also E. C. Brooks to W. K. Boyd, May 29, 1924, Ernest Seeman to E. C. Brooks, May 27, 1924, State College Papers.

held by its alumni. One of the major tasks of the new president was to eliminate the basis for such notions by improving the professional status and physical plant of State College.[9]

The Zook Report was the basic outline for Brooks's reorganization of the college. It suggested that the college be organized into four divisions: agriculture, engineering, general sciences, and social sciences and business administration. Each division would be headed by a dean. Zook emphasized the need for an expansion of the curriculum to provide students of technology with more instruction in "cultural" subjects and to attract a "more varied clientele" through new courses in teacher training, journalism, textile manufacturing, and agricultural and engineering administration. He also recommended an expansion in library facilities, buildings, and laboratories as well as an increase in the quality and salaries of the teaching staff.[10]

Brooks realized that implementing the reorganization program would require the full co-operation of the faculty. Thus, in his first general faculty meeting in September, 1923, he declared:

I am not an autocrat and I believe in a democratic form of government. I shall expect from each of you a frank statement as to your ideas in regard to every phase of the college and its work, and it shall be my privilege to exchange as frankly mine with you. It is only through this frank interchange of ideas that I can become the spokesman of the best thought of this institution and this I conceive to be one of the chief duties of your president.[11]

Through the application of this policy, Brooks not only maintained cordial relations with the faculty during the period of reorganization but throughout his career at State College. The members of the faculty offered valuable suggestions on such questions as course content, credit requirements, and rearrangements of existing courses. In fact, they did much of the actual work in executing the recommendations of the Zook Report. On questions of general policy, however, Brooks worked more closely with the Faculty Council, a group composed of deans and members elected by the general faculty. The

9. Lockmiller, *History of State College*, pp. 135, 287; Faculty Committee, "Student Morale at North Carolina State College," State College Papers; interview with Mr. A. S. Brower, Oct. 2, 1956.
10. George F. Zook, *Report on a Survey of the North Carolina College of Agriculture and Engineering* (Raleigh, 1923), pp. 3-22.
11. *Alumni News*, VI (Sept., 1923), p. 2.

council and the president shared in the power of policy-making, and the chairman of the council, called Chairman of the Faculty, was in effect vice-president of the college. The Faculty Council included a group of able and energetic men whose advice and co-operation enabled the new president to revamp the college with speed and relative ease.[12]

On February 27, 1924, Brooks reported to the trustees that the initial phase of the reorganization program had been completed. The college had been divided into four schools, namely agriculture, engineering, general science, and graduate. Each school was subdivided into departments. The School of Agriculture was headed by Dr. B. W. Kilgore as Dean with three administrative subordinates called directors of research, extension, and instruction. The School of Engineering under former president Riddick was organized along similar lines and included an Engineering Experiment Station created in 1923. Both schools added new courses and modified or eliminated old ones in order to provide several programs of study "with definite vocational aims." The new courses furnished instruction in such fields as marketing, management, and industrial relations. All graduate training previously carried on in a decentralized manner by the several departments was co-ordinated within a Graduate School under Dean Carl C. Taylor, one of Brooks's closest advisers, who also served as the Director of the Bureau of Economic and Social Research and as Chairman of the Faculty for several years.[13]

Brooks was particularly concerned about the establishment of the division that subsequently became the School of Science and Business headed by Dean B. F. Brown. Brooks insisted that all students at State College, after selecting a profession or vocation, should pursue a program of study that would "already be determined" rather than being given a certain number of credits for a group of courses without a definite vocational aim. This prescribed program would include courses in the School of Science and Business, such

12. Minutes of the General Faculty of North Carolina State College, Sept. 26, 1923, May 28, 1924, Minutes of the Faculty Council of North Carolina State College, Feb. 28, May 28, 1924, Archives of North Carolina State College of Agriculture and Engineering, Raleigh.

13. E. C. Brooks, "To the Board of Trustees," Feb. 27, 1924, Brooks Papers (BLS); *News and Observer*, Jan. 20, 1924; *State College Record*, XXII (May, 1924), 5; Minutes of the Faculty Council, Dec. 6, 1924.

as languages, literature, and the social sciences, in order to "give young men trained for technical service a higher conception of their duties as citizens and leaders." The school also embodied the natural sciences, business administration, and courses for training teachers of science and vocational subjects. Throughout his administration Brooks bent every effort to provide the students with an education that combined preparation "in the art of making a living" with "the best thought pertaining to human relationships."[14]

From the outset he manifested a keen interest in the scholastic standards and physical welfare of the students. In 1923 he set in motion a revised system of points for meritorious work that reduced class absences by 50 per cent and raised the average scholarship by 7 per cent within a year. He believed that additional courses in English would greatly enhance the general scholastic status of students by providing adequate means for the expression of their ideas. Consequently, he encouraged the expansion of the English department. At the same time he inaugurated changes in student government and physical education, both of which he considered closely related to intellectual development. The innovations in student government produced a noticeable improvement in student morale. The new Student Council first proved its efficiency by a swift and judicious solution of a hazing episode in April, 1924. Another boost to student morale was Brooks's emphasis on physical fitness of all students rather than the production of a few athletic heroes. He reorganized the department of physical education and made its courses an integral part of the college curriculum.[15]

Brooks fully realized that the standards of the college depended in large measure upon the quality of the faculty. In one of his first meetings with the faculty he emphatically stated: "We *must raise* the academic level of this institution." He believed that the first step in this direction was the elimination of that portion of the teach-

14. Brooks's Memorandum, 1924, Brooks, "To the Board of Trustees," Feb. 27, 1924, Brooks Papers (BLS); Minutes of the Faculty Council, Jan. 12, 1924; *State College Record*, XXII (April, 1924), 10, 38-39; *News and Observer*, Jan. 21, 1924.

15. Minutes of the General Faculty, Sept. 26, 1923, Nov. 21, 1924; Minutes of the Faculty Council, March 15, 1924, April 6, 1925; *News and Observer*, Jan. 21, 22, 1924, April 6, 1925; "Annual Report of the President of the College, 1924-1925," *State College Record*, XXIV (May, 1925), 20-21; *Alumni News*, VII (Dec., 1923), 1; Report of *The Wataguan*, 1926-1928, Minutes of the Faculty Committee on Athletics, Sept. 18, 25, Oct. 9, 1923, Jan. 24, 1924, State College Papers.

ing force possessing only bachelor's degrees or the equivalent. His intention was that the college should assist such instructors in studying for advanced degrees and employ no one who could not be considered for an assistant professorship. Brooks was especially eager for members of the faculty to pursue research and disseminate their findings through classroom instruction and publication. To encourage research, the teaching load for the individual instructor was reduced by several hours per week. In 1924-1925 a general increase in the salary scale provided a maximum salary of $2,000 for the instructor and $4,500 for the full professor. Brooks also urged faculty members to participate in the activities of national organizations in their fields and promised them liberal financial assistance to attend professional meetings.[16]

Under Brooks the college gradually achieved a higher status in the public estimation, and echoes of the trade school idea grew faint after the initial phase of the reorganization. His policy, however, elicited unexpected reactions in the General Assembly of 1925. When he appeared before the legislators to plead for larger appropriations for the college, they questioned him closely on the real purpose of his changes in the college curriculum. Many legislators believed that engineering and agriculture had been minimized by Brooks in his efforts to build "a liberal arts college similar to the University." Brooks not only sought to correct this misconception by a thorough explanation of his program, but invited a group of prominent farmers to visit the college to "see what is being done to improve agriculture in North Carolina." He requested officials of the School of Science and Business to revise the published description of the school in order to show its relation to technical training. The complaints voiced by the legislators did not affect his educational policy for the college, and several months later he again told the faculty: "We are going to give the men who enter the professions from State College the same opportunity for general culture that any man has graduating from any other institution."[17]

16. Minutes of the General Faculty, Sept. 26, 1923, May 28, Nov. 21, 1924; Minutes of the Faculty Council, Sept. 19, Oct. 1, 25, 1923, March 6, Dec. 16, 1924; E. C. Brooks to Herman Taylor, March 21, 1927, Brooks Papers (DUL); memorandum by Mr. B. F. Brown, Oct. 1, 1956; *News and Observer,* Jan. 20, 1924.
17. Memorandum by Mr. B. F. Brown, Oct. 1, 1956; Minutes of the General Faculty, March 4, 14, Oct. 22, 1925; Minutes of the Faculty Council, March 11, 17, 1925.

One of the most perplexing problems that confronted Brooks at the college was the confused situation regarding the joint control of the Agricultural Experiment Station and Extension Service by the State Department of Agriculture and the college. In brief, the history of the joint control since 1913 had been marked by the rise of petty jealousies and antagonistic cliques that had greatly reduced the effectiveness of the work in agricultural experimentation and extension services. The public was generally unaware of the divided administrative responsibility and gave the Agriculture Department all credit for compiling and disseminating agricultural data to farmers. Yet, federal funds for extension work provided by the Smith-Lever Act of 1914 were paid to the college, then transferred to the Department of Agriculture. In February, 1923, Secretary of Agriculture Henry Wallace ruled that agricultural research and extension supported by federal funds had to be conducted by the land-grant colleges. Despite an agreement to place the Extension Service at the college, it remained in the office of the Agriculture Department. Moreover, the Experiment Station, though located on college property, was actually controlled by the Department and rarely used by college professors or students. As a result, the college was forced to duplicate the research of the Station for instruction in agriculture. Friction between the officials of the college and the Agriculture Department precluded a rearrangement of the Station and Extension Service under the system of joint control.[18]

Upon assuming the presidency of the college, Brooks immediately initiated negotiations for a permanent solution to the problem. The Zook Report had strongly recommended that the college assume complete control of both the Station and the Extension Service. Brooks personally deplored the duplication, the "lost motion," and the "aimless experiments and futile research" in agriculture resulting from the existing situation. His intention was to unify all agricultural research, extension, and instruction under the authority of the college in order to render more effective and practical service to the people of the state. The Agriculture Department would co-operate

18. I. O. Schaub, *North Carolina Experiment Station: The First Sixty Years, 1887-1937* (Raleigh, 1955), pp. 95-97, 104-108; *News and Observer*, June 10, 12, 13, 1923; E. C. Brooks, "The Relation of North Carolina State College to the State Department of Agriculture, 1924," State College Papers.

only in its statutory capacity as a "regulatory and law enforcement agency." Brooks's arguments were supported by Governor Morrison, the college trustees, and the ruling by the federal Secretary of Agriculture. But the opposition of Commissioner of Agriculture W. A. Graham created a difficult situation, since the successful operation of the proposed arrangement necessitated his co-operation. Brooks overcame this obstacle with characteristic skill and tact by direct negotiations with Graham, and as if to seal his victory, he appointed the Director of the Experiment Station, B. W. Kilgore, as Dean of the School of Agriculture. Thus, by May, 1924, Brooks had successfully executed one of the most difficult phases of the college reorganization program.[19]

In 1925 his plan came into full operation when the legislature abolished the old system of joint control. The Extension Service and Experiment Station were then transferred to the college and placed under Kilgore as Dean of the School of Agriculture. The State Department of Agriculture appropriated $60,000 annually for extension and research at the college. The Purnell Act, passed by Congress in 1925, provided an additional $20,000 for the Experiment Station, an amount that was to be increased by $10,000 annually until the total annual appropriation reached $60,000. At the same time, Brooks created a committee representing the college and the Agriculture Department in order to eliminate duplication in research and to promote co-operation which was almost necessary in view of the fact that the Agriculture Department still owned and operated test farms related to the Experiment Station. Largely as a result of this co-ordinating body, relations between the college and the Department of Agriculture generally remained harmonious throughout Brooks's administration.[20]

19. E. C. Brooks, "The School of Agriculture, 1924," E. C. Brooks, "To the Joint Committee For Agricultural Work," E. C. Brooks, "To the Board of Trustees of State College, Feb. 24, 1924," E. C. Brooks to W. A. Graham, July 8, 1924, State College Papers; Schaub, *North Carolina Experiment Station*, pp. 106-109; Minutes of the Trustees, May 26, 1924; interview with Mr. Clarence Poe, July 6, 1956; *News and Observer*, June 13, July 19, 1924.

20. Schaub, *North Carolina Experiment Station*, p. 108; Mumford, *Land Grant College Movement*, pp. 107-110; *Agriculture and Industry*, II (April 23, May 21, June 4, 18, 1925); E. C. Brooks, "Report of the Research and Other Work Conducted by State College From Funds Derived From the Department of Agriculture, June 23, 1925," "Recommendations Adopted by the Joint Committee on Agricultural Work, July 6, 1926," E. C. Brooks to O. Max Gardner, June 22, 1926, W. A. Graham to E. C.

A major difficulty did arise, however, from the appointment of Kilgore as Dean of the School of Agriculture. Two main considerations had influenced Brooks's decision to appoint Kilgore: first, he was eminently qualified for the position both by training and experience; and second, his presence in the school would speed up the transfer of the Experiment Station to the college. On both points Brooks's reasoning proved to be valid. But Brooks and Kilgore soon drifted apart, and in the spring of 1925 they "clashed regarding the administration of the teaching work in the School of Agriculture." Brooks was unhappy because Kilgore refused to become a "teaching dean" and was generally dissatisfied with the state of affairs in the School of Agriculture. Kilgore, on the other hand, complained that administrative subordinates and faculty members who "went over his head to Brooks" crippled his efforts to strengthen the school. On May 29, 1925, Kilgore offered his resignation, which, upon Brooks's recommendation, was accepted by the trustees.[21]

The resignation precipitated the first serious controversy of Brooks's administration, mainly because of Kilgore's personal popularity and influence in agricultural circles. The press generally agreed with the *News and Observer* that Kilgore's resignation was "nothing short of tragedy." Conflicting versions of the whole affair circulated throughout the state. Some charged that Brooks had "conspired" with the faculty of the School of Agriculture to get rid of Kilgore; others described the whole college as a "hotbed of intrigue." The college alumni aired the episode at their annual meeting in June, 1925, where a small, vociferous minority severely criticized Brooks. However, the General Alumni Association voted overwhelmingly in favor of a resolution endorsing his administration. Undoubtedly, friction and jealousy existed between Kilgore and his subordinates, but all evidence indicates that Brooks was fair and candid in his dealing with him. The trustees strongly supported Brooks throughout the controversy, and O. Max Gardner, a prominent trustee, complimented his handling of "the delicate situation

Brooks, May 12, 1932, E. C. Brooks to W. A. Graham, May 23, 1932, State College Papers.

21. *News and Observer*, May 27, 29, 1925; Minutes of the Trustees, June 8, 1925; B. W. Kilgore to E. C. Brooks, May 29, 1925, E. C. Brooks to B. W. Kilgore, May 30, 1925, State College Papers; interviews with Mr. I. O. Schaub, June 28, 1956, and Mr. Clarence Poe, July 6, 1956.

with regard to Dr. Kilgore." At Brooks's request his old friend Ira O. Schaub succeeded Kilgore as Dean.[22]

[3]

Although by 1925 Brooks had implemented the main recommendations of the Zook Report, he continued to perfect the organization and curriculum of the college throughout the remainder of his administration. Every phase of the college work, whether it was research in strawberry fungi, building a dairy barn, or instruction in history, aroused his interest and received his careful attention. Brooks was determined that State College should participate directly in the social and economic development of the state. Through his efforts the College Extension Service, the Bureau of Economic and Social Research, and the Agricultural Extension Service were expanded and brought in more direct contact with a larger segment of the state's population. The short courses in agriculture and annual farmers' conventions were utilized as a means to make the college a potent force in agricultural life. In 1923 Brooks initiated a campaign to publicize the work of the college in various technical, economic, and social fields. At his request the trustees created an official publicity bureau in 1928. He also encouraged the alumni to organize local chapters throughout the state in order to provide vehicles of communication between the college and the public. He personally addressed numerous gatherings and in 1928 secured a more elaborate alumni magazine called *N. C. State Alumni News*.[23]

By the end of his administration in 1934, the curricula of the three undergraduate schools had undergone remarkable expansion. In many instances, Brooks himself suggested and actually introduced new courses and departments in these schools. He and Schaub con-

22. Various rumors claimed that Dr. Carl Taylor was angling for Kilgore's position, but Taylor stoutly denied them. Minutes of the Trustees, June 8, 1925; C. L. Newsome to T. T. Horne, June 1, 1925, O. Max Gardner to E. C. Brooks, June 11, 1925, State College Papers; B. B. Higgins to E. C. Brooks, June 3, 1925, Governors' Papers (McLean); *News and Observer*, June 9, 1925; "Annual Report of the President of the College, 1925-1926," *State College Record*, XXV (May, 1926), 18.

23. Lockmiller, *History of State College*, p. 160; Minutes of the Faculty Council, Sept. 13, 1924, June 7, Sept. 5, 1928; Minutes of the General Faculty, Nov. 7, 1923; *News and Observer*, July 29, Aug. 1, 1923, July 26, 1927, July 25, 1929; Brooks, "Tentative Organization of N. C. State College, 1923," State College Papers; *The Technician*, Jan. 30, 1925; *N. C. State Alumni News*, I (Nov., 1928), 222-223.

tinually readjusted the curriculum of the School of Agriculture in order to place the "proper" emphasis upon farm management, organization, and production. By 1927 the school provided adequate instruction "on the business side of farming." The additions to the agricultural curriculum after 1924 included forestry, agricultural administration, farm crop seed improvement, landscape gardening, and game bird preservation.

Brooks wished especially a broad program of studies in forestry, since forest products formed a significant portion of North Carolina industry. In 1925 he persuaded the trustees to co-operate with the State Department of Conservation and Development in appointing a specialist in forestry who would offer certain courses in the School of Agriculture. Four years later, the instruction in forestry was reorganized and expanded under the competent supervision of Dr. J. V. Hoffmann, former professor in the Pennsylvania Forest School. The School of Agriculture, then, became the School of Agriculture and Forestry. Brooks secured three tracts of forest land for experimental and demonstration work. These tracts, located in the piedmont and coastal plains, were known as the Poole Woods, the MacLean Forest, and the George Watts Hill Demonstration Forest.[24]

Under Brooks the School of Engineering witnessed an extraordinary expansion in its curriculum, faculty, and enrollment. He was, in large measure, responsible for introducing courses in construction, ceramic, chemical, sanitary, and aeronautical engineering. One of his main objectives was to place the School of Engineering in a position of leadership in the development of the state's economic and natural resources. Brooks was particularly interested in the work of the department of ceramic engineering, organized in September, 1924, under Professor A. F. Greaves-Walker, a recognized authority on ceramics. Through the combined efforts of Brooks and Greaves-Walker, this department came into close co-operation with

24. "Annual Report of the President of the College, 1925-1926," *State College Record*, XXV (May, 1926), 18-21; Minutes of the Faculty Council, Nov. 2, 1926, Jan. 28, 1928; "Annual Report of the President of the College, 1926-1927," *State College Record*, XXVI (June, 1927), 6-7; "Annual Report of the President of the College, 1928-1929," *State College Record*, XXVIII (June, 1929), 11-14; E. C. Brooks to John Huntington, Nov. 26, 1920, Brooks Papers (DUL); E. C. Brooks to A. W. McLean, Aug. 31, 1925, Governors' Papers (McLean); Report of the Director of Instruction, School of Agriculture, April 1, 1927, Report of the Department of Forestry, 1929-1930, E. C. Brooks to J. V. Hoffmann, May 14, 1932, Report on the Tract of Land Offered to State College as a Forest Laboratory by A. D. MacLean, State College Papers.

the North Carolina Clayworkers Association and contributed to the development of the relatively untapped clay resources of the state. With comparable enthusiasm Brooks promoted research and instruction in the departments of sanitary and chemical engineering. The expanded curriculum of the Engineering School quite naturally attracted a larger enrollment, and in 1926 Brooks reported that it was the largest school in the college, enrolling "more students than all the other schools combined."[25]

Throughout his administration Brooks kept a jealous vigil over the School of Science and Business, which was primarily his own handiwork. He continually reminded the faculty, trustees, and alumni that one purpose of the school was to provide students of technology with "the essentials of culture." The occasional complaints of the trustees regarding the "undue" emphasis on liberal arts merely resulted in a forceful restatement of this purpose by Brooks. In 1926 the school organized departments of geology and history under Professors J. L. Stuckey and Hugh T. Lefler, respectively. The same year Brooks himself offered a senior-graduate course in the "science of government." The School of Science and Business was also designed to train men in business administration, industrial management, and other fields related to the "business side" of agriculture, engineering, and textiles. In addition, the school contained a department of military science, and all students were required to participate in the Reserve Officers Training Corps. On several occasions the question of compulsory military training aroused strong opposition from students and professors. Though Brooks felt that the ROTC possessed "educational value," he gradually shifted it to a voluntary basis in order to quiet the existing criticism.[26]

25. "Annual Report of the President of the College, 1924-1925," *State College Record*, XXIV (May, 1925), 45-47; "Annual Report of the President of the College, 1925-1926," *State College Record*, XXV (May, 1926), 25; Lockmiller, *History of State College*, p. 160; *News and Observer*, Jan. 20, 1924, June 8, 1925, Sept. 16, 1927, May 23, 1929; Minutes of the Faculty Council, April 19, 1926, Oct. 2, 1928; Report of the Dean of the School of Engineering, 1929-1930, Report of the Department of Ceramic Engineering, 1929, State College Papers.

26. Minutes of the Trustees, June 6, 1927; Minutes of the General Faculty, Sept. 16, 1926; *The Technician*, Nov. 27, 1925; *News and Observer*, May 13, 1928, April 26, 1929; E. C. Brooks to B. F. Brown, June 27, 1929, E. C. Brooks to Fred Bushey, March 25, 1927, E. C. Brooks to Walter Lingle, April 3, 1930, E. C. Brooks to E. C. Early, Oct. 22, 1930, E. C. Brooks to Pat J. Hurley, Aug. 30, 1930, State College Papers; Holland Thompson, "Report on the Dismissal of Dean Carl C. Taylor," *Bulletin of the American Association of University Professors*, XVIII (March, 1932), 229. Hereinafter cited as *AAUP Bulletin*.

The School of Science and Business afforded Brooks an opportunity to bring State College into closer co-operation with the public
schools. At his direction John F. Miller, chairman of the department
of physical education in this school, established model programs of
physical training and recreation in several county school systems.
Moreover, Brooks worked with State Superintendent A. T. Allen to
develop a major sphere of co-operation in vocational education. The
training of vocational teachers at the college was shared by the School
of Science and Business and the Summer School. In 1923-1924,
Brooks reorganized the summer school under the supervision of T.
E. Browne, who was also director of the Division of Vocational Education of the State Department of Public Instruction. The summer
school no longer enrolled elementary teachers, but concentrated
upon instruction for teachers and principals in service in rural high
schools. By 1926 the enrollment in the regular six-week summer
session had increased to 249 persons, including 150 high school
teachers. During the same period the department of vocational education in the School of Science and Business attracted an increasingly larger number of students.[27]

After consulting Allen and other public school officials, Brooks
requested the college trustees to establish a School of Education by
expanding the faculty and curriculum of the department of vocational education. In September, 1927, the School of Education,
headed by T. E. Browne, was organized for the purpose of training
"teachers of agriculture, industrial arts, and high school subjects,
principals of rural high schools, home demonstration agents, home-
makers, vocational guidance counselors, and farm agents." During
its first year the school enrolled 150 students, of whom 118 registered
in the department of agricultural education. The students were provided opportunities for practice teaching in the Wake County
schools. Contrary to State College tradition, the School of Education admitted women as regular students. Although Brooks was largely responsible for this revolutionary policy, he insisted that "the im-

27. *N. C. Alumni News*, I (Dec., 1928), 37; E. C. Brooks to A. T. Allen, Nov. 19, 1923,
A. T. Allen to E. C. Brooks, Nov. 21, 1923, A. T. Allen to E. C. Brooks, Nov. 20, 1924,
E. C. Brooks to A. T. Allen, Nov. 19, 1924, Brooks Papers (DUL); *Alumni News*, VI
(Oct., 1923), 4; E. C. Brooks to A. W. McLean, Aug. 10, 1925, Governors' Papers
(McLean); *Alumni News*, VIII (Jan., 1925), 5; *News and Observer*, Feb. 5, 1924; Report
of the Director of the Summer School, 1926, State College Papers; "Annual Report of
the President of the College, 1925-1926," *State College Record*, XXV (May, 1926), 36-37.

pression should not be created that women students could come to this institution for a general liberal arts course, but that women students as well as men should select some definite vocational aim, and their schedule of studies should be made out with that in view." Brooks maintained a personal interest in the School of Education and co-operated with its chairman in its expansion to meet the increasing demands for vocational teachers.[28]

The fifth undergraduate division of the college established during Brooks's administration was the Textile School. In 1923 the departments of textile engineering and manufacturing in the Engineering School were sadly lacking in modern textile machinery and laboratory facilities for research in cotton fabrics. For years Brooks had been interested in the development of cotton mills in the South, and he clearly recognized their importance in the economic life of North Carolina. Thus, he believed that State College should become a center of textile research "extending from the field to the fabric" and should provide courses in the technical and management side of the industry. He was appalled by the meager facilities for textile education at the college and immediately set out to remedy the situation. Not only did he seek advice on the reorganization of textile education from various local sources; he traveled to New England to observe reputable textile schools at first hand. At his suggestion several alumni who were prominent textile executives donated various types of equipment to the college. Finally, in 1925, Brooks induced the trustees to organize a Textile School under Dean Thomas Nelson by consolidating the departments of textile engineering and manufacturing. During the next three years the curriculum of the Textile School underwent considerable expansion, especially in regard to its offerings in fabric design, chemical analysis, bleaching, and dyeing.[29]

28. *News and Observer,* June 28, 1927, Nov. 15, 1929; Minutes of the Executive Committee of the Trustees, May 26, 1927; Minutes of the Faculty Council, May 29, 1929; "Annual Report of the President of the College, 1927-1928," *State College Record,* XXVII (June, 1928), 33; "Annual Report of the President of the College, 1925-1926," *State College Record,* XXV (May, 1926), 36-37; Report of the Director of Instruction, School of Education, 1929, State College Papers.

29. Proposal to President Brooks, Sept. 15, 1924, State College Papers; *News and Observer,* June 3, 1924, Jan. 2, Feb. 7, 1925, May 14, 1927; E. C. Brooks, "Industry and Social Progress," E. C. Brooks, "The Importance of the Technical Man to the Textile Industry," Brooks Papers (BLS); "Annual Report of the President of the College, 1925-1926," *State College Record,* XXV (May, 1926), 41-42; *The Technician,* Jan. 9, 1925; Minutes of the Trustees, June 8, 1925; Minutes of the Executive Committee of the Trustees, Dec. 19, 1929.

Brooks, however, believed that the school had two serious weaknesses: first, it failed to place students in direct contact with the textile industry; second, its curriculum was almost devoid of instruction in such socio-economic factors as the health, education, and working conditions of the laborers. In 1929 he initiated another reorganization of the Textile School in order to eliminate these two defects, but the decrease in state funds for the college resulting from the economic depression delayed the full implementation of his plans. Despite the financial obstacles, he continued his efforts to build a reputable Textile School through close co-operation with such trustees as S. B. Alexander, David Clark, and Arthur Dixon, all prominent in the textile industry. In 1931 an investigation of the school by an independent textile authority corroborated the two defects pointed out by Brooks earlier. In the following year Brooks, Governor Gardner, and the trustees unanimously agreed that the reorganization of the Textile School necessitated the retirement of Dean Nelson, whose methods and ideas had apparently become obsolete.[30]

Before selecting a new dean, Brooks himself studied the organization and curricula of various textile schools. In February, 1933, he received an opportunity for wider studies of this kind through an appointment to the Advisory Committee of Three on Textile Education sponsored by the Textile Foundation. The other two members of the committee were Karl T. Compton, President of the Massachusetts Institute of Technology, and Robert E. Doherty, Dean of the Engineering School in Yale University. The job of the committee was to outline a curriculum in textile education that would meet the existing demands in the textile industry. At the request of the Textile Foundation, Brooks studied textile and industrial education in Great Britain during the summer of 1933. He spent most of his time in schools in London, Manchester, and Glasgow, taking copious notes that were to be a partial basis for reorganizing the Textile School at State College. Brooks was particularly

30. "Annual Report of the President of the College, 1926-1927," *State College Record*, XXVI (June, 1927), 11; *News and Observer*, Nov. 24, 1929, June 8, 1930; Minutes of the Executive Committee of the Trustees, Sept. 4, 1929, June 16-17, 1932; S. B. Alexander to E. C. Brooks, March 20, 1931, E. C. Brooks to S. B. Alexander, March 25, 1931, Albert Palmer to S. B. Alexander, May 7, 1931, S. B. Alexander to E. C. Brooks, Aug. 31, 1931, State College Papers. See also W. J. Cash, *The Mind of the South* (New York, 1941), p. 326.

impressed by three aspects of British textile education: the reliance upon scientific research; the emphasis upon economics and management; and the instruction in design, patterns, and colors. His findings were included in *The Training of Men for the Textile Industry*, published by the Advisory Committee of Three in 1934. Brooks had just begun to revamp the Textile School at State College in accordance with the views of the committee, when he retired as president of the college, leaving the task to his successor.[31]

In his efforts to improve the curricula of the five undergraduate schools, Brooks kept clearly in focus the importance of academic standards. In fact, one of the primary considerations underlying the whole reorganization program was the elevation of State College to a position of academic and professional respectability. Brooks never encouraged broadening the curriculum merely for the sake of appearances. That all courses should have a "definite vocational aim" and be taught by qualified instructors were his chief concerns. A large portion of his discussions with the faculty centered upon course contents, teaching load, entrance requirements, library facilities, and other questions affecting academic standards. Under Brooks, students were admitted on the basis of graduation from a standard high school or the completion of fifteen high school units and the passage of a college entrance examination. At his suggestion each school within the college appointed a faculty committee to insure the maintenance of reasonable standards by its students "in scholarship, honesty, and courtesy." Under this system the quality of student scholarship showed marked improvement.[32]

While the scholastic standards of the student body were rising, the resident student enrollment increased rapidly, reaching its peak

31. Edward T. Pickard to E. C. Brooks, Feb. 27, 1933, E. C. Brooks to Stuart Cramer, March 27, 1933, "Purpose of the Textile Survey, 1933," E. C. Brooks to Edward T. Pickard, June 13, 1933, E. C. Brooks to A. M. Dixon, May 5, 1934, Minutes of the Textile Foundation's Advisory Committee, June 16, 1933, E. C. Brooks, Preliminary Report on Textile Education in England and Scotland, 1933, State College Papers; E. C. Brooks to Mrs. E. C. Brooks, Aug. 5, 1933, E. C. Brooks to Mrs. E. C. Brooks, Aug. 16, 1933, Brooks Papers (DUL); Brooks's Notebooks, Brooks Papers (BLS); *News and Observer*, March 29, 1933; *The Training of Men For the Textile Industry* (Washington, 1934).

32. Minutes of the Faculty Council, Nov. 10, 1925, March 24, May 8, July 26, 1926; Report of the Dean of Students, 1926-1927, State College Papers; "Annual Report of the President of the College, 1927-1928," *State College Record*, XXVII (June, 1928), 7-8; Lockmiller, *History of State College*, p. 169.

in 1930 with 1,944 students. Likewise, the teaching staff increased from 109 in 1923 to 265 in 1933. In selecting new faculty members, Brooks consistently emphasized graduate training and doctoral degrees. Closely related to higher academic standards was his work to improve the college's meager library facilities. Brooks personally directed the reorganization of the departmental libraries into one central library housed in the D. H. Hill Library Building, completed in 1926. Largely through his influence in securing the necessary funds, the number of volumes in the college library increased from about 18,000 in 1923 to 31,000 in 1932, not including 42,000 government publications. The improvement in standards and facilities under Brooks resulted in the election of State College to membership in the Southern Association of Colleges and Secondary Schools on December 4, 1928.[33]

Brooks by no means restricted his attention and interest to the five undergraduate divisions of the college. Indeed, one of his favorite projects was the Graduate School, headed by Dean Carl C. Taylor. The faculty of the school was generally drawn from the undergraduate divisions, and its curriculum was designed to provide advanced study in agriculture, engineering, industry, business administration, science, sociology, and education. Brooks envisioned a bright future for the Graduate School and hoped that it would eventually supply "the highly trained teachers and experts" so desperately needed in the South.[34] In 1924 the college had fifteen candidates for graduate degrees and two years later conferred its first Doctor of Philosophy degree. At the same time Brooks requested the trustees to expand the graduate work in agricultural and industrial management, business law, economic and social history, economics, and other courses "that lie at the base of technical training."[35]

33. *News and Observer*, May 28, 1924; "Annual Report of the President of the College, 1924-1925," *State College Record*, XXIV (May, 1925), 2-3; Minutes of the Faculty Council, Sept. 11, 1926, Jan. 4, 1929; Report of the Librarian, March 2, 1926, State College Papers; Lockmiller, *History of State College*, p. 164; memoranda by Mr. B. F. Brown, Oct. 1, 1956, and Mr. W. L. Mayer, Sept. 12, 1956.

34. Brooks, "To the Board of Trustees, Feb. 27, 1924," Brooks Papers (BLS). From its founding until 1923 the college granted 125 graduate degrees. During Brooks's administration it conferred 326 graduate degrees. The largest number of graduate degrees in any single field was in education. See Clyde Cantrell, "Graduate Degrees Awarded and Titles of Theses, 1894-1940," *State College Record*, XL (Aug., 1941), 35-46.

35. "Annual Report of the President of the College, 1925-1926," *State College Record*, XXV (May, 1926), 48.

The bright hopes that Brooks held for the Graduate School in 1924 became eclipsed by grave doubts three years later. The static enrollment must have been disappointing to him, but his main concern was that graduate students "were not always required to measure up to our published standards." He feared that the school was overstepping the bounds of its resources in granting doctoral degrees. Such fears were evidently well founded in view of the meager library facilities and the paucity of advanced training among professors offering graduate instruction. Moreover, the Graduate School suffered from a rift that was growing between Brooks and Dean Taylor. At any rate, Brooks halted the granting of doctoral degrees in 1927 until the standards of the master's degree could be raised.[36]

In the following year he began to seek ways of raising the level of graduate instruction. After conferring with the officials of the Bureau of Education, he decided that the Graduate School should become a school of technology "centering around agriculture, engineering, and textile manufacturing." This plan presumably placed considerably less emphasis upon social studies than did the existing curriculum. The sharp reduction in college funds resulting from the economic depression delayed the reorganization of the Graduate School on "a technological basis." Nevertheless, Brooks managed to raise the requirements for the master's degree and to reduce the undergraduate teaching load of graduate professors. In 1931 Dean Taylor was "dismissed" and a faculty committee headed by Dr. R. F. Poole, professor of plant pathology, was placed in general charge of graduate instruction, although students registered "in the school in which their major work is found" and were "immediately under the direction" of the appropriate dean. This decentralization of the graduate program was precipitated by further decreases in college funds rather than any implementation of Brooks's plans.[37]

36. Minutes of the General Faculty, Sept. 15, 1927; "Annual Report of the President of the College, 1927-1928," *State College Record,* XXVII (June, 1928), 54-55; Report of the Librarian, March 2, 1926, State College Papers.

37. Minutes of the Faculty Council, Dec. 11, 1929, Nov. 10, 1931; Minutes of the Executive Committee of the Trustees, December 19, 1929; "Biennial Report of the President of the College, 1930-1932," *State College Record,* XXXII (Jan., 1933), 18; Minutes of the General Faculty, Jan. 4, 1930; E. C. Brooks, "The Graduate School, June, 1931," State College Papers. Also see below, pp. 248-249.

[4]

A significant factor in the growth of State College between 1923 and 1934 was Brooks's success in dealing with financial problems. One of his first acts as president was the inauguration of a budget system in every department of the college and the creation of a central purchasing office. He also co-ordinated all financial agencies of the college under a business manager, later called comptroller, and persuaded A. S. Brower, his former assistant in the State Superintendent's office, to accept the position. Brooks not only perfected an efficient financial organization within the college, but secured larger appropriations from the legislature. He personally presented the college's needs to the legislators and demonstrated the same political acumen in behalf of the college that had characterized his success as State Superintendent. Largely as a result of his efforts, the annual appropriations for the operating expenses of the college increased from $275,000 in 1922 to $450,025, in 1929, the last year of prosperity. Other sources of income included institutional receipts, large federal funds, and $60,000 per year from the State Department of Agriculture.[38]

Shortly before Brooks assumed office, the legislature of 1923 appropriated $1,350,000 for buildings and permanent improvements at State College, an amount larger than the total building expenses of the Riddick administration. This appropriation, however, was wholly inadequate for the expansion program that Brooks desired. His activities during the next three sessions of the legislature were largely responsible for additional appropriations totaling $1,230,000 by 1930. With these building funds Brooks produced an extraordinary transformation in the physical plant of State College. Several old buildings were renovated and enlarged, walks and drives paved, and campus lights installed. Thirteen new structures included classroom and dormitory buildings, a gymnasium and athletic stadium, and a library. Brooks was interested in each item of the construction

38. Minutes of the General Faculty, June 2, Sept. 26, 1928; *News and Observer,* Oct. 30, 1923, May 28, 1924; E. C. Brooks to A. T. Allen, Nov. 1, 1923, Brooks Papers (DUL); "Appropriations and Expenditures of the University, N. C. State College, and N. C. College for Women, 1917-1933," Governors' Papers (Gardner); *Annual Report of the Auditor of the State of North Carolina, 1923,* pp. 104-105.

program and insisted that the location and design of each building contribute to the beauty of the campus.[39]

The two buildings that attracted his greatest attention were the D. H. Hill Library and the President's home. Securing adequate funds for their construction required all the political skill and convincing arguments at his command. The library building, modeled after Jefferson's Monticello, was completed in 1926, and Brooks selected his former teacher, Edwin Mims, to deliver the dedicatory address. Four years later, the President's home was constructed at a cost of $30,000. Brooks had long insisted that the college president should reside on the campus, rather than receive an annual stipend for renting a house several miles away. He closely followed every detail in the construction of the house, and in 1930 the Brooks family moved into the spacious President's home on the college campus.[40]

As the Great Depression settled upon the state, building funds, indeed all college finances, were sharply curtailed. After 1929 Brooks was preoccupied with the financial problems of the college and the somewhat related question of University consolidation. He was forced to reduce the college's operating expenses and at first attempted to absorb the reductions through economies that would not jeopardize the curriculum and quality of instruction. His first economy measures concerned alumni work, telephone services, and faculty travel expenses. Even the heavily engraved stationery of the president's office gave way to cheaper paper with printed letterheads. Such economies, however, would not cover the increasingly drastic reductions in the college budget. In 1931 Brooks therefore began reducing faculty salaries, and for the next two years he seldom went before the Faculty Council without announcing further cuts in the budget. Between 1929 and 1933 the state appropriations to the col-

39. Lockmiller, *History of State College,* p. 150; "Appropriations and Expenditures of the University, N. C. State College, and N. C. College for Women, 1917-1933," Governors' Papers (Gardner); Report of the Comptroller, 1926-1927, State College Papers; *News and Observer,* July 26, 1925, March 30, 1927, June 17, 1934; *Alumni News,* IX (April-May, 1926), p. 1.

40. Minutes of the General Faculty, March 14, 1925; *News and Observer,* June 8, 1926, Jan. 19, 1927; *The Technician,* Jan. 19, 1927; see Folder marked "Matters Relating to the President's house," State College Papers. After the completion of the President's house, the trustees added the annual allowance of $1,500 for rent to Brooks's salary, which then became $10,000. See *The Budget of the State of North Carolina, 1929-1931,* p. 268.

lege declined by more than 40 per cent. When Comptroller A. S. Brower resigned in 1931 to become State Purchasing Agent, Brooks assumed direct charge of the college's finances. His urgent appeals to the legislature of 1933 produced only a subsistence budget, but he nevertheless managed to steer the institution safely through the darkest period of the depression.[41]

In addition to tedious financial questions, Brooks encountered other difficult and sometimes unpleasant problems during his career at State College. He was always deeply concerned about the reputation of the college and reckoned public opinion as a pertinent factor in the welfare of the institution. Thus he took into account the sentiments expressed by the press and the alumni. The newspapers in the state were usually generous in their treatment of State College. Occasionally, however, they embarrassed Brooks by publishing erroneous accounts of campus activities and by capitalizing on unfortunate incidents within the college. The alumni generally rallied to his defense whenever the need arose and vigorously supported his policies, but a few zealous sports fans among them periodically created disturbances about the athletic program and clashed with the faculty committee on athletics. Their primary concern for a "winning team" irritated Brooks and on one occasion led him to remark: "I will be glad when I can retire and let someone else wrestle with this athletic problem."[42]

Brooks was ever mindful, too, of the reaction of the General Assembly to any question affecting State College. He could scarcely be otherwise in view of its control over the college purse-strings. This factor, coupled with his understanding of legislative psychology, partially accounted for his position in the controversy between the

41. Minutes of the Faculty Council, May 6, 1930, Sept., 1931-Sept., 1933; Minutes of the General Faculty, April 23, 1933; The President's Report, 1931-1932, State College Papers; News and Observer, March 8, 1932, March 18, 1933. In 1933 Brooks sought to interest W. N. Reynolds of Winston-Salem, the tobacco magnate, in establishing a Reynolds Foundation for improving rural life. This multi-million dollar foundation would presumably have aided State College, but the plans never went beyond the preliminary stages. See E. C. Brooks to W. N. Reynolds, March 14, 1933, State College Papers.

42. Interview with Mrs. E. C. Brooks, May 9, 1956; Minutes of the Athletic Committee, Sept. 18, 25, 1923, Carl C. Taylor to E. C. Brooks, Jan. 16, 1924, Minutes of the Faculty Committee on Athletics, March, 1930-Jan., 1932, Minutes of the Special Athletic Committee, Nov. 14, 1930, David Clark to E. C. Brooks, Oct. 13, 1931, State College Papers; Lockmiller, History of State College, pp. 179-183; memorandum by Mr. W. L. Mayer, Sept. 12, 1956.

so-called fundamentalists and modernists concerning Darwin's theory of biological evolution. The controversy reached its apogee in North Carolina in 1925 and 1927, when the fundamentalists carried their fight to the floor of the legislature. In 1925 Representative D. Scott Poole, proclaiming that "the Lord Jesus is on trial," introduced a bill to bar the teaching of evolution in public schools. The opposition to the bill, led by President Harry Chase of the University and President William Louis Poteat of Wake Forest College, resulted in its defeat by a vote of 67 to 46. Nevertheless, the fundamentalists reorganized their forces, refilled their coffers, and prepared for a showdown in the Legislature of 1927. In that year Poole again introduced an anti-evolution bill that died in the committee.[43]

Brooks did not join Chase and Poteat in their fight in the General Assembly of 1925, but B. W. Wells and Z. P. Metcalf, two professors of science, represented State College and voiced strong objections to the Poole Bill. At the time Brooks was seeking a large appropriation from the legislature and fighting charges that he was building a "liberal arts college." He probably considered it unwise to antagonize certain legislators by openly casting his lot with Chase and Poteat. His first lengthy statement on the evolution controversy appeared in June, 1925, in an address entitled "The Need of Cooperation between Teachers and Ministers," clearly a plea for moderation. Brooks stoutly defended academic freedom and denounced attempts by "jealous denominationalists" to apply "religious tests to those whose orthodoxy may be questioned." But he insisted that even academic freedom had "its metes and bounds and does not presuppose that a college teacher has license to propagate any noxious doctrines that may dribble from the vagaries of an unwholesome mind." For him the "simple faith of our devout people" still contained a valuable truth that warranted respect. He maintained his position in the face of various demands by the so-called Committee of One Hundred, a fundamentalist group predominantly Presbyterian in membership. In a discussion with the Faculty Council in February, 1927, he accurately predicted that the

43. Edgar Knight, "Monkey or Mud in North Carolina," *The Independent,* CXVIII (May 14, 1927), 515-516, 523; *The Technician,* Feb. 13, 1925; Norman Furniss, *The Fundamentalist Controversy, 1918-1931* (New Haven, 1954), pp. 84-86.

second Poole Bill would die in the committee, but "urged that
unless it became absolutely necessary State College should not be
drawn into a discussion on the bill."[44]

By 1929 the evolution controversy had faded from the legislative
arena only to be replaced by a discussion of more immediate concern to Brooks. The outburst was touched off by the so-called
"Apple Orchard Affair," in which a State College student, while
stealing apples from the horticultural department's orchard, was
shot and seriously wounded by a Negro watchman on October 3,
1928. Brooks publicly deplored the shooting and immediately undertook a thorough investigation to determine the persons responsible
for supplying the watchman with live ammunition. The incident
precipitated an emergency meeting of the trustees, a widely publicized court trial, and the dismissal of the superintendent of the
horticultural grounds. The clamor had barely subsided when Senator W. M. Persons provoked a discussion of the affair in the legislature in February, 1929. In concluding his tirade against Brooks and
his "political activities," the Senator shouted: "I understand it [the
college] even keeps a nigger to shoot boys for taking an apple or
watermelon." Person's colleagues, however, squelched his attempt
to inaugurate a full-scale investigation of State College by a legislative commitee.[45]

The most severe criticism leveled against Brooks during his
career at the college was precipitated by the "dismissal" of Dr. Carl
C. Taylor, Dean of the Graduate School and an outstanding sociologist. The two men worked together closely during the first two
years of Brooks's administration, and each respected the abilities
of the other, but for various reasons they began to drift apart after
1925. Finally, Brooks recommended the abolition of Taylor's posi-

44. *The Technician*, Feb. 13, 1925; Minutes of the General Faculty, March 4, 14,
1925; E. C. Brooks, "The Need of Cooperation between Teachers and Ministers, June,
1925," Brooks Papers (BLS); *News and Observer*, April 2, 1926; "Annual Report of
the President of the College, 1925-1926," *State College Record*, XXV (May, 1926), 11-
13; W. P. Few to E. C. Brooks, March 29, 1926, E. C. Brooks to W. P. Few, April 1,
1926, Few Papers; R. A. McLeon to E. C. Brooks, Feb. 5, 1926, State College Papers;
Minutes of the Faculty Council, Feb. 1, 1927.

45. Minutes of the Called Meeting of the Executive Committee of the Trustees,
Oct. 6, 1928; Clarence Poe to Members of the Board of Trustees, Oct. 10, 1928, E. L.
Cloyd to E. C. Brooks, Oct. ?, 1928, E. C. Brooks to L. S. Brassfield, Nov. 27, 1928, J.
W. Bailey to E. C. Brooks, Jan. 30, 1929, D. G. Brummitt to E. C. Brooks, Jan. 30,
1929, State College Papers; *News and Observer*, Oct. 4, 5, 6, 7, 13, 21, 28, 1928, Feb. 9,
12, 1929.

tion as Dean of the Graduate School in June, 1931. He characterized this recommendation as an economy measure and placed it upon an impersonal level by requesting the abolition of an office rather than the firing of an individual. He also argued that Taylor as a sociologist could not give the proper direction to the reorganization of the Graduate School on a technological basis. The approval of his recommendation by the trustees unleashed a storm of bitter criticism of Brooks and provoked an unfortunate public discussion of the affair. Finally, the American Association of University Professors initiated an investigation of the episode to determine whether academic freedom and tenure had been violated. After a thorough inquiry, the investigators largely rejected Taylor's liberal views, the suggestions of a power struggle between Brooks and Taylor, and the need for economy as significant factors in the case. They concluded that "the fundamental reason for the action seemed to be the tension that had developed between able men differing widely in aims and temperament."[46]

Amid his many duties as a college president Brooks managed to satisfy his taste for writing by completing his seventh and final major work. *Our Dual Government: Studies in Americanism for Young People* was published in 1924. The initial stimulus for such a book was the passage of a legislative act in 1923 requiring instruction in Americanism in all North Carolina public schools. The act was largely the handiwork of the American Legion, then busily engaged in patriotic activities. When the measure was passed, Brooks as State Superintendent was keenly interested in securing the adoption of the "proper" book for the Americanism courses, but he could hardly afford to present his own work. With his transfer to State College in June, 1923, he at once began preparation of a volume that would incorporate a broad view of Americanism and

46. Thompson, "The Dismissal of Dean Carl C. Taylor," *AAUP Bulletin*, XVIII (March, 1933), 224-232; interviews with Dr. Carl C. Taylor, Feb. 19, 1957, Mrs. E. C. Brooks, May 9, 1956, Mr. Clarence Poe, July 6, 1956, Mr. E. C. Brooks, Jr., July 12, 1956, Dean E. L. Cloyd, July 6, 1956; memoranda by Mr. B. F. Brown, Oct. 1, 1956, and Mr. W. L. Mayer, Sept. 12, 1956; *Southern Textile Bulletin* (Dec. 11, 1930); John Lawrence to E. C. Brooks, March 3, 1925, R. Murphy Williams to E. C. Brooks, Aug. 5, 1926, Brooks, "The Graduate School, 1931," E. C. Brooks to H. W. Tyler, June 16, 1931, State College Papers; *News and Observer*, June 9, 12, 16, 1931; *Greensboro Daily News*, June 10, 1931; *Durham Morning Herald*, June 11, 1931; Virginius Dabney, *Liberalism in the South* (Chapel Hill, 1932), pp. 343-344; Cash, *Mind of the South*, p. 326.

at the same time satisfy the requirements of the law. A year later, the State Board of Education adopted as a public school textbook *Our Dual Government,* which was also approved by the American Legion.[47]

During his eleven years at State College Brooks found time for numerous activities beyond the pale of college administration. He devoted much time and energy to the county government commissions and the North Carolina Park Commission. He served as chairman of the Public School Equalizing Fund Commission, vice-president of the State Literary and Historical Association, and president of the North Carolina College Conference. He was also a director of the North Carolina State Fair and worked closely with Governor McLean in reorganizing the fair under state control. In 1925 Brooks was among eight prominent educators appointed to the Commission on the Length of Elementary Education, sponsored by the Commonwealth Fund and headed by Charles H. Judd of the University of Chicago. For two years Brooks gave generously of his time to the investigations of the commission, and many of his suggestions were incorporated in its published report. Throughout his career at State College he played an active role in the affairs of the Association of Land Grant Colleges and Universities.[48]

Governors McLean and Gardner frequently called upon Brooks for advice on various economic and social questions. During the 1920's he studied the agricultural depression and offered numerous suggestions for improving the farmers' plight. The major points in his farm program were: diversification of crops, co-operative purchasing and marketing organizations, sound farm management, and county-wide systems of practical agricultural education for adults as well as youths. From 1929 to 1933 Brooks stumped the

47. *Public School Law, Codification of 1923,* p. 120; A. L. and Mae Fletcher, *History of the American Legion and American Legion Auxiliary, Department of North Carolina, 1919-1929* (Raleigh, 1930), pp. 269-270; *News and Observer,* June 24, Oct. 4, 1924; A. T. Allen to E. C. Brooks, June 16, 1924, Brooks Papers (DUL); E. C. Brooks, *Our Dual Government: Studies in Americanism for Young People* (Chicago, 1924).

48. *News and Observer,* April 7, May 5, 1925, Aug. 9, Sept. 13, 1927, March 13, Oct. 21, 1928, Oct. 31, 1929; *The Papers of Walter Clark,* ed. Aubrey L. Brooks and Hugh Lefler (Chapel Hill, 1950), II, 472-473; Charles Judd to E. C. Brooks, July 24, 1925, E. C. Brooks to Charles Judd, July 27, 1925, E. C. Brooks to Charles Judd, Feb. 17, 1927, Report of the Commission on the Length of Elementary Education, Brooks Papers (DUL); *Report of the Commission on the Length of Elementary Education* (Chicago, 1927); A. W. McLean to R. L. McMillan, Oct. 21, 1927, Governors' Papers (McLean).

state in behalf of Governor Gardner's Live-At-Home campaign and threw the full support of State College behind this movement to alleviate the acute economic distress of North Carolina farmers. He also headed the Governor's Agricultural Advisory Committee, accompanied Gardner to several important meetings with federal officials, and served on the Committee of Five Hundred of the Southeastern Economic Council. In 1931-1932 he was president of the Association of Southern Agricultural Workers. His presidential address, entitled "How Shall Agriculture Survive the Depression?," won wide acclaim and was published in several national farm journals.[49]

As early as 1928 Brooks began to feel the physical strain of his intensely active life. In January, 1928, he suffered "attacks of dizziness" caused by hypotension and underwent a rest cure at a sanitarium in Battle Creek, Michigan. But no sooner had he returned to North Carolina than he again plunged into several activities with his characteristic vigor. As a result his former ailment returned with complications. In 1931 he suffered further attacks of vertigo and was forced to spend several days in Duke Hospital. His examination there showed "marked" signs of arteriosclerosis in addition to hypotension and an "improved" diabetic condition. For the next two years Brooks obviously did not get the amount of rest prescribed by his physicians, and even though he may have slowed down his pace, the cares and responsibilities of his office increased.[50]

The need for rest and diversion was the principal reason for a trip to Europe in 1928. Brooks accepted an invitation from the Agricultural Foundation of the International Potash Syndicate to join a group of American educators and agricultural specialists

49. A. W. McLean to E. C. Brooks, Oct. 7, 1926, E. C. Brooks to A. W. McLean, Oct. 11, 1926, E. C. Brooks to A. W. McLean, Oct. 28, 1926, E. C. Brooks to A. W. McLean, Dec. 3, 1926, A. W. McLean to E. C. Brooks, Feb. 8, 1928, O. Max Gardner to E. C. Brooks, April 4, 1930, Hugh McRae to E. C. Brooks, Jan. 15, 1932, Brooks Papers (DUL); *Public Papers and Letters of Governor Gardner*, pp. 505-506; O. Max Gardner to E. C. Brooks, Dec. 18, 1930; Minutes of the Agricultural Advisory Committee, Jan. 28, 1929, State College Papers; E. C. Brooks, "How To Make Permanent What Is Begun under the Gardner Regime," Brooks Papers (BLS); *News and Observer*, June 22, 1927, Sept. 22, Oct. 1, 1929, Dec. 18, 1930, Feb. 3, 1932; *The National Grange Monthly* (Nov., 1932), p. 4; *Proceedings of the Annual Convention of the Association of Southern Agricultural Workers, 1932*, pp. 3-6.

50. Medical Record of Dr. E. C. Brooks, Hist. No. 5162, 5/11/31, Duke Hospital; *The Technician*, Jan. 21, 1928; E. C. Brooks to Charles Gold, March 7, 1928, Brooks Papers (DUL).

in a tour of several European countries. Although he did find time for bridge games and relaxation aboard ship, the journey could otherwise have scarcely contributed much to the restoration of his health. He became the spokesman for the group and delivered addresses at various points in France, Germany, Holland, and England. The group concentrated its attention upon model farms and agricultural research centers. Brooks was particularly impressed by the scientific agriculture practiced in Germany, and the German agricultural schools furnished him ideas that he intended to utilize at State College. In fact, the whole tour, including the Folies Bergère, proved to be thoroughly "enlightening" to him.[51]

Brooks made his second trip abroad in the summer of 1930 at the invitation of the government of Chile. The occasion was the centennial celebration of the opening of the Chilean nitrate mines. The invitation was extended to twenty-two outstanding Americans, whose visit would strengthen "the friendship between the United States and Chile through a better understanding of their industries, educational methods, and national policies." The tour included brief visits in Cuba, Panama, and Peru before reaching the final destination. In Chile Brooks manifested especial interest in the social welfare and agricultural programs of President Ibáñez as well as in the nitrate mines. He again acted as spokesman for his party and responded to numerous toasts and addresses of welcome. On July 17, 1930, the University of Chile elected him an honorary member of the faculty. The following day at the Catholic University of Santiago Brooks delivered a formal address on "Educating an Agricultural Class," which was printed as a pamphlet and distributed among the students. The Catholic University conferred upon him a doctor's degree *honoris causa*. After his departure, the United States ambassador to Chile, W. S. Culbertson, wrote him: "I assure you that your visit to Chile contributed very materially to the extension of good will between the two peoples. I only wish that all missions might be as successful as yours."[52]

51. *News and Observer*, Aug. 27, 1928; E. C. Brooks to Mrs. Brooks, July 8, 1928, E. C. Brooks to Mrs. Brooks, July 12, 1928, E. C. Brooks to Mrs. Brooks, July 14, 1928, E. C. Brooks to Mrs. Brooks, July 21, 1928, E. C. Brooks to Mrs. Brooks, July 31, 1928, E. C. Brooks to Mrs. Brooks, Aug. 4, 1928, Brooks Papers (DUL).
52. *News and Observer*, June 2, Aug. 24, 1930; E. C. Brooks to Mrs. Brooks, July 10, 1930, E. C. Brooks to Mrs. Brooks, July 15, 1930, E. C. Brooks to Mrs. Brooks, July 21, 1930, E. C. Brooks to Mrs. Brooks, July 22, 1930, E. C. Brooks to Mrs. Brooks, July 23,

As president of State College Brooks went about his work with the same enthusiasm, energy, and tenacity of purpose that characterized his previous career. Only the crippling effect of ill health forced a slight change of pace in 1931. By that date Brooks had already accomplished his major tasks at State College. He had brought the institution into intimate relationship with the economic and social life of the state. The "art of living well at home" became in reality a guide for every aspect of the college program, whether it concerned experiment station research or courses in sociology. In eleven years at State College Brooks broadened the curriculum, produced an efficient administrative organization, raised academic standards, and transformed the physical plant almost beyond recognition. In fact, he lifted the college from what some called a trade-school status to a technological and professional institution of recognized standing.

His outstanding achievements aroused interest and admiration in educational quarters outside North Carolina and brought attractive offers to employ his talents elsewhere. The only offer that Brooks seriously considered was an invitation to become Commissioner of Education in New Jersey in 1925. During the next three years he declined the presidencies of Louisiana State University, Oklahoma Agricultural and Mechanical College, and Alabama Polytechnic Institute. His "unfinished task" at State College was the principal reason that he gave for rejecting these offers. But just as Brooks was completing this task, the legislature in 1931 passed an act merging State College, the University, and North Carolina College for Women into the Greater University of North Carolina.[53]

1930, W. S. Culbertson to E. C. Brooks, Sept. 10, 1930, Brooks Papers (DUL); E. C. Brooks, "Some Impressions of South America and the State College Men I Met," *N. C. State Alumni News,* III (Sept., 1930), 9-10, 22.

53. F. M. P. Pearse to E. C. Brooks, May 25, 1925, E. C. Brooks to F. M. P. Pearse, May 28, 1925, F. M. P. Pearse to E. C. Brooks, June 30, 1925, F. M. P. Pearse to E. C. Brooks, July 8, 1925, R. O. Young to E. C. Brooks, July 2, 1926, E. C. Brooks to R. O. Young, July 8, 1926, E. C. Brooks to R. O. Young, July 23, 1926, W. A. Milton to E. C. Brooks, May 5, 1928, Fred Dummond to E. C. Brooks, May 14, 1928, E. C. Brooks to Fred Dummond, May 22, 1928, H. V. Hanson to E. C. Brooks, Feb. 9, 1928, E. C. Brooks to H. V. Hanson, March 2, 1928, Brooks Papers (DUL).

Ten: UNIVERSITY CONSOLIDATION
AND RETIREMENT, *1931-1947*

[1]

The idea of a consolidated University of North Carolina embracing the state-supported colleges at Chapel Hill, Raleigh, and
Greensboro was by no means new in 1931. In fact, it had been advocated by various individuals for more than fifteen years. One of the
most persistent champions of a consolidated university was Josephus Daniels, who as a member of the Watauga Club was a founder
of State College. In an address to the legislature in 1919, Daniels,
then Secretary of the Navy, pleaded for a state university that
would include the University at Chapel Hill, North Carolina College for Women, State College, and the teachers' colleges at Boone
and Greenville. His plan called for "one institution, one board of
trustees, and one president" for the purpose of eliminating "duplication of effort" among the various state-supported institutions of
higher learning.[1]

In 1922 Governor Cameron Morrison espoused a similar proposal that excluded the teachers' colleges. President Harry Chase of
the University vehemently opposed the project and assured the
Governor that "any joint board of control" for the three institutions
would "be very dangerous in practice." Chase added that he was
aware of the "matter of duplication," but that it was "practically
confined to the work in engineering." In view of this opposition
Morrison apparently decided to drop his own plans for a consolidated university.[2]

1. E. S. Millsaps to O. Max Gardner, Dec. 27, 1930, Governors' Papers (Gardner);
N. C. State Alumni News, III (Jan., 1931), 101; *News and Observer*, Feb. 14, 1919.
2. Harry W. Chase to Cameron Morrison, March 27, 1922, Governors' Papers
(Morrison).

At the time of the Morrison proposal, Brooks as State Superintendent was a member of the board of trustees of the University, but there is no evidence that he entered the discussion on university consolidation. When he became president of State College, the question of duplicate curricula in the three state institutions was still provoking criticism in certain quarters. In June, 1923, he confidentially expressed a desire to discuss the whole problem with Chase and Julius I. Foust, president of North Carolina College for Women, but apparently the three men never held the discussion. In the meantime, Brooks reorganized State College, placing strong emphasis upon the new School of Science and Business that not only provided basic "cultural" subjects, but offered work in business administration and the social sciences leading to the bachelor's degree. In the General Assembly of 1925, certain legislators charged that Brooks was attempting to "build a liberal arts college" to compete with the University. They talked about a consolidated university in order to erase duplications, but no such bill was introduced in the legislature. On January 21, 1925, however, a joint committee from the University and State College, including Brooks, Chase, Clarence Poe, and Judge N. A. Townsend, had presented a report of its investigation of curricular duplications in the two institutions. In short, the committee found "no real duplication resulting in an unnecessary expense." Not even the two engineering schools in Raleigh and Chapel Hill formed unnecessary duplication. With such assurances Brooks continued to strengthen his School of Science and Business, and in 1927 organized a School of Education that was opened to women students.[3]

In that year O. Max Gardner, an alumnus of both State College and the University, who had been a trustee of the former institution since 1907, began to express apprehension about Brooks's educational program. He feared that State College was straying too far from its original purposes, especially in the School of Science and Business. He also felt that Brooks's expansion of courses in liberal arts and education had placed State College in a competitive race

3. E. C. Brooks to Harry Chase, June 19, 1923, Brooks Papers (DUL); Minutes of the Faculty Council, March 4, 14, 1925; David Lockmiller, *The Consolidation of the University of North Carolina* (Chapel Hill, 1942), pp. 9, 12; Report of the Joint Committee on Duplication, Jan. 21, 1925, State College Papers.

with the University. On several occasions he voiced grave concern about this problem to the college trustees.[4]

Gardner became Governor of North Carolina in 1929, and in the following year he was forced to consider drastic measures to meet the crisis precipitated by the Great Depression. Thus, he prepared a legislative program whose outstanding features included economy and "centralization of power." He employed the Brookings Institution to conduct a survey of state government and to recommend changes to "promote increased efficiency and economy." The report of the survey group, presented to Gardner on December 15, 1930, strongly suggested a merging of the University, North Carolina College for Women, and State College "into one large University of North Carolina." The report's indirect references to unnecessary duplications in the curricula of the schools apparently confirmed the Governor's worst fears.[5]

In any case, Gardner began to consider seriously the question of a consolidated university that would eliminate this duplication and produce economy in the long run. He discussed the project with Foust and Frank Graham, who succeeded Chase as president of the University in 1930. Foust was at first cool to the proposal and frankly told Gardner that the Brookings Institution had overlooked "the fact that they are dealing with people and not material things." Aware that "the spirit of the age is along the line of mergers," he still insisted that Gardner could "accomplish everything" that he desired simply by requesting the heads of the three schools to co-operate in eliminating unnecessary and costly duplications in their curricula. Within two months, however, Foust had completely reversed his position, probably because he realized that North Carolina College for Women would not be as seriously affected by the merger as the other two institutions. Moreover, he apparently considered himself the logical choice for the presidency of the consolidated university. Frank Graham supported Gardner's consolidation project only after assurances that general education would

4. Lockmiller, *Consolidation of the University*, p. 12; Minutes of the Trustees, June 6, 1927; E. C. Brooks to B. F. Brown, June 27, 1929, State College Papers; memorandum by Mr. W. L. Mayer, Sept. 12, 1956.

5. *Papers and Letters of Governor Gardner*, pp. xxvii, xxxv-xxxvi; *Report on a Survey of the Organization and Administration of the State Government of North Carolina*, pp. vii, 171-173.

remain in all three institutions for the freshman and sophomore years; that duplicate curricula (not courses) in upper classes and professional and graduate schools would be eliminated; and that economy would mean "economy in the highest sense"—that money saved by erasing duplication would be spent to raise the standards of all three schools. Apparently, Brooks alone among the presidents of the three institutions was not consulted by the Governor about consolidation.[6]

On December 24, 1930, Gardner publicly announced his intention to recommend the establishment of a consolidated university in the forthcoming session of the General Assembly. The Consolidation Bill was drafted by his special legal counsel, Judge N. A. Townsend, who had served on the joint committee on duplication in 1925. Brooks was "never consulted about the merger bill until after it was drawn," although Foust and Graham apparently assisted in its preparation in advisory capacities. The measure was presented to the legislature on February 13, 1931, in a special message from the Governor. The outstanding features of the bill included: changing the name of North Carolina State College of Agriculture and Engineering to North Carolina State College of the University of North Carolina; the creation of one board of trustees for the consolidated university, consisting of one hundred members chosen by the legislature; the appointment by the governor of a commission on university consolidation that would select experts to study the three institutions and recommend changes in organization and curricula; and the approval of the commission's recommendations by the consolidated board of trustees. The economy supposedly envisioned by the Consolidation Bill was undoubtedly the most attractive feature for a large portion, if not a majority, of the legislators in 1931. Certainly, Gardner and his cohorts employed shrewd strategy in securing the passage of the act.[7]

6. J. I. Foust to O. Max Gardner, Dec. 23, 1930, J. I. Foust to O. Max Gardner, Feb. 4, 1931, J. I. Foust to O. Max Gardner, Sept. 27, 1932, Governors' Papers (Gardner); Lockmiller, *Consolidation of the University*, p. 29; *Durham Morning Herald*, March 4, 1931; interview with Dr. Frank Graham, Dec. 21, 1956. Foust reversed his position on consolidation again in 1932 about the time it became known that Graham would be chosen the president of the consolidated university.

7. *News and Observer*, Dec. 25, 1930, Feb. 14, 1931; Lockmiller, *Consolidation of the University*, pp. 20-34; E. C. Brooks to David Clark, August 29, 1932, Proposed Bill to be Entitled An Act to Consolidate the University of North Carolina, North Carolina State College of Agriculture and Engineering, and North Carolina College for Women, State College Papers.

Meanwhile, Brooks had voiced strong objections to certain features of the Townsend measure. In fact, he would have been happier had the Consolidation Bill never been drafted at all. In the Gardner-Townsend plan, however, he saw passages that made him anxious about the future of State College. He fought every move to change the name of the institution and finally managed to retain "Agriculture and Engineering" as a part of its title—a significant accomplishment in view of the subsequent controversy over the location of the engineering school in the consolidated university. Brooks was unsuccessful in securing changes in other sections of the bill in accordance with his own ideas. For example, he wanted to maintain three separate boards of trustees and establish a correlating body to represent all three schools. He also insisted in vain that the recommendations of the consolidation commission be approved by each board of trustees rather than the consolidated board. The basic consideration underlying these proposals was his realization that the University alumni through their control of the legislature would dominate the consolidated board of trustees. Furthermore, Brooks was convinced that economy in terms of dollars and cents would not be achieved by merging the three colleges. Despite his opposition, the Consolidation Bill was enacted into law on March 27, 1931, with E. C. Brooks, Jr., of Durham casting the only negative vote in the House of Representatives, a vote that undoubtedly reflected his father's attitude.[8]

After the passage of the law, Brooks decided to make the best of what he considered an unfortunate situation, but the students, alumni, and certain trustees of State College refused to follow his example. They generally looked upon consolidation as a nefarious plot by a "few" University alumni to strengthen their own *alma mater* at the expense of State College. They flatly denied that any economy would result from the measure and insisted that the elimination of duplicate curricula could be more easily achieved without

8. Brooks, "Amendments Memo—Consolidation Bill," State College Papers; *Durham Morning Herald*, March 4, 1931; *News and Observer*, March 4, 1931; Clarence Poe to O. Max Gardner, Feb. 23, 1931, Governors' Papers (Gardner); interviews with Mr. E. C. Brooks, Jr., July 12, 1956, and Mr. A. S. Brower, Oct. 2, 1956. Both at the time and later many individuals questioned the validity of the economy argument used to support consolidation. Lefler and Newsome (*North Carolina*, p. 555) wrote that university consolidation was "*ostensibly* to save money and prevent overlapping educational functions" (italics mine).

consolidation. The Mecklenburg Chapter of the State College alumni, led by David Clark and Malcomb Hunter, went on record as "unanimously and unalterably opposed to consolidation," a position that was undoubtedly shared by a majority of their fellow alumni. The *Alumni News* claimed that the legislators had been "caught flat-footed" by the report of the Brookings Institution and concluded: "O Economy, Economy, we hope no sins will be committed in thy name." The campus newspaper, *The Technician,* criticized Brooks for his failure to speak out vehemently against consolidation, which it considered a move "by the University to keep from being outstripped" by Duke University. At their annual meeting in June, 1931, the State College alumni voiced strong protests against the merger and quietly planned their strategy for securing the repeal of the act by the next legislature. Several prominent alumni believed that if State College traded its School of Science and Business and Graduate School for the engineering school at Chapel Hill, the legislators would see that the major duplications had been removed and would therefore repeal the Consolidation Act. Although their strategy failed, these alumni at least realized that the location of the engineering school in the consolidated university would pose a difficult problem.[9]

Despite his opposition to consolidation, Brooks neither led a movement against it nor lent himself to the various resistance groups formed by the alumni. He was extremely cautious in both his public and private statements about the matter. He was so discreet, in fact, that his close associates at State College sometimes disagreed about his attitude toward consolidation. One believed that he remained "absolutely neutral," while another declared: "My impression was that Dr. Brooks did not like the idea of consolidation, but I never heard him say so." Brooks felt that a strong negative attitude would only further jeopardize State College. He was convinced that the Consolidation Act would not be repealed, and feared that continued outbursts by alumni and certain trustees would cripple his efforts to maintain the integrity of State College and prevent the emasculation of its curriculum. Thus, by tempering

9. Watson Powell to O. Max Gardner, Feb. 27, 1931, Governors' Papers (Gardner); *N. C. State Alumni News,* III, (April, 1931), 150; *The Technician,* March 13, 1931; *News and Observer,* June 9, 1931; J. W. Harrelson to S. B. Alexander, June 23, 1931, State College Papers.

their bitterness he sought to remove what he considered a major obstacle to the welfare of the college during the process of consolidation.[10]

On July 16, 1931, the Commission on University Consolidation held its first meeting in the Governor's office. The commission consisted of thirteen members, with Governor Gardner as chairman and Fred Morrison as secretary. Brooks, Riddick, and S. B. Alexander represented State College, while Foust, Graham, and four of their colleagues represented North Carolina College for Women and the University. Under the law the commission was to present a plan for the executive control and co-ordinated educational program of the consolidated university to the board of trustees by July 1, 1932. This plan was to be based on the findings of a survey of the three institutions by prominent educational experts. The commission was to have $12,900 to finance the survey. Brooks was appointed to a subcommittee of four to select these experts. Dr. Fred J. Kelly, specialist in higher education in the Office of Education, consented to aid the commission in an advisory capacity. Dr. George Works of the University of Chicago was chosen director of the survey, and he in turn selected Dr. Frank McVey of the University of Kentucky and Dr. Guy Stanton Ford of the University of Minnesota as his associates. In addition, a host of experts investigated various phases of the curricula of the three institutions. From October, 1931, to May, 1932, Brooks spent considerable time in conference with these specialists and in other work relating to the affairs of the consolidation commission.[11]

In May, 1932, the survey team distributed its findings to the members of the commission. The most sweeping recommendation in this report was the proposal to transfer State College to Chapel Hill or reduce it to a junior college offering only general education. Other sections of the report suggested: one chief executive of the

10. Interviews with Dr. Frank Graham, Dec. 21, 1956, Mr. E. C. Brooks, Jr., July 12, 1956, and Mr. A. S. Brower, Oct. 2, 1956; memoranda by Mr. W. L. Mayer, Sept. 12, 1956, and Mr. B. F. Brown, Oct. 1, 1956.
11. Minutes of the Commission on University Consolidation, July 16, 1931, Fred Morrison to E. C. Brooks, July 22, 1931, George Works to E. C. Brooks, Jan. 2, 1932, J. I. Foust to E. C. Brooks, Jan. 22, 1932, State College Papers; Minutes of the Faculty Council, Oct. 12, 1931; Lockmiller, *Consolidation of the University*, pp. 40-43. The other members of the Commission on University Consolidation were Louis R. Wilson, N. A. Townsend, B. B. Kendrick, F. L. Jackson, Mrs. E. L. McKee, and Miss Easdale Shaw.

consolidated university with an administrative head in each of three units; one comptroller, one director of extension, one director of graduate work, and one director of summer school for the consolidated university; and the dissolution of the School of Science and Business at State College. The report also strongly favored centering all engineering education at Chapel Hill. Finally, the survey group declared that it had "not been able to point to any large financial economies that could be affected immediately," but consolidation would "make for increased efficiency in the state's program of higher education."[12]

Brooks was "greatly disturbed" by the report, which confirmed all his anxieties for the future of State College. The structure that he had so painstakingly built during the previous decade seemed to be crumbling all about him. The proposed dissolution of the School of Science and Business was especially distasteful to him. He believed, however, that any suggestion to move State College to Chapel Hill was not only ridiculous, but impossible under the law. In fact, he disliked all the major recommendations of the survey team and hoped that the whole report would be shelved. Governor Gardner also had misgivings about portions of the report, and needless to say, the State College alumni and trustees were near open rebellion. Brooks persuaded Gardner to speak to the General Alumni Association early in June, 1932, regarding consolidation. The Governor opened his address by declaring: "Despite reports to the contrary, State College will always remain North Carolina State College of Agriculture and Engineering, and will always be located at Raleigh if I have any influence left, and. . . ." At this point a storm of applause drowned out his words and, according to one observer, "he need not have said another word." Brooks then assured the alumni that several of the more drastic recommendations of the survey group were illegal under the Consolidation Act. These statements by Brooks and Gardner temporarily relieved the fears of the alumni.[13]

12. *Report of the Commission on University Consolidation* (Raleigh, 1932), pp. 6-7, 11-90. Cf. Report to the North Carolina Commission on University Consolidation, State College Papers.

13. The President's Report, 1931-1932, E. C. Brooks to J. I. Foust, May 30, 1932, E. C. Brooks to Mark Squires, May 23, 1932, O. Max Gardner to E. C. Brooks, May 24, 1932, State College Papers; E. C. Brooks to O. Max Gardner, April 25, 1932, Governors' Papers (Gardner); *N. C. State Alumni News*, IV (June, 1932), 131-132.

Several days later, on June 13-14, 1932, the full Commission on University Consolidation considered the report presented by Dr. Works and his assistants. The proposal to transfer State College to Chapel Hill was promptly rejected. The commission delayed action on the location of the engineering school, but approved almost all other recommendations of the survey team. Brooks and Foust argued that the executive control of the consolidated university should be placed in the hands of the presidents of the three institutions; but despite their protests, the commission voted for a single executive to be selected by the consolidated board of trustees. The recommendations of the commission were filed with the new board of trustees on June 30, 1932, and accepted with few changes. Brooks, Foust, and Graham formed a Presidential Directorate that performed the executive functions of the consolidated university until the trustees selected a president.[14]

The recommendations of the Commission on University Consolidation renewed all the fears of the State College alumni. A majority of them apparently believed that although their *alma mater* would remain in Raleigh, the most attractive and popular features of its curricula would be gradually "absorbed" by the Chapel Hill unit. By this time some of the University alumni had also become skeptical of the consolidation program, and for a while it seemed that they would join forces with the State College alumni. Although this possibility soon faded, the State College alumni, led by the so-called "Charlotte group," decided to make a "showdown" fight, which proved to be almost wholly ineffective except to arouse the ire of the Governor. Gardner deplored their efforts "to create the impression that there is some monstrous force . . . trying to crush State College" and plainly stated that the college had "never occupied in the legislative mind the same degree of power or prestige or position as has the University." But through consolidation, he concluded, the Chapel Hill unit would "no longer have any advantage in the legislative program."[15]

14. Minutes of the Commission on University Consolidation, June 13-14, 1932, State College Papers. Among the changes made by the trustees was the substitution of "president" for "chancellor" as the title of the chief executive of the consolidated university. *News and Observer*, July 12, 1932.

15. *News and Observer*, July 8, 1932; S. B. Alexander to O. Max Gardner, Aug. 2, 1932, O. Max Gardner to S. B. Alexander, Aug. 3, 1932, Governors' Papers (Gardner); David Clark to E. C. Brooks, July 26, 1932, J. L. Becton to E. C. Brooks, July 2, 1932,

On July 22, 1932, Brooks issued his first public statement on consolidation since the passage of the act in the previous year. In an address to the summer school students, he insisted that State College would be "the technological branch of the Consolidated University" located in Raleigh. According to him, the policy of the consolidated board of trustees was "to develop three coordinate institutions under one administration for the purpose of eliminating needless duplication and promoting educational advantages more economically." Brooks considered this statement necessary "on account of the faculty and alumni" who looked to him to guide State College "safely" through consolidation. He consistently maintained that according to the law there should be "three coordinate institutions" on equal footing and sought to impress this idea upon a board of trustees containing approximately sixty University alumni. He urged the board to adopt a policy that would maintain the integrity of each institution or, in any case, to establish a "definite policy to guide the administration of the new university."[16]

In spite of his reassuring statements, Brooks was far from happy. He was accustomed to long-term planning, but the uncertainties of consolidation forced him to work on a day-to-day basis. The fluctuating state of affairs caused him no little worry and placed an additional strain upon his weakened physical constitution.[17]

On November 14, 1932, the board of trustees took a major step toward stabilizing the consolidation program by establishing the executive control of the university. Frank Graham was elevated to the presidency of the consolidated university against his wishes, while Brooks and Foust became vice-presidents in charge of the Raleigh and Greensboro units. In his association with Graham in the Presidential Directorate, Brooks had come to appreciate his "ability and sense of fairness." The relationship between the two men was "always cordial," and they worked together harmoniously for the

Kemp P. Lewis to S. B. Alexander, June 22, 1932, Kemp P. Lewis to E. C. Brooks, July 5, 1932, State College Papers; Malcomb Hunter, *Facts about the Consolidation of the University of North Carolina, N. C. State College, and N. C. College for Women; The Technician,* Oct. 28, 1932.

16. E. C. Brooks, "The Effect of Consolidation on North Carolina State College, July 22, 1932," E. C. Brooks to J. I. Foust, July 21, 1932, E. C. Brooks, "The Need of Defining a Policy to Guide the Administration of the New University, Sept. 28, 1932," State College Papers.

17. Interviews with Mrs. E. C. Brooks, June 19, 1956, and Mr. E. C. Brooks, Jr., July 12, 1956.

next two years. They co-operated fully in initiating a study of State
College by several faculty committees in order to assist in carrying
out the recommendations of the consolidation commission. Graham
never issued executive orders to Brooks and Foust, but conferred
with them in person on all important matters.[18]

Brooks, however, still faced perplexing, sometimes disagreeable
problems in shifting State College to its new status. Undoubtedly,
one of his most distasteful tasks was the dissolution of the School
of Science and Business. Although the college was to retain fundamental courses in general education, all business administration was
to be transferred to Chapel Hill. Brooks insisted upon keeping
certain courses in management and the "business side" of engineering and textile manufacturing at State College. He therefore persuaded the trustees to create a department of industry under Professor Theodore Johnson in the Textile School in order to absorb
part of the curriculum of the School of Science and Business. By
this device he salvaged at least a few remnants of the school in
which he had always manifested a special pride.[19]

Perhaps the most difficult and controversial problem confronting
Brooks was the location of the engineering school in the consolidated
university. Although the survey group considered the engineering
school at Chapel Hill far superior to the one at Raleigh, Brooks
insisted that State College as the technological branch of the university should possess all work in engineering. He had sought to
remove any doubt about the location of the school in 1931 by retaining "Engineering" as a part of the title of State College. Nevertheless, the controversy regarding this problem gained momentum
in the fall of 1932. The students and alumni of State College envisioned another attempt by the University "lawyers" to transfer
one of the most attractive curricula of their *alma mater* to Chapel
Hill. They felt that since the Chapel Hill unit had already profited
by the abolition of their School of Science and Business, it should

18. Frank Graham to the Executive Committee of the Trustees, Nov. 2, 1932, Governors' Papers (Gardner); Lockmiller, *Consolidation of the University*, pp. 55-56;
E. C. Brooks to J. I. Foust, Oct. 5, 1932, E. C. Brooks to Frank Graham, Nov. 15,
1932, State College Papers; interviews with Dr. Frank Graham, Dec. 21, 1932, and
Mr. E. C. Brooks, Jr., July 12, 1956.

19. E. C. Brooks to E. R. Johnson, June 23, 1932, E. C. Brooks to W. A. Wickenden,
June 23, 1932, E. C. Brooks to S. B. Alexander, Dec. 8, 1932, State College Papers;
Minutes of the Executive Committee of the Consolidated Board of Trustees, No. 119,
Governors' Papers (Gardner); *News and Observer*, Oct. 9, 11, 1932.

be willing to sacrifice its engineering school. So loud were their complaints that the board of trustees assured them on November 14, 1932, that "there is no intention . . . to discontinue the schools of engineering at Chapel Hill or Raleigh." This resolution, apparently condoning the existence of the major duplicate curricula in the two colleges, completely failed to pacify the State College alumni, and bitterness continued to mount. Throughout the spring of 1933, the trustees continually postponed action on the engineering schools, thereby precipitating additional anxieties among the friends of State College. In June, 1933, the new governor, J. C. B. Ehringhaus, attempted to mitigate their fears by assuring them that State College would "not become the red-headed stepchild of the consolidation."[20]

Brooks persisted in his efforts to have all engineering concentrated at State College. He was fully aware that in the final analysis President Graham and the University alumni who dominated the board of trustees would determine the location of the engineering school. For this reason he preferred to fight for the State College site without the aid of belligerent alumni, who had already antagonized the friends of the Chapel Hill unit. The next three years proved the wisdom of his tactics, for in 1936, after a hard-fought contest, President Graham persuaded the trustees to place all engineering curricula at State College.[21]

The perplexities of university consolidation coupled with other difficult problems that Brooks encountered at State College placed a severe strain upon his failing health. He was continually apprehensive about the future of the college under consolidation and felt that his work was restricted on all sides by a board of trustees whose actions he was unable to anticipate. Since his days at Kernersville Academy, Brooks had formulated the policies and his trustees had adopted them. For nine years the State College trustees had con-

20. Report to the North Carolina Commission on University Consolidation, E. C. Brooks to W. D. Faucette, Aug. 23, 1932, David Clark to E. C. Brooks, Feb. 14, 1933, R. R. Eagle to Josephus Daniels, Jan. 4, 1933, David Clark to E. C. Brooks, March 1, 1933, R. R. Eagle to E. C. Brooks, April 29, 1933, Jonathan Daniels to R. R. Eagle, April 15, 1933, E. B. Hunter to O. Max Gardner, Nov. 13, 1932, State College Papers; *News and Observer*, July 22, 1932, June 13, 1933; *The Technician*, Oct. 28, 1932; *N. C. State Alumni News*, V (Nov., 1932), pp. 23, 30; *N. C. State Alumni News*, V (Dec., 1932), 37; Lockmiller, *History of State College*, p. 199.

21. Interview with Dr. Frank Graham, Dec. 21, 1956; David Clark to E. C. Brooks, Feb. 14, 1933, State College Papers.

sistently followed his recommendations. But Brooks lost his cherished independence in the consolidated university and did not adjust to the new circumstances without difficulty. He was disturbed by various decisions that he considered detrimental to the welfare of State College and at his own inability to change or compensate for them. These worries caused him many sleepless nights and soon produced noticeable effects upon his physical strength. For this reason his wife urged him to leave State College and accept an offer by President William P. Few to become Lecturer in Education in Duke University. He rejected this idea because the friends of State College looked to him to guide the institution safely through consolidation. Moreover, he felt that his resignation would be interpreted as an easy escape from a difficult situation and as evidence of his unwillingness to occupy a subordinate position in the consolidated university. Thus, he remained at State College even though he recognized that the burdens of the office were detrimental to his health.[22]

On November 18, 1933, Brooks became ill in Washington en route home from a meeting of the Association of Land Grant Colleges in Chicago. He suffered a severe attack of arterial thrombosis that paralyzed the right side of his body. He was too ill to be moved from his room in the Hotel Raleigh to a hospital. His family rushed to Washington immediately and were joined shortly afterward by President Graham and Professors W. C. Riddick and Theodore Johnson of State College. Graham assisted the family in securing the services of Dr. Sterling Ruffin, former physician to Woodrow Wilson. For days Brooks's life hung in an uneasy balance, and those attending him feared for the worst. Then, he began to rally and by late November was "thinking of the things he meant to do." Dr. Ruffin, however, confided to Graham that Brooks could probably live many years if he were relieved of his executive duties at State College—information that Graham kept strictly confidential.[23]

In February, 1934, Brooks returned to his office at the college for the first time in three months. He appeared "much thinner"

22. Interviews with Mrs. E. C. Brooks, May 9, June 19, 1956, and Mr. E. C. Brooks, Jr., July 12, 1956.
23. *The Technician,* Nov. 24, 1933; *News and Observer,* Nov. 21, 25, 1933; interview with Mrs. E. C. Brooks, June 19, 1956; Mrs. E. C. Brooks to W. P. Few, Nov., 1933, Few Papers; interview with Dr. Frank Graham, Dec. 21, 1956.

and leaned heavily upon a cane. As late as April he was still unable to use his right hand even for signing correspondence. In his absence Graham had carried on the executive work of the college, even though he had been authorized by the trustees to select a dean of administration to serve during Brooks's illness. Throughout the spring of 1934 Brooks was barely able to attend to the routine duties of his office. Nevertheless, he was continually planning the reorganization of the Textile School that he had already begun and gave no indication of any intention of resigning his post. Late in the spring he did request the trustees to grant him "a leave of absence" in order to regain his physical strength. Brooks was still unwilling to concede that his days of intense activity were over; he looked forward to the future with the same optimism that had characterized his past.[24]

In the meantime, the board of trustees had decided to retire both Brooks and Foust, who had also suffered a stroke of paralysis. Graham was not responsible for this action nor had he divulged Dr. Ruffin's advice regarding Brooks to the trustees. But he was assigned the delicate task of notifying Brooks and Foust of the trustees' decision. Rather than going directly to Brooks, Graham persuaded Brooks's physician to break the news to him. This quite naturally created an awkward situation between the two men; but whatever bitterness Brooks may have entertained was soon replaced by a "feeling of relief and satisfaction."[25] Certainly he harbored no enmity toward Graham. On June 8, 1934, he wrote George W. Connor: "I feel quite sure that the right move has been made and that I ought to have quit before now. I think perhaps I would not have had the stroke in Washington if I had been relieved of the strain that I have been carrying."[26] Brooks became President Emeritus of State College and Research Professor of Education with an annual stipend of $4,000. Graham "saw to it" that he always had an office

24. *N. C. State Alumni News,* V (Feb., 1934), 69; E. C. Brooks to Francis Winston, April 5, 1934, E. C. Brooks to A. C. Davis, June 27, 1934, E. C. Brooks to I. O. Schaub, June 9, 1934, Brooks Papers (DUL); *News and Observer,* Nov. 25, 1933; *The Technician,* Feb. 2, 23, 1934; Minutes of the General Faculty, May 12, 1934; E. C. Brooks to Frederick Feiker, March 8, 1934, E. C. Brooks to A. M. Dixon, May 5, 1934, State College Papers.

25. Interview with Dr. Frank Graham, Dec. 21, 1956; E. C. Brooks to F. H. Perry, June 8, 1934, Brooks Papers (DUL).

26. E. C. Brooks to George W. Connor, June 8, 1934, Brooks Papers (DUL).

at the college. Under the new policy of the consolidated university
his successor, John W. Harrelson, held the title of Dean of Administration.[27]

[2]

In 1934, Brooks began his retirement with a long vacation in
the North Carolina mountains. Mrs. Brooks, of course, was constantly at his side to make sure that he obeyed the doctor's orders.
His health gradually improved, but he still had to avoid all strenu-
ous activities. Though his physical handicaps proved to be permanent, Brooks maintained his mental alertness and his keen sense
of humor. His vacation at the mountain resorts provided him an
opportunity to employ his talents as a raconteur, a role that had
won him wide popularity. So enjoyable was the stay in the mountains
in 1934 that he and his wife returned to the Boone-Blowing Rock
area during several succeeding summers. Because of Brooks's precarious health, these summer vacations were about the extent of their
travels except for occasional visits with their three children, who
had all married and established homes of their own.[28]

Upon their return to Raleigh in 1934, Brooks and his wife
decided to move to the Sir Walter Hotel rather than to their own
home on North Blount Street. This decision was undoubtedly
prompted by Brooks's desire to remain in close touch with individuals conducting the affairs of North Carolina. In any case, he was
frequently visited by state officials, members of the General Assembly, and former students and associates during his eight years at
the Sir Walter. One of his favorite pastimes was talking to friends in
the lobby of the hotel, where "he always had a crowd around him."
In describing Brooks one observer declared that he still maintained
his traits of "cordiality, friendliness, and courtesy" that had made
him such a popular "personality." Certainly his facile conversation
and ready wit still fascinated those who heard him. One day late in
the spring of 1937 a friend jokingly remarked to Brooks: "I see you
have lost a finger on your left hand." Brooks raised his hand and

27. Memorandum by Mrs. E. C. Brooks, Jan. 24, 1957; Brief Report Covering the
College Activities, 1933-1934, State College Papers.
28. Interviews with Mrs. E. C. Brooks, Jan. 25, 1957, and Mrs. Travis (Martha
Brooks) Callum, Jan. 25, 1957; Brooks Family Bible.

looked at it as if he were surprised to find the appendage missing. "Well, bless my soul," he declared, "so I have." Then, he proceeded in his own inimitable way to tell the story of severing his finger with a hatchet when he was four years old.[29]

Brooks, however, was not sought after solely because of his entertaining conversation and extensive repertoire of humorous stories. Many friends and former colleagues came to him for advice on a wide variety of questions, and, as one of his associates later said, "he continued to offer his wise counsel to those who sought it." He was still able to participate in the activities of the Watauga Club, and his "wise counsel" undoubtedly proved to be valuable to the members of the club who were directing the affairs of the state. In 1936 Brooks became a consultant to the Educational Policies Commission, a body established by the National Education Association for outlining an educational program adapted to "social needs." Similarly, he served various other organizations in an advisory capacity.[30]

The nature of Brooks's ailment forced him to spend a large part of his time in restful seclusion. Nevertheless, he managed to keep himself well-informed about national and state affairs through listening to the radio and reading extensively in current literature. He became an ardent admirer of President Franklin Roosevelt and followed the course of the New Deal with enthusiasm. Brooks, of course, was primarily interested in events in North Carolina, especially the educational and economic developments. He was able to watch the public schools that he had reorganized in 1919 expand their enrollment, terms, facilities, and corps of qualified teachers until the annual operating expense of the school system reached $72,655,102 in 1947. The Brooks School Code still remained the basic law for public education.[31]

Quite naturally, Brooks maintained a keen interest in the affairs

29. Memorandum by Mrs. E. C. Brooks, Jan. 24, 1957; "Dr. E. C. Brooks," *The State* (June 19, 1937), pp, 20, 30.

30. Brower, "Eugene Clyde Brooks" (an address, 1951); interview with Mrs. E. C. Brooks, Jan. 25, 1957; Clarence Poe to E. C. Brooks, March 2, 1938, James K. McClure to E. C. Brooks, Dec. 8, 1936, E. C. Brooks to Clarence Poe, Jan. 14, 1936, A. J. Stoddard to E. C. Brooks, Feb. 13, 1936, E. C. Brooks to A. J. Stoddard, Feb. 21, 1936, E. C. Brooks to B. L. Smith, Feb. 14, 1936, Brooks Papers (DUL).

31. Interviews with Mrs. E. C. Brooks, June 19, 1956, Jan. 25, 1957; Brower, "Eugene Clyde Brooks" (an address, 1951); Medical Record of Dr. E. C. Brooks, Hist. No. 5162, 7/12/38, Duke Hospital.

of State College and regretted that his physical condition prevented him from spending much time in his campus office. J. W. Harrelson, his friend and successor at the helm of the college, respected his judgment and undoubtedly found his advice valuable. In 1935 Brooks wrote President Graham: "I wish to congratulate you particularly because of the statesmanlike way in which you have handled the consolidation problems. I do not think as I look back across the years that they could have been handled better. . . . It is needless for me to tell you that we at State College are pleased."[32] Brooks, therefore, came to believe that Graham would prevent the emasculation of the State College curricula in the process of consolidation. His conviction was strengthened by the decision in 1936 to concentrate all engineering work of the consolidated university in the Raleigh unit. On his seventy-fifth birthday in 1946 Brooks declared: "I rejoice that one of my big dreams has come true: State College now ranks among the best land grant colleges in the nation."[33]

Upon his retirement in 1934 Brooks began work on the history of North Carolina that he had wanted to write since his days as principal of the Kinston Graded School. He collected a large quantity of material on the subject, and his extensive notes indicate that he used many pertinent primary sources. Despite continued ill health and a clumsy right hand, he managed to write in long hand a large portion of the work that he entitled "North Carolina: A History of Government, Agriculture, Industry and Education." His manuscript contains a rather complete account of the period from 1790 to 1860, but the remaining chapters are little more than sketches. Unfortunately, Brooks did not complete the work or revise those sections that he had written. Recognizing that the research and writing of a sound historical work placed too much strain upon him, he abandoned the project and began to prepare his autobiography, which he called "The Education of a North Carolinian." Through this account he intended to relate certain aspects of North Carolina history that he had observed at first hand. The autobiography, like the state history, was never completed, and, in fact, covered only the period of his youth in Lenoir County.[34]

32. E. C. Brooks to Frank Graham, June 12, 1935, Brooks Papers (DUL).
33. *News and Observer,* Dec. 4, 1946.
34. The voluminous notes and the manuscripts of his state history and autobiography are in the Brooks Papers (BLS).

His failure to finish these works suggests the gradual weakening of his physical strength. Brooks still suffered attacks of vertigo, but according to his wife, he was "always the perfect patient." In 1938 his physician described him as "an obese jolly gentleman . . . in acute distress" and as "an old man for his sixty-six years of age." In 1942 Brooks and his wife decided to move to their own home, because the bustling activity in the hotel was no longer conducive to his comfort and welfare. He spent the last five years of his life in the large white house near the Governor's Mansion that he had purchased while State Superintendent. During this period there was little visible change in his health until the first week in October, 1947, when he became critically ill from a return of old ailments compounded by new ones. After a two-week struggle, he died quietly on October 18, 1947, within three months of his seventy-sixth birthday, and was appropriately buried in Maplewood Cemetery in Durham—the town in which he had spent the happiest period of his life.[35]

In spite of Brooks's retirement for thirteen years, his services to North Carolina during more than three decades had not been forgotten. Citizens throughout the state mourned his death, and the press attempted to do justice to his contributions. The *Winston-Salem Journal,* expressing the sentiments of numerous newspapers, declared:

The death of Dr. Brooks marks the passing of another of those intellectual and moral giants of the Aycock-McIver era who made possible the progress of educational and social enlightenment in this commonwealth which has pushed North Carolina into the national limelight as the most progressive state in the South. North Carolina owes more to him than it can now know.[36]

In 1948, the year after his death, the North Carolina Education Association placed his name in the Educational Hall of Fame over the citation, "inspiring teacher, masterful speaker, intrepid leader."[37]

35. Medical Record of Dr. E. C. Brooks, Hist. No. 5162, 7/12/38, Duke Hospital; memorandum by Mrs. E. C. Brooks, Jan. 24, 1957; interview with Mrs. E. C. Brooks, June 19, 1956; *News and Observer,* Oct. 19, 1947.
36. *Winston-Salem Journal,* Oct. 21, 1947. See also *New York Times,* Oct. 20, 1947; *Charlotte Observer,* Oct. 21, 1947; *Greensboro Daily News,* Oct. 20, 1947; *Durham Morning Herald,* Oct. 20, 1947.
37. Citation of Dr. Eugene Clyde Brooks to the North Carolina Educational Hall of Fame (mimeographed copy), Brooks Papers (BLS).

Three years later, at the dedication of the Eugene Clyde Brooks School in Greensboro, City Superintendent B. L. Smith perhaps best described the personal qualities underlying the achievements of his former college teacher when he remarked: "Dr. Brooks was endowed with extraordinary native ability, an enquiring mind, great energy, indefatigable effort, a keen sense of humor, 'the gift of people,' and a far vision. He was a born leader. Through his inspiration you caught his enthusiasm, his devotion to a cause, and were challenged with his sense of mission."[38]

38. B. L. Smith, "Eugene Clyde Brooks" (an address, Nov. 14, 1951), Brooks Papers (DUL).

Index